SCALE SIXTH-INCH TO MILE

0 1 2 3 4 5 6   12

© – John Bartholomew & Son.Ltd.Edinburgh

D1577142

Scottish Mountaineering Club
District Guide Books

THE SOUTHERN HIGHLANDS

General Editor: W. B. SPEIRS

DISTRICT GUIDE BOOKS

Southern Highlands
Central Highlands
Western Highlands
Northern Highlands
Islands of Scotland
Island of Skye
The Cairngorms
Southern Uplands

Munro's Tables

SCOTTISH MOUNTAINEERING CLUB
DISTRICT GUIDE BOOKS

THE
Southern Highlands

by Donald Bennet

THE SCOTTISH MOUNTAINEERING TRUST
EDINBURGH

First published in Great Britain in 1972 by
THE SCOTTISH MOUNTAINEERING TRUST

Copyright © 1972 by the Scottish Mountaineering Trust

First Edition (Wilson) 1949
First Edition New Series 1972

Designed for the Scottish Mountaineering Trust by
West Col Productions

TRADE DISTRIBUTORS
West Col Productions
1 Meadow Close
Goring on Thames
Reading Berks RG8 OAP

SBN 901516 64 3

Set in Monotype Plantin Series 110 and Grotesque 215
and printed in Great Britain by Cox & Wyman Ltd,
London, Reading & Fakenham

CONTENTS

ILLUSTRATIONS

ILLUSTRATIONS

8

Photos by Tom Weir: 6, 10, 11, 12, 45, 56, 68, 77. By Douglas Scott: 48, 55. All other photos by the author.

FOREWORD

THE Southern Highlands Guide Book edited by J. D. B. Wilson was published in 1949 and has been out of print for some time. A revised edition was therefore necessary to meet the decision of The Scottish Mountaineering Trust to keep all the Guide Books as up to date as possible.

The district covered is close to the densely populated Lowlands of Scotland, and is therefore popular for day outings and short weekends, although it does not offer the opportunities for the more challenging expeditions which are available in the Glencoe and Ben Nevis regions.

The Trust have been fortunate in obtaining the services of Donald Bennet, Honorary Secretary of the Scottish Mountaineering Club, to rewrite this Guide Book. His wide experience in climbing and ski touring at home and in Greenland, and his recent visits to all parts of the Southern Highlands, have enabled him to produce a Guide Book which is at the same time accurate in detail and balanced in outlook. All those visiting the area will be indebted to him for the information which will enable them to plan expeditions to suit their abilities.

W. B. Speirs, *Glasgow*, August, 1972.

ACKNOWLEDGEMENTS

WRITING a guide book is like climbing Mount Everest—in one respect at least. The author, like the climber, depends greatly on the efforts of his predecessors, and adds his own contribution to theirs. Thus my first acknowledgement is to John Wilson, the previous author of the Southern Highlands Guide Book. Those who read this guide after reading his, will realise the extent to which I have made use of his earlier material.

In doing the 'field-work' for the present guide book I have been greatly helped by my wife and many fellow members of the Scottish Mountaineering Club who have accompanied me with forbearance to unfrequented corners of the Southern Highlands in fair weather and foul. They can now all relax, we will go somewhere else next year.

I am grateful to Ian Fulton for information about climbs on Dumbarton Rock, to Doug Lang for information about Craiglug and to Robin Campbell for information about climbs elsewhere; I also thank Tom Weir and Douglas Scott for providing photographs.

Dr. D. J. Fettes of the Institute of Geological Studies, Edinburgh has written a section on the Geology of the Southern Highlands, and this valuable contribution is acknowledged.

Information about climbs at the Whangie has been based on a private publication by J. Cullen and C. Vigano of the Creag Dhu Mountaineering Club. Information about climbs on Dumyat, Ben Ledi and Leum an Eireannaich is based on a similar publication of the Ochils Mountaineering Club edited by T. Low; permission to use this information is gratefully acknowledged.

Finally, the patience and co-operation of the General Guide Books Editor, Willie Speirs, has helped to lighten the author's work.

PROPRIETARY AND
SPORTING RIGHTS

THE Scottish Mountaineering Trust desire to impress upon all those who avail themselves of the information given in their Guide Books that it is essential to consider and respect proprietary and sporting rights.

During the shooting season, from about the beginning of August to the middle of October, harm can be done in deer forests and on grouse moors by people tramping through them. During this period walkers and climbers should obtain the consent of the local stalkers and gamekeepers before walking over shooting lands. At times it is not easy to recognise what constitutes shooting lands. In cases of doubt it is always wise to ask some local resident.

It should also be noted that many of the roads in the upper glens were made and are maintained by the proprietors, who do not acknowledge a public right to motor over them, though they may follow the lines of established rights-of-way. It is, however, frequently possible to obtain permission to motor over some of them, but, as the situation is liable to change, local enquiries should be made in advance.

INTRODUCTION

THE area covered by this volume of the Scottish Mountaineering Club's series of General Guide Books extends from the line of the Forth–Clyde canal across the centre of Scotland northwards to the line of the River Awe, Glen Orchy, the southern edge of the Moor of Rannoch, Loch Rannoch and Loch Tummel. The eastern boundary of the area follows the Rivers Tummel and Tay to the sea, and includes the Kingdom of Fife. On the west the area is bounded by the much-indented coastline round the Cowal peninsula, Kintyre and up the west coast to Oban and the lower reaches of Loch Etive. Thus the area covered includes the counties of Dunbarton, Stirling, Clackmannan, Kinross and Fife, and parts of Argyll and Perthshire.

The area defined above is not entirely mountainous, and in fact practically all the high mountains of our area are in Argyll and Perthshire. Elsewhere there are ranges of low hills such as the Campsie Fells in Stirlingshire and the Lomond Hills in Fife, and these have been included because their proximity to centres of population makes them popular. On the west coast the districts of Kintyre, Knapdale and Lorne have only low hills, and being rather remote they are unfrequented by climbers and walkers.

North of the low hills, which are close to the southern boundary of our area, there are several groups of hills between two and three thousand feet high. These include the Cowal and Ardgoil hills on the north-west of the Firth of Clyde, the Luss Hills on the west side of Loch Lomond, the Trossachs in the centre of Scotland and the Ochil Hills in the east.

North of these hills the Scottish Highlands achieve their full stature, and the heights of the main mountains rise to over three thousand feet, and in one or two cases almost four thousand feet. Forty-six mountains in the Southern Highlands are classified as 'separate mountains' over three thousand feet in Munro's Tables, and a further twenty-four summits over three thousand feet are classified as 'tops'. All these mountains and tops are listed in Sections

1, 2 and 3 of Munro's Tables. With only seven exceptions, all the 3000 ft. mountains in the Southern Highlands lie wholly or partly in the catchment area of the River Tay and its tributaries, so the area is dominated geographically by the upper glens and straths of this river, which lie in a roughly west to east direction.

Hill-Walking

The mountains of the Southern Highlands are notable for the absence of massive rock features such as buttresses, ridges, gullies and steep-walled corries that characterise the mountains further north. Although many of the hills are quite rugged and have outcrops of rock, these outcrops tend to be small and vegetatious and it is probably true to say that there is no comparable area of high mountains in Scotland with so little rock-climbing. There are of course exceptions such as The Cobbler, which is justly famous for its rock-climbing, and some of its neighbours in the Arrochar Alps, but apart from these there is not much more than small crag and outcrop climbing. As a result the Southern Highlands are (in summer at least) mainly hill-walkers' mountains, and this is therefore mainly a hill-walkers' guide book.

In dealing with hill-walking routes on the mountains it is the author's policy to describe no more than two or three routes on any mountain. The routes chosen are those with climbing or scenic interest, routes following well defined mountain features such as prominent ridges, routes following tracks and paths and other short and easy routes. Practically every mountain in the Southern Highlands can be climbed by any one of several different routes, and the experienced hill-walker with a good map and good judgement can plan a route to suit his own wishes and capability.

There are also many good low-level walks through the mountains following paths, tracks, old drove roads and glens. Many of these are also described in this book. The reference in the text to paths or tracks does not necessarily imply a right-of-way (unless specifically stated). The Forestry Commission usually permit access through their land by marked paths and tracks, and most landowners readily grant permission for walkers to use stalking paths and other paths at times outwith the stalking and shooting season. Walkers and climbers should, however, always be prepared to seek permission to use paths through private land.

Rock-Climbing

As already mentioned, the Southern Highlands are not noted for their rock-climbing potential. The principal rock-climbing area is the Arrochar Alps where The Cobbler and, to a lesser extent, Beinn Narnain, Beinn Ime, Creag Tharsuinn and The Brack have some good but rather short routes of all standards. None of the climbs exceeds 400 ft. in length. The climbs in the Arrochar Alps are described in detail in the Scottish Mountaineering Club's Climbers' Guide to *Arrochar* by J. R. Houston, and only brief descriptions of some of these climbs are given in this book.

There is a fine granite crag on Dunleachan Hill on the west side of Loch Fyne which is also described in the Climbers' Guide to *Arrochar*. The Leum an Eireannaich, north of Balquhidder, is an impressive but neglected crag which deserves to be better known.

Further north in the hills around Bridge of Orchy there are some fair crags in the corries of Beinn Dorain, Beinn an Dothaidh and Beinn Udlaidh, but these have never become popular, presumably because one only has to go fifteen miles further north to reach the very much better climbs on the Glen Coe mountains.

Elsewhere in the Southern Highlands there are many small crags, of which mention may be made of Ben A'n (Trossachs), Dumyat (Ochils), The Whangie (Kilpatrick Hills), Dumbarton Rock, the Lomond Hills (Fife) and some pinnacles on Ben Ledi.

The grading system for rock-climbs used in this book is the adjectival system at present common in British climbing. The abbreviations are: Easy – E., Moderate – M., Difficult – D., Very Difficult – V.D., Mild Severe – M.S., Severe – S., Hard Severe – H.S., Very Severe – V.S. The grading of artificial routes, A1, A2 and A3 is also used.

Winter Climbing

The Southern Highlands have more to offer by way of winter climbing. Crags which in summer are loose and vegetatious, and corries which are unpleasant slopes of scree and steep grass can in winter give excellent climbs when they are bound by frost and covered with snow and ice. The hardest winter climbs are to be found in the Arrochar Alps, usually following summer routes in gullies, chimneys and grooves. Unfortunately, because of their modest height and closeness to the western seaboard, the Arrochar

Alps cannot be relied upon to give good winter climbing conditions for more than three or four weeks in an average winter.

In general, the winter climbs of the Southern Highlands are of the gully variety, most of them being straightforward climbs of no great difficulty. The best known climbs are the Central Gully of Ben Lui and the Y-Gully of Cruach Ardrain. Elsewhere there are winter climbing possibilities in the north corrie of Ben Lomond, on the Tarmachan Hills near Killin, Ben Lawers, Beinn Chaluim, Beinn Udlaidh, Beinn an Dothaidh and several other mountains.

The usual grading system for winter climbs is used, namely:

Grade I – Easy snow climbs with no pitches and little or no cornice difficulty.

Grade II – Snow climbs with short ice pitches or difficult cornices. Snow bound ridge and buttress climbs of moderate difficulty.

Grade III – Serious climbs with difficult ice pitches. Hard snow and ice bound ridge and buttress climbs.

Grade IV – Gully and chimney climbs with long, hard ice pitches and sustained difficulty. Snow and ice covered rock-climbs of sustained Severe or less sustained Very Severe standard.

Ski-Mountaineering

Because so many of the Southern Highland mountains are smooth and evenly weathered, there are considerable possibilities for ski-mountaineering. In this respect the Southern Highlands are probably second only in Scotland to the Cairngorms. Mountains which in summer may be rather uninteresting or featureless for the hill-walker can in winter provide the ski-mountaineer with excellent sport of all standards of skiing difficulty.

It is a common misconception that one must be an accomplished downhill skier to enjoy ski-mountaineering. This is not so, in Scotland at least, and skiers of intermediate standard can take to the mountains on their skis provided that they know their limitations. It is much more important that the ski-mountaineer should be first and foremost a competent mountaineer in winter conditions, able to choose a good route, judge snow and ice conditions and generally use his 'mountain sense' to keep out of trouble. On skis the selection of the right route, both uphill and downhill, is all-important. This is particularly true going downhill, where the skier must always ski well within his limits. Mountain skiing is very different from piste skiing, and there are no rescue teams standing by.

On the other hand the rewards of ski-mountaineering are great. Going uphill the skier can achieve a rhythm of movement which the walker cannot hope for, and although the skier's progress may be no faster, he may well arrive at the top fresher. This is particularly true when the snow is deep and soft. Going downhill, of course, the skier has all the advantages.

The enjoyment of ski-mountaineering depends to a large extent on having the correct equipment in good working order. Skins, bindings and touring attachments should be carefully checked before each outing. A badly fitting binding or a broken strap on one's skins can completely spoil the day.

Finally a word about the right snow conditions. Ideally, of course, the snow should be lying right down to the foot of the mountains to avoid the need to carry skis at the beginning of the day. It is probably advisable to avoid the temptation to get out on the hills on skis as soon as the first snow falls, as the resulting conditions – soft snow on a base of grass, heather or rocks – are not conducive to good skiing. Another condition to be avoided, or at least treated with care, is that which is usual when hard frost follows a period of thawing conditions. Then, when the snow becomes hard and icy, the climber would be better advised to take out his ice axe and crampons rather than his skis.

Maps
The best maps for the climber and hill-walker are without doubt the Ordnance Survey One-inch Series. They show the detail that the climber and walker needs, and are essential for accurate navigation through the mountains in bad visibility. At the time of writing this guide book some of the current Seventh Series Maps are not fully up-to-date in showing reservoirs and enlarged lochs created by the North of Scotland Hydro-Electric Board, and some roads and aqueducts built by the Board are also not shown. Not surprisingly, many newly planted forests are not shown, and consequently access routes to the hills which look possible on the map may turn out to be impossible because of newly planted forest. However, because of their superiority for the climber, this guide book uses place names, spellings, heights and map references taken from the Ordnance Survey One-inch Maps.

Bartholomew's Half-inch Series of maps is very suitable for the tourist and walker who does not require the detail shown by the One-inch Maps, and their colour contouring gives a very clear impression of the country at a glance.

In certain cases names or heights on the One-inch and Half-inch maps are at variance, and the One-inch versions are preferred except where noted in the text.

The following sheets of the Ordnance Survey One-inch Series cover the Southern Highlands area: 47, 48, 49, 52, 53, 54, 55, 56, 59, 60 and 61. The following sheets of Bartholomew's Half-inch Series cover the area: 44, 45, 47, 48, 49.

Access and Transport

Access to all parts of the Southern Highlands is easy by public roads, and there are very few hills more than four or five miles from the nearest point on a public road. There are also many private roads, Forestry Commission roads and Hydro-Electric Board roads which lead into the mountains; however, the fact that they are mentioned in this book should not be taken to imply that the public can drive along them. Generally speaking the public are allowed to use Forestry Commission and Hydro-Electric Board roads for walking but not driving, but occasionally permission can be obtained to drive along these roads, and keys to locked gates may be obtained by arrangement with local officials, foresters or keepers.

As in many parts of the country, public transport services tend to have deteriorated in recent years, and the closure of the railway line from Stirling to Crianlarich through Callander and Lochearnhead, with branch lines to Comrie and Killin, has robbed the Southern Highlands of one of their two traditional rail arteries. In the days before the motor car this line was the trade route for climbers from Edinburgh on their way to the Southern and Central Highlands. Now the only rail route through the area that is of use to climbers is the Glasgow to Oban and Fort William line which passes through Helensburgh, along the east side of Loch Long, the west side of Loch Lomond and up Glen Falloch to Crianlarich where the line divides. The Oban line continues westwards by Tyndrum (Lower) and Dalmally, while the Fort William line goes north by Tyndrum (Upper) and Bridge of Orchy. The only other rail services in the Southern Highlands area, those in Fife and between Edinburgh, Stirling, Perth, Pitlochry and Blair Atholl, are very much on the periphery of the mountains.

There are bus services throughout the area covered by this book; however in some cases remote country services operate on only one or two days a week, and a few services do not operate during school holidays. Although the information given at the end of each chapter about bus services is correct at the time of writing, changes of routes and timetables will doubtless make some of this information out-of-date before long. The timetable published by W. Alexander and Sons (Midland) Ltd. covers almost all the bus services in the Southern Highlands and can be obtained from bus stations in most towns in the area and from The Travel Press and Publicity Co. Ltd., 114/116 George Street, Edinburgh.

Accommodation

There are hotels throughout the area covered by this book, and in summer at least there is a hotel within walking distance of all the mountains in the area with the possible exception of those at the head of Glens Lyon and Lochay. Many hotels close during the winter months, and at that time it may be more difficult to find suitable accommodation of this type.

Bed and breakfast accommodation is also widely available throughout the area during the summer months only. Full information about hotels, boarding houses and bed and breakfast establishments can be found in *Where to Stay in Scotland*, published by the Scottish Tourist Board, 2 Rutland Place, Edinburgh.

There are about twenty Youth Hostels in and close to the Southern Highlands. The following hostels are in the mountain areas and are particularly suitable for climbers and walkers: Ardgartan, Inverbeg, Rowardennan, Crianlarich, Loch Ard, Fintry, Trossachs, Glendevon, Balquhidder, Killin and Garth. Other hostels on the fringe of the mountains are: Glasgow, Loch Lomond, Tighnabruaich, Inveraray, Cruachan, Strathtummel, Birnam, Perth and Falkland. Full details of membership and facilities of the Scottish Youth Hostels Association can be obtained from the Association's Head Office, 7 Glebe Crescent, Stirling.

A number of bothies and other mountain shelters are noted in this book, however the mention of a bothy does not imply that permission exists for climbers and walkers to use it. Permission to stay in bothies should always be sought beforehand. The Mountain Bothies Association exists to repair and restore bothies and other shelters in the mountains, and the Bothy Handbook published by the Association contains a list of bothies in hill and mountain country in the U.K.

In most mountainous parts of the Southern Highlands there are few restrictions on camping. Exceptions include private land, cultivated farm land and Forestry Commission land, and permission should always be sought before camping on such land. There are many organised camp sites low down in the glens and near towns and villages; however, most climbers prefer to camp in more remote areas, and there is no shortage of peaceful campsites high in the glens, by lochside and in mountain corries.

Parks and Conservation

There are a number of Forest Parks and other areas under protection in the Southern Highlands which are listed below.

Queen Elizabeth Forest Park. This park is administered by the Forestry Commission and includes Ben Lomond, the forest south of Loch Ard, the eastern half of Ben Venue and the Trossachs. There are many pleasant low-level walks in this park as well as three popular mountains, Ben Lomond, Ben Venue and Ben A'n.

Argyll Forest Park. This park is also administered by the Forestry Commission and includes Ardgoil, part of Cowal and most of the Arrochar Alps. It is an area of very fine mountains, forests and lochs which has a lot to offer the climber and walker.

Guides to the two Forest Parks mentioned above are published by H.M. Stationery Office, Edinburgh and can be obtained from some booksellers.

Ben Lawers. Ben Lawers is noted for its great variety of alpine flowers and plants, and the southern side of the mountain overlooking Loch Tay is under the care of the National Trust for Scotland. The Trust has an Information Centre at the car park on the Loch Tay to Glen Lyon road (MR 609376), and a short nature trail just above the car park takes the visitor through several of the different vegetation zones on the hillside.

Ben Lui, Fionn Choirein. It is understood at the time of writing that the Nature Conservancy has plans to create a small reserve on the north-west side of Ben Lui in the lower part of the Fionn Choirein.

Sporting and Proprietory Rights and Access

It has always been the policy of the Scottish Mountaineering Club that sporting and proprietory rights of landowners should be respected by climbers. There are two times of the year when climbers and walkers should be particularly careful before going on the hills, namely the lambing season from March to May and the stalking and shooting season from August to October. At these times permission and advice should be sought from gamekeepers, farmers or shepherds concerning hills on which climbers and walkers can go without infringing local interests.

With the extensive planting of forests in several parts of the Southern Highlands it is important for climbers to avoid damaging and destroying young trees by walking indiscriminately through them, and also to avoid damaging boundary fences by climbing over them. Where access routes have been provided through forests, and stiles or gates provided at fences, these should be used. Unfortunately there are some areas where access routes do not appear to have been provided for climbers and walkers, and care should be taken when it is necessary to go through such areas.

Mountain Rescue

(The following information is correct at the time of writing, but may in time become outdated.)

Mountain rescue in Scotland is effected by the co-ordinated action of voluntary Mountain Rescue teams, the Police and R.A.F. Mountain Rescue teams. Climbers in the vicinity of an accident are expected to offer their help. Official Mountain Rescue Posts provide a nucleus of rescue equipment for teams in the more popular climbing areas.

In the event of an accident, help should be sought from the local rescue organisation which alone has the equipment, can summon the manpower and knows the system of medical aid and evacuation to hospital. In general it may be quickest and simplest to contact the Police (dial 999). Alternatively a Rescue Post should be alerted.

Mountain Rescue Posts in the Southern Highlands (with the names of the supervisors and telephone numbers).

Succoth, Arrochar	Mr. J. Paterson, Succoth Farm, Arrochar	Arrochar 241
Crianlarich Police Station, Perthshire.	Officer in Charge	Crianlarich 222

Scottish Ski Club Hut,	Officer in Charge,	Tel. Police
Ben Lawers	Police Station,	
	Killin	
Drymen,	Dr. McLaren,	Drymen 203 or
Stirlingshire	Creitendam,	Police, Drymen 300
	Drymen.	

The position of a Post is sometimes changed and should be verified.

Mountain Rescue Teams
Area Organiser, Hamish MacInnes, 'Ice Axes', Glencoe, Tel. Ballachulish 230.
Argyll Police Mountain Rescue Team.
Perth and Kinross Police Mountain Rescue Team
R.A.F. Leuchars Mountain Rescue Team
Arrochar Mountain Rescue Team
Lomond Mountain Rescue Team (Drymen)
Rannoch School Mountain Rescue Team
Benmore Adventure Centre Mountain Rescue Team (Dunoon)
Ochils Mountain Rescue Team
Glencoe Mountain Rescue Team

Advice for climbers
The routes described in this guide book range from simple walks on well marked tracks to serious climbs demanding skill, knowledge and the right equipment. However, it must be stressed that any expedition which in good weather is perfectly safe and simple may become very different if the weather becomes bad or mist comes down, and such weather changes can occur very suddenly. Similarly routes, which in summer conditions present no difficulty, may become difficult or dangerous in winter conditions – especially to a party not experienced in winter climbing. To generalise, practically any expedition on the mountains is potentially dangerous should severe weather or snow conditions occur, and the party lack the necessary experience to deal with such conditions.

In many cases accidents are caused by a combination of events, no one of which singly would have been serious. Ample time should be allowed for expeditions, especially when the route is unknown. Before setting out on an expedition a party should leave information at its hotel, hostel, hut, tent or car as to its objective, route and estimated time of return. This may save valuable hours of searching in the event of an accident.

A party should always stay together, particularly in misty weather, and three is the minimum number to ensure safety in the event of an accident. The pace of a party should be dictated by the slowest member, and the party should be prepared to turn back if weather conditions become very bad or if any member is going very slowly or is exhausted.

Whilst care should be exercised at all times, this is most important on the descent, particularly if the route is unknown. During and after rain, rocks, boulders and even grass may become very slippery if one is wearing rubber soled boots. Do not run downhill. A minor slip or fall might result in a sprained ankle, and a mountain rescue team might have to be called out.

In the event of an accident requiring a rescue team at least one member of the party should stay with the injured climber, while one or two go down for help. If there are only two in the party, the injured climber should be left with all spare clothing, food, whistle and torch while his companion goes for help. The location of the injured climber should be marked by reference to some conspicuous landmark. The person descending to the valley should inform the police as quickly as possible.

Some common causes of difficulty are:

Underestimation of time required for expedition.
Slow or untried companions or members who are in poor training.
Illness caused through unwise eating or drinking.
Extreme cold or exhaustion through severe conditions.
Poor, soft snow; steep hard snow; snowstorms; mist.
Change in temperature rapidly converting soft snow into ice – involving step cutting.
Rain making rock slippery or snow filling the holds when rock-climbing.
Frost after snow or rain glazing rocks with ice.
Sudden spates rendering the crossing of burns dangerous or impossible and necessitating long detours.

Hints – Equipment:

All parties should carry:
Simple First Aid equipment, torch, whistle, watch, Ordnance Survey One-inch Map, compass, and be able to use them.
Except in a few spots in Skye where the rocks are magnetic, the

compass direction is certain to be correct even if it differs from one's sense of direction.

Ice-axes should be carried if there is any chance of snow or ice, and a rope unless it is certain not to be required.

Clothing: At all times reserve clothing should be carried. Temperatures change rapidly, especially at high levels. Clothing should be warm; in winter a Balaclava helmet and thick woollen gloves should be carried. Well-shod boots should always be worn.

Food: Each member of a party should carry his own food. Climbers will find from experience what kind of food suits their individual need. Normally, jams and sugar are better than meat and are rapidly converted into energy. Most people will find it advisable to avoid alcohol on the hills, but a flask may be carried for emergencies. Light meals at frequent intervals are better than heavy meals at long intervals. In winter it may be advisable to make an early stop for food if shelter is found.

The Geology of the Southern Highlands

D. J. FETTES

Anyone looking northwards across the Midland Valley of Scotland will be impressed by the abruptness of the 'Highland Boundary' with rolling, grassy land giving way to heather covered, craggy hills. This sudden change in topography marks one of the fundamental features of Scottish geology – the Highland Boundary Fault – a huge shatter zone which brings together the ancient crystalline schist of the Highlands with the softer, younger sediments of the south. The fault runs from Bute in the west to Stonehaven in the east through such well marked features as Glen Artney. The major movements of this great fault took place hundreds of millions of years ago, but tremors are still felt at the present day.

South of the Highland Boundary Fault lies a wide expanse of sandstone and lava belonging to the Old Red Sandstone, overlain to the south by the mixed sediments and lava of the Carboniferous. Sedimentary rocks such as limestone and sandstone are relatively soft, thus the sediments of the Midland Valley have been planed by the forces of erosion to a smooth profile. This feature has been enhanced by the glaciers of the Ice Age which (some twenty thousand years ago) scoured the rocks and then in their dying stages plastered them with the debris scraped from the Highland hills. Lava, however, is tougher and more resistant to erosion, and in consequence the lavas of the Old Red Sandstone are preserved in the Ochil Hills which stand out prominently from the surrounding land. Similarly the lavas of the Carboniferous period are preserved in the Kilpatrick and Campsie Hills. When lava is erupted, the base of the flow becomes cold and broken and mixed with the debris on the ground. The surface of the flow cools and cracks, and before being covered by the subsequent flow it may be badly weathered and covered by ash, dust and possibly sediment. Consequently, hills formed by an accumulation of lava flows are marked by a succession of rotten and broken layers. Thus, although lava hills present steep features and impressive scarps, they seldom offer rock-climbing of any length or quality.

At the same time as the Carboniferous lavas were pouring out onto the surface, molten igneous rock was intruding the underlying sediment at depth. Dark, basic rock (dolerites) thus formed now lie exposed at the top of the Lomond Hills in Fife. This capping of tough, igneous rock has protected the sediments below from erosion so that the Lomonds stand out from the denuded plains around them. Similar rocks outcrop on the coast of Fife and on the Isle of May.

To the north of the Highland Boundary Fault lie two great rock assemblages, the Dalradian and the Moine. The former is a mixed group of schists, quartzites and marbles, and the latter is a monotonous series of flaggy quartzitic rock which stretches from the northern part of Perthshire to Sutherland. These two assemblages were once sediments very similar to those now found in the Midland Valley; however, during the Caledonian Orogeny (some four or five hundred million years ago) these rocks were subjected to great stresses, and were thrown into a series of gigantic folds to become greatly deformed and cleaved. The accompanying high pressures and temperatures re-crystallized and metamorphosed the rocks. In general the degree of metamorphism increases northwards so that shale bands near the Highland edge have been changed to slate, whilst further north they have re-crystallized to give the well-known micaschist which is often characterised by large, pink garnets. Sandstones have been fused to form quartzites, and intercalated lavas and intrusive igneous rocks are now found as the dark green hornblendeschists so typical of the south-west Highlands. The structure of the area is complex, with folds of all sizes deforming and twisting the rocks; however, one huge fold dominates the area, rising from the ground to the north of Ben Lawers, stretching horizontally southwards and dipping steeply downwards near the Highland Boundary. This great structure has given the majority of the rocks in the area a predominantly flat-lying attitude, although large, rolling folds locally steepen the dip and repeat different rock groups on the ground. These rock groups lie as bands roughly parallel to the Highland Boundary Fault, and often stretching the entire breadth of Scotland. The youngest rocks are found adjacent to the Highland Boundary Fault, and become progressively older northwards.

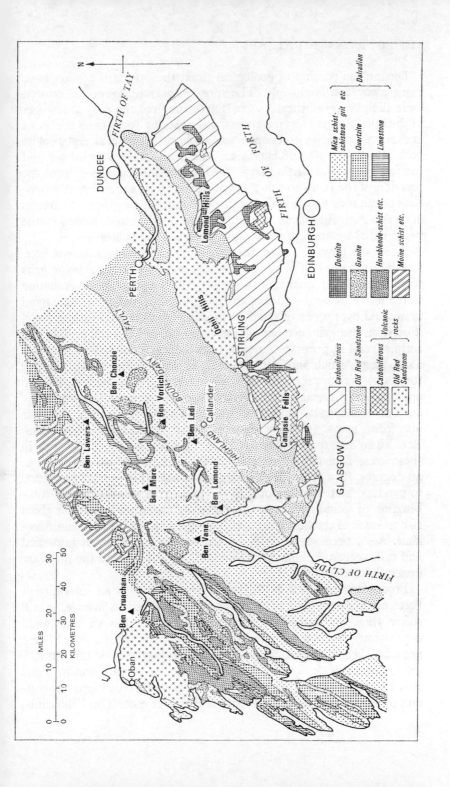

N

FIRTH OF TAY

DUNDEE

FIRTH OF FORTH

EDINBURGH

PERTH

FAULT

Lomond Hills

Ochil Hills

STIRLING

Ben Chonzie

Ben Vorlich

HIGHLAND

BOUNDARY

Ben Lawers

Ben Ledi

Callander

Ben More

Campsie Fells

GLASGOW

Ben Lomond

Ben Vane

FIRTH OF CLYDE

Ben Cruachan

Oban

MILES
0   10   20   30
KILOMETRES
0 10 20 30 40 50

Dolerite

Granite

Hornblende-schist etc.

Moine schist etc.

Carboniferous

Old Red Sandstone ⎫
                  ⎬ Volcanic rocks
Carboniferous   ⎭

Old Red Sandstone etc.

Mica schist-schistose grit etc.

Quartzite ⎫
          ⎬ Dalradian
Limestone ⎭

During the passing of geological time, the forces of erosion have worn away the Highlands. The most important agents of erosion were the glaciers of the Ice Age. These sculpted the rugged features of the hills, gouging out the valleys and plucking rocks from the backs and sides of corries to deepen and enlarge them. Soil and broken rock which had accumulated over the aeons were scraped off and carried away down the valleys. Two important features control the reaction of the rocks to this great abrasive force, the inherent toughness of the rock type and the degree and attitude of planes of parting, such as schistosity planes. Gullies and cracks are often formed by the preferential weathering out of igneous dykes and shatter zones.

The rocks forming the southern half of the Dalradian Assemblage, i.e. the southern half of the Highlands, are a series of schistose grits with intercalated quartz-mica-schists, the mica-schists dominating in the north. Near the edge of the Highlands an important slate band is marked by a series of quarries running from Birnam to Aberfoyle. The schistose grits are one of the toughest of the rock groups and form several impressive summits such as Ben Venue, Ben A'n, Ben Ledi, Ben Vorlich and Ben Chonzie, as well as many lesser craggy tops. On the lower northern slopes of Ben Venue bands of green epidotic grit can be seen which may represent the ash thrown out by ancient volcanoes. The quartz-mica-schist to the north of the grits also forms many well-known summits such as Ben Lomond, Ben Lui, Ben More and the Crianlarich hills. The schistosity of the rock in these areas is usually relatively flat, the dip seldom exceeding 30 or 40 degrees. As a result, weathering along the schistosity planes tends to produce 'step-like' features in the rock. It is this favourable combination of sound rock type and flat-lying structure which has given rise to some of the best climbs of the region in the hills around Arrochar. Also, because the grits do not readily break down into sand and soil, vegetation finds little foothold on the cliffs and the rocks are generally clean.

Proceeding northwards from this group there is an intermittent band of limestone which, although re-crystallized to marble, is still softer than the surrounding rock and usually lies in unexposed depressions. North again, calcareous mica-schists predominate. These are relatively soft rocks, easily weathered so that they do not produce the dramatic rock scenery of the mountains further south. Thus Ben Lawers, formed of this type of rock, although the highest mountain of the area is relatively smooth and free of rock. The Killin hills, such as Meall nan Tarmachan and Beinn nan Eachan, show some impressive cliffs although they are also formed of calcareous-mica-schists. The rock, however, is crumbly and soft and does not form the 'steps' of the tougher grits. The crumbled and rotten rock provides a good foothold for vegetation and in consequence climbs where they exist are of poor quality. The junction between this calcareous-mica-schist and the quartz-mica-schist of the south passes near the foot of the main corrie on Ben Lui.

The northernmost and oldest significant rock group of the Dalradian is a thick band of quartzite. One of the hardest rocks, quartzite has little or no schistosity and is more homogeneous. In consequence, it weathers uniformly and although forming prominent hills such as Schichallion and Carn Mairg, it does not form spectacular cliffs. Rock-climbs on quartzite are usually short but of good quality.

The Dalradian is succeeded northwards by the flaggy quartz-mica-schists of the Moine. Many of the hills around Glen Orchy, such as Beinn a' Chaisteal, lie wholly within the Moine; others such as Beinn Udlaidh and Beinn Dorain straddle the boundary between the two groups. The lower slopes of Beinn Dorain and Beinn an Dothaidh are composed of Moine quartz-mica-schists, with limestone and mica-schists of the Dalradian forming the last few hundred feet. A north-east trending fault passing through the summit of Beinn Udlaidh brings a small patch of Dalradian mica-schist to the south-east into contact with quartz-mica-schist of the Moine.

One reason why the hills of the Southern Highlands do not have more good rock-climbing areas is the absence of large igneous complexes such as those of the Cairngorms, Glencoe, Ben Nevis and Skye. Although small patches of diorite and granite occur around Comrie and on the north side of The Cobbler, they do not provide notable rock features. The Lorne plateau lavas belong to the Old Red Sandstone, but as the name suggests, there are no prominent summits.

Notable faults occur in the area with a north-east to south-west trend. Large faults pass through Loch Tay and also from the head of Loch Fyne via Tyndrum into the Spey Valley. The latter fault, at Tyndrum, brings Moinian rocks against Dalradian schists. Lead and silver mineralised rocks on this fault have been mined and the scars of the old mines can still be seen on the hillside south of the Oban road near Tyndrum. Sporadic mining has also been carried out at various points in the region during the 18th and 19th centuries, but the only other notable mines are the copper mines at Tomnadashan on the south side of Loch Tay and at Kilfinan on Loch Fyne.

1

The Kilpatrick, Campsie
and Fintry Hills

Maps: Ordnance Survey One-inch Series, Sheets 54, 60, 61 and Loch Lomond and
the Trossachs Tourist Map.
Bartholomew's Half-inch Series, Sheet 45.

These groups of low hills form a more or less continuous range across
the centre of Scotland between Dumbarton and Stirling. The
Kilpatricks overlook Dumbarton and the north shore of the River
Clyde as far upstream as Clydebank. North-east of them, across the
wooded Strath Blane, are the Campsie Fells which extend eastwards
to the Kilsyth Hills and are the highest and most extensive of the
hills described in this chapter. North-east again, across the forested
Carron Valley with its large reservoir, are the Fintry and Gargunnock
Hills which present an almost continuous escarpment to the north
overlooking the villages of Kippen and Gargunnock.

These hills are composed of lava sheets worn down by ice in past
ages. Some of the prominent rounded tops such as Dumgoyne are
the vent plugs of ancient volcanoes whose hard lava cores have
weathered slowly.

The principal characteristics of all these hills are similar. Their
tops, with one or two notable exceptions such as Dumgoyne and
Meikle Bin, are flat and grassy with considerable areas of eroded peat
bog. These plateaus are intersected by many small streams. The
flanks of the hills on the other hand are in many places steep, and
there are quite considerable escarpments and cliffs overlooking
Blanefield, Lennoxtown, Fintry and Gargunnock. Generally speaking
the hills give rather rough and tiring walking as the grass of their
summits is very tussocky and the peat bogs are in places extensive.

c

It is probably true to say that the most interesting features of these hills are to be found not on their summits, but on their flanks. For example the strange rock formation at the Whangie on the edge of the Kilpatricks, the Corrie of Balglass on the north side of the Campsies and the beautiful burns of Ballagan and Finglen have more interest for the walker and climber than the rather featureless tops. At the Spout of Ballagan the hillside is cut away steeply, and the geological strata are exposed in a series of clearly defined layers.

The southern slopes of the **Kilpatrick Hills** rise quite steeply above the River Clyde between Dumbarton and Clydebank. The interior of the hills is dotted with about a dozen reservoirs, and towards the north the hills drop gradually towards the rather featureless expanse of Dumbarton Muir and Stockie Muir beyond which lie the wide valleys of Strath Endrick and Strath Blane.

Most of the hills are mere swellings in the undulating moorland which characterises the Kilpatricks, and only the highest of them, Duncolm, 1314 ft., is in any way outstanding. Its circular summit rises for about two hundred feet above the surrounding moor, and on the north-east side there are some steep basalt rocks. Fynloch Hill, 1313 ft., is just less than a mile south-west of Duncolm, but it is rather featureless.

The Kilpatricks are mainly of interest as providing good moorland walks within easy reach of Glasgow. There is access to the hills by good tracks and private roads which strike northwards from Milton, Old Kilpatrick and Duntocher on the north side of the River Clyde, and westwards from Craigton, Carbeth and Auchengillan on the A809 road from Glasgow to Drymen. For example there is a good cross-country walk starting at Auchengillan and following a good private road to Burncrooks Reservoir. From there rough going across gradually rising moorland leads south-west to Duncolm. The descent can be made southwards to Greenside Reservoir, and finally down a delightful road by the Loch Humphrey Burn to Cochnohill Farm and Duntocher. There are many other similar walks in these hills.

The most-frequented corner of the Kilpatricks is the Whangie, a remarkable rock feature on the west side of Auchineden Hill, 1171 ft., the northernmost hill of the Kilpatricks. A good path starts at the Queen's View car-park on the A809 road (MR 511808) and contours round the north side of Auchineden Hill for just over a mile. The Whangie is a long, narrow flake of rock which has split off the parent hillside to leave a deep and narrow cleft between it and the hillside. The flake is about a hundred yards long, and is vertical on both sides. The crest is very narrow, generally less than a yard wide, and can be reached by easy scrambles at both ends and at an intermediate point. The traverse along the crest of the flake is an airy scramble. At the northern end of the Whangie there is a much smaller flake known as the Gendarme, whose top can be reached by a Moderate scramble.

The Whangie is probably the most popular rock-climbing practice crag within easy reach of Glasgow. The climbs are all rather short, only two or three on the outside of the main flake exceeding forty feet, and the rock is in places very unreliable. Nevertheless, there are thirty or forty very enjoyable short climbs of all standards on good rock, and the bizarre rock scenery gives the Whangie a character all of its own. A complete graded list of rock climbs at the Whangie is contained in Appendix 1.

The **Campsie Fells** are the highest and most extensive of the groups of hills described in this chapter. The southern slopes of the hills drop steeply to Strath Blane and the valley of the River Kelvin, and the northern side of the hills is bounded by the Endrick Water and the Carron Valley Reservoir. At the western end Dumgoyne, 1402 ft., is a prominent conical hill, certainly the most distinctive of the Campsies. The highest hill, Earl's Seat, 1896 ft., is about two miles east-north-east of Dumgoyne, but being the highest point of an undulating plateau it is not very distinctive.

The Campsies are bisected by the B822 road from Lennoxtown to Fintry, (known locally as the Crow Road), which reaches over a thousand feet at its highest point. East of this road Meikle Bin, 1870 ft., is the highest point, and it is distinctive when seen from a long way off to the north or south. Its northern slopes dropping towards the Carron Valley Reservoir are densely forested. Eastwards from Meikle Bin the fells drop gradually to the Kilsyth–Carronbridge road.

The south side of these hills have some steep, rocky escarpments overlooking Blanefield and Lennoxtown, and on the north side the Corrie of Balglass and the smaller corrie to its west are fine features. The undulating plateau which extends for more than ten miles from west to east without dropping below a thousand feet is for the most part featureless and devoid of tracks save for those made by sheep. The walking across this plateau is very rough in places.

Dumgoyne is probably the most popular of the Campsies by virtue of its isolated position and characteristic appearance. It commands a very fine view of Loch Lomond and the hills beyond. A very pleasant approach to Dumgoyne from Blanefield takes the private road along the line of the Loch Katrine aqueduct. After a mile or so the cottage at Cantywheery is reached and one strikes up the hillside northwards and then north-west towards the summit whose final slopes are best climbed on the west as the south and east sides are steep and rocky. Slackdhu, 1624 ft., can also be climbed easily from Cantywheery, or more directly and steeply from Blanefield.

Earl's Seat is more or less equidistant between Blanefield and the B818 road near Ballikinrain Castle. The possible routes to this hill include the Ballagan Burn from Strathblane, the road to Canty-wheery and an ascent over Clachertyfarlie Knowes, or the Ballikin-rain Burn from the north.

The Corrie of Balglass is a beautiful semi-circular corrie with a lovely little waterfall at its head. The Balglass Burn actually flows out of the next corrie to the west, and is another possible route to Earl's Seat. Both these corries are best approached from the B818 road a mile east of Ballikinrain Castle.

The Crow Road gives easy access to the central part of the Camp-sies, and three tops, Holehead, Dungoil and Lecket Hill can each be climbed in less than three quarters of an hour from the nearest points of the road. Meikle Bin is further afield, and the shortest route to this hill starts at Waterhead Farm a mile and a half north-east of the summit of the Crow Road. From the farm the Bin Burn is followed until the forest is passed and one can strike south-eastwards directly to the top.

A pleasant but much longer route to Meikle Bin starts at Queenzie-burn on the A803 road from Kirkintilloch to Kilsyth. A narrow road leads up into the hills at Corrie Farm, and from there a good track leads on to the Birken Reservoir. The last mile and a half north-westwards to Meikle Bin is trackless and involves a slight drop, but the going is quite easy to the top of the hill.

In winter under a covering of snow the Campsies can give good skiing, although a fair depth of snow is needed to smooth out the tussocky grass. At such times the summit of the Crow Road is the ideal starting point for tours both westwards and eastwards, the best being the traverse to Earl's Seat and descent to Strath Blane.

There is not much rock-climbing to be had in the Campsies, the best being on the face of Slackdhu above Blanefield. The biggest line of cliffs is under the summit of Slackdhu and is bounded on the north-west by Long Gully, a Moderate scramble in summer, but promising better things in winter. In the centre of the face there is another gully known as Coffin Gully. Its first pitch is deeply cut and obvious, but higher up the gully is more like a scoop in the cliffs. *Coffin Gully Buttress* bounds the gully on the left (north-west) and offers a rather scrappy climb of 250 ft., Very Difficult. The first pitch is fairly well defined and overlooks the gully; thereafter there is a section of very bad rock and grass leading to a short vertical crack; the final section is the most difficult, being steep, exposed and none too sound, however it can be avoided by traversing to left or right along grassy ledges.

The best climbing in the Campsies is on a rather insignificant looking cliff about six hundred yards south-east of Coffin Gully. A small stream comes over the edge of the hill and in wet weather there is a little waterfall down a 40 ft. chimney called Jenny's Lum. The cliff to the left of the Lum, although only 40 ft. high is impressively steep and its north-western edge is *Jenny's Lum Arête*, a very fine little climb and the classic problem of the Campsies. The Arête is vertical, the holds good but small, and the climb is not one to linger over as the strain on fingers and arms is great. The standard is Hard Severe. Round the corner on the left of the Arête, *Wallace's Chimney* is a mild Difficult by comparison. The Lum itself is seldom dry, and is lined with slippery green moss; however, when it does dry out it gives a good climb.

A few yards to the right of the Lum is a detached pinnacle. Easy chimneys on both sides of this pinnacle lead to its top from which a stride and scramble leads to the top of the cliff, (Moderate). There are two better climbs on the outside face of the pinnacle. The *Pinnacle Arête* starts at the lowest point and there are a few awkward moves until a mantelshelf is surmounted, (Severe). Left of the Arête, near the left-hand chimney, a steep crack gives a Very Difficult variation. A few yards to the right of the pinnacle there is another smaller pinnacle called *Jacob's Ladder* which gives a short, steep climb on good holds, (Very Difficult).

Elsewhere on Slackdhu the rock is of doubtful quality, often being completely unreliable. There is a two-tier climb between Coffin Gully and Jenny's Lum. The lower half is near a prominent tree, and the upper half (reached after crossing a wide grass terrace) is a little pinnacle followed by a scoop from which a direct exit may be made. Several hundred yards south-east of Jenny's Lum there is a prominent crag on the right of an open gully. The crag is called Black Craig, but this is something of a misnomer as the rock is whitish due to a covering of lichen. There is a grass ledge about one third of the way up the crag, whose total height is about 150 ft. The crag has been climbed several times, but the rock is very loose and vegetatious and in places appears to be held together by ivy. C. M. Allan, who in 1934 made one of the earliest ascents, pronounced it 'barely justifiable', and few would disagree. The crag was the scene of a tragedy in 1935.

On the left of Black Craig the gully forms a little amphitheatre with two smaller gullies above it, both watercourses in wet weather. The left-hand one is narrow and well-defined, being a narrow chimney at its top. The right-hand one is wider. Both have been climbed, but cannot be recommended as they are loose and vegetatious.

Elsewhere in the Campsies there is little of rock-climbing interest. North of Lennoxtown there is a line of cliffs above the Crow Road. The most prominent feature is a dark chimney in the centre of the lowest tier of rock. This is *Moabite Chimney*, and it gives a rather dirty climb ending with a pull-up over a chockstone which appears to be embedded in mud, (30 ft., Very Difficult). The upper tiers of rock appear to be very unsound.

Above Ballikinrain and a little east of Earl's Seat there is a short cliff of columnar basalt on which there are one or two climbs on sound rock. In the Corrie of Balglass there is a big slab of which the only recorded ascent has been made with the help of a top-rope.

The **Fintry** and **Gargunnock Hills** are less interesting than the Campsies. The features of these hills are the almost continuous escarpments along their northern sides, and the fine waterfall at the Spout of Ballochleam. Elsewhere the hills are little more than elevated moorland which drop away gradually towards the south-east. The highest point is Stronend, 1677 ft., at the north-west corner of the Fintry Hills. It can be reached from several points on the Fintry to Kippen road by a short, steep climb. The view from Stronend to the north and north-west across the flat expanse of Flanders Moss is very fine.

There are few tracks and paths through the hills, of which only one will be mentioned. From the west end of the Carron Valley Reservoir a good track leads north through the forest to the farm at

Cringate; thereafter a faint path continues past the deserted cottage at Burnfoot towards the watershed at the head of the Endrick Water. A good track is joined, and this leads over the col and down past the Spout of Ballochleam towards Kippen. These are desolate and featureless hills whose lonely character is epitomised by the deserted cottages at Cringate and Burnfoot.

Transport and Accommodation
There are bus services along most of the roads around the hills described in this chapter. The south side of the Kilpatrick Hills is served by regular buses and trains between Glasgow and Dumbarton. The Glasgow to Drymen and Aberfoyle bus service passes along the A809 road on the north-east side of these hills. There are regular services by bus from Glasgow to Killearn, Strathblane, Lennoxtown, Kilsyth and Stirling which give access to the Campsie Fells. There is a service on school days only between Balfron and Fintry.

There are many hotels in the area covered by this chapter. Possibly the most convenient from the point of view of the hill-walker are those at Killearn, Strathblane, Lennoxtown, Fintry, Carronbridge and Kippen.

There is a Youth Hostel at Fintry.

BIBLIOGRAPHY

Practice Scrambles, G. Thomson, *S.M.C.J.*, Vol. 2, p. 8.
The Whangie, G. Thomson, *S.M.C.J.*, Vol. 2, p. 139.
Hills near Glasgow, H. B. Watt, *S.M.C.J.*, Vol. 2, p. 206.
Saturday Hill Walks near Glasgow, W. W. Naismith, *S.M.C.J.*, Vol. 15, p. 35.
The Campsie Fells, J. N. Orr, *S.M.C.J.*, Vol. 21, p. 18.

2

The Lomond and Ochil Hills

Maps: Ordnance Survey One-inch Series, Sheets 55 and 56.
Bartholomew's Half-inch Series, Sheet 45 or 49.

The Lomonds and the Ochils, together with a few smaller hills near them, lie between the Forth and Tay valleys in the counties of Fife, Kinross, Clackmannan and part of Perthshire. This is not by any stretch of the imagination a mountainous part of the country, and the hills are much lower than their Highland neighbours. They owe their popularity to their nearness to the central part of Scotland, and their main interest is for hill-walkers. Although there is a little rock-climbing on the Lomonds and on Dumyat in the Ochils, rock-climbers living in this part of Scotland are more likely to look to the Hawcraig near Aberdour and Craig-y-Barns near Dunkeld for their climbing practice. (Climbs on these crags are described in the *Climbers' Guide to Creag Dubh and the Eastern Outcrops* published by Graham Tiso and will not be mentioned here.)

The Lomond Hills are rather a modest trio when judged by their height alone; however, they are fine little hills, rising steeply above Loch Leven and the Howe of Fife, and they are conspicuous features in the Fife landscape. The characteristic rounded summits of the East and West Lomond can be recognised from many distant viewpoints.

The three hills, East and West Lomond and Bishop Hill, form a semicircular group. The outer side of the semicircle, facing north and west, forms a steep and fairly continuous hillside, craggy in places, while within the semicircle formed by the tops there is an extensive area of high moorland and hill farms which drops gradually to the south-east and holds several reservoirs. On the north the rich farmland of the Howe of Fife reaches right to the foot of the steep scarp of West Lomond.

Access to these hills is very easy from all sides as they are ringed by roads. In addition, a minor road from Falkland to Leslie crosses the pass between East and West Lomond at a height of almost 1000 ft., and there are many tracks and paths over the hills.

West Lomond, 1713 ft., is the highest of the three hills. Its summit is a grassy dome rising above the long escarpment of the north face. The easiest ascent can be made from the Falkland–Leslie road; from a point on it two miles due east of the summit of the hill a track leads westwards, becoming grassy as it climbs gradually across the moor to end near Miller's Loch. Thereafter it is an easy climb to the top. This is a very easy approach, and it is quite possible to use a bicycle for part of the way.

From the north-east the hill can be climbed from Strathmiglo by a minor road (becoming a track) through the Drumdreel woods; this brings one below the steep north-east side of West Lomond and the ascent can be made by the wide, easy gully in the middle of the Craigengaw cliffs.

From the north-west one can ascend by way of a track south of the Glen Burn to reach Glenvale, a beautiful little valley with miniature waterfalls, bathing pools and white sandstone cliffs. This glen is also known as the Covenanters' Glen, and a niche at the foot of one of the sandstone cliffs is John Knox's Pulpit. From Glenvale an easy climb northwards up grassy slopes leads to West Lomond in about half an hour.

East Lomond, 1394 ft., (1471 ft. on Bartholomew's Map) stands immediately above the old town of Falkland with its famous Palace. The hill can be climbed in a very short time from Falkland by the track through the woods on its north side. Alternatively, one can leave the A912 road a mile and a half south-east of Falkland and follow the hill road by Purin Den. This road, which crosses East Lomond a short distance south of the top, is followed to a little wood high up on the eastern shoulder whence a path leads towards the summit where there is a fine indicator.

Bishop Hill is the southernmost of the three Lomonds, and its summit is a long, undulating, grassy plateau, steep-sided to the west. The One-inch Map does not give a height, and indicates that it is just less than 1500 ft.; Bartholomew's map gives the highest point, near the north end of the hill, as 1510 ft.

The south end of the plateau, White Craigs, 1492 ft., is most quickly climbed from Kinnesswood, there being a track for most of the way. From the east a hill road climbs to an old limestone quarry just north of White Craigs.

The 1510 ft. top near the north end of the plateau can be climbed from Glenvale (q.v.), there being a grassy track for part of the way. A more direct route from the west side is to take the minor road from Balgeddie towards Glenlomond Hospital. The road is left just before reaching the hospital and a track through the fields can be followed directly towards the hill. The final steep ascent leads past the weird pinnacle known as Carlin Maggie which stands in front of a small dolerite cliff. The grassy, cairnless top is close at hand above this crag.

The traverse of the three Lomond tops is a good walk, and with adequate bus services and hostelries on the surrounding roads it need not be too exhausting. There are grand views from these hills on a fine day, and one can see from the snows of Ben Macdhui to the smoke of Auld Reekie, with many a lower hill and valley besides. The contrast between the mountainous north and the industrial south is striking.

The Lomond Hills also have their little offerings for the rock-climber, although whether or not these are appreciated will depend on the preferences of the climber himself. If he is interested only in firm, clean rock he should look elsewhere, for it must be admitted that the dolerite of the Lomonds is in a state of continual decay. J. H. B. Bell, who pioneered the early climbs, recommended crampons for dealing with the vegetation and advised seconds to wear goggles to protect their eyes from the sand and grit dislodged by their leaders. If one is prepared to overlook these shortcomings in exchange for the grand views, the following notes may be of help:

Bishop Hill. There are minor crags on the south-west side of this hill, but the best rocks overlook Glenlomond Hospital. Carlin Maggie is the centre of attraction, but it seems that the ascent of this elegant pinnacle has only been accomplished with the aid of a shoulder on the inside, or wooden wedges on the outside. Several of these wedges (at the time of writing) remain in the crack on the outside face of the pinnacle in a state of decay.

The cliffs behind Carlin Maggie offer a variety of problems on columnar dolerite – mostly chimneys and cracks about 30 ft. high. N. Macniven has reported about twenty routes here and elsewhere, but written records are absent, and probably unnecessary. In one or two places decaying wooden wedges indicate the lines of some of the harder routes; elsewhere the routes are easier, as for example a chimney near the north end of the crag. There is another similar crag a few hundred yards south of Carlin Maggie.

Glenvale. The largest of the white sandstone outcrops on the north side of this glen gives some short climbs. John Knox's Pulpit is a niche at the bottom of the cliff, and a 15 ft. climb on its left leads to the next ledge. This is overhung, and forms a large cave or amphitheatre from which a very hard pitch leads to the top of the cliff. There is also a rather hard climb on the true right of the waterfall a short distance upstream from John Knox's Pulpit.

West Lomond. The main feature is Craigengaw, a cliff about half a mile north-east of the summit and a few hundred feet below it. A broad, easy-angled gully – the Great Gully – runs up through the cliffs, and all the climbs are very close to it. The east wall of Great Gully is particularly loose and nasty, even by Lomond standards, as a result of a recent landslide. There are two chimneys which have been climbed, the deeper one being *Professor's Chimney* (30 ft., S); a small pinnacle has also been climbed, but most of the rock on this side of Great Gully is quite rotten.

On the other side of Great Gully the angle between its west wall and the north face of Craigengaw forms a steep nose of rock which is split in its lower half by a grassy groove. This is *The Split Nose*, the most notorious of Lomond climbs (130 ft., V.S., J. H. B. Bell). For the first 25 ft. there is a choice of two difficult cracks; then a 60 ft. groove follows, vegetatious to start with and ending as a vertical chimney with a sensational move leftwards at its top to reach the Copestone, a large boulder on the Nose. A traverse right and a short ascent lead to the Nettleshelf, beyond which some cracked slabs lead to the Outlook Slab which forms a fitting end to the climb.

There are no recorded climbs on the main face to the west of the Split Nose. On the west wall of Great Gully there is a narrow, grassy gully – *Moonshine Gully*, (125 ft., D., J. H. B. Bell) – which gives an interesting climb for botanists. From a point about half way up this gully one can traverse rightwards to the Copestone of the Split Nose; this is the *Lateral Split Nose*, (30 ft., V.D., J. H. B. Bell). The continuation up the upper part of the Split Nose is Severe. To the left of Moonshine Gully, and close to it, there is a conspicuous block of rock projecting from the cliff; this is the Anvil. The ascent can be made from directly below, and a difficult pull up is needed to reach the sloping ledge just below the Anvil. This ledge is traversed leftwards to reach the top from the south-east, (50ft., S., J. H. B. Bell).

A short distance west of the Split Nose, and almost at the same level, there is a small pinnacle – the Corboff Pinnacle – just below the main line of crags. It is really a double pinnacle as a vertical crack splits it in two, and the ascent from the downhill side is made by this crack. The uphill side of the pinnacle is short and easy.

To the north of West Lomond, and situated at about 700 ft. near the foot of the escarpment, there are the curious rock formations of the Maiden's Bower and the Bannetstane. The Bower is a circular cave with the floor at ground level, and a vaulted roof 8 or 9 ft. high. On the other side of the rock is the Bannetstane, a mushroom-shaped block of sandstone perched on a narrow stalk. The top is gained by a stride from the main rock and a good hand pull. On the east side, above the Bower, there are one or two entertaining traverses and a circular rock window, and the rocks below the Bannetstane facing north-west give a good little climb.

Three other minor climbing grounds in east Fife may be mentioned. Probably the best of the three is Craiglug at Dairsie (MR 404183). To approach the crag, one leaves the A91 road from Cupar to St. Andrews at the Cupar end of Dairsie village; take the road past the school and some cottages and follow the track signposted 'Fingask'. Craiglug is then obvious across a field on the right. The crag faces west and is ideal for an evening visit as it gets the last rays of the sun. The rock is dolerite and fairly sound. The routes, which vary in length from 20 to 50 ft., are numbered with paint on the rock for easy identification; however, these man-made marks may disappear in time. The early climbs on Craiglug were probably made by climbers from the R.A.F. Leuchars Mountain Rescue Team and St. Andrews University Mountaineering Club; more recently some hard routes have been done by G. Farquhar and R. Farquhar. Starting at the north end of the crag, the following routes are recommended: 8 (V.D.), 9 (S.), 10 (V.D.), 11 (V.S.), 12 and 13 (both S.). There is a gap as the crag diminishes, and the next noteworthy route is 17 (S.). Finally, there are some very good and hard problems on the short, overhanging wall at the south end of the crag. The best climb of all, however, is the 400 ft. Girdle Traverse.

The other areas of rock-climbing interest in east Fife are near St. Andrews. Three-quarters of a mile south-east of the town along the bay there is a thin tower of sandstone – the Maiden Rock. Seen end on it appears as a true pinnacle with steep sides, but it is in fact more like a flake with a level summit ridge. There are over a dozen routes on sound rock of 25 to 35 ft., and a girdle traverse of 75 ft. Half a mile further along the coast the Rock and Spindle gives one route, easy to within 12 ft. of the top and then involving a disagreeable traverse rightwards before the last part of the ascent.

The Buddo Rock is 3½ miles south-east of St. Andrews near Buddo Ness, and is reached from the coast road by a farm track and across fields. There are several obvious routes to the top, which is grassy and flat. The rock is split and one can walk through from one side to the other. The most entertaining route – Arch Traverse (30 ft., S.) – starts from near the rock arch at the south-east side and goes right, up greasy sandstone, to the top. The main difficulty is half way up.

South-west of the Lomonds there are some low hills of minor interest. Benarty Hill stands on the south side of Loch Leven, and the Saline and Cleish Hills form an area of high moorland further west. Benarty, 1167 ft., like the Lomonds, has a steep north face with a small dolerite crag. It can be quickly climbed from Vane on Loch Leven where there is a wildfowl observatory and a short nature trail. The view from the top across Loch Leven to the Lomonds is very pleasant.

The **Cleish Hills** are rather featureless, and the tops are rough and marshy. Dumglow, 1241 ft., is the highest point and it can be ascended in half an hour from the B9097 road on its north side. Two miles to its west, Wether Hill, 1100 ft., is close to the highest point of the A823 road from Dunfermline to Rumbling Bridge from which it can be climbed in quarter of an hour. West of this road lie the **Saline Hills**, with its two highest points, Knock Hill, 1189 ft., and Saline Hill, 1178 ft., both easily accessible from the old coal mine at Steelend, 2 miles east of Saline village. The traverse of the four hills just mentioned gives a good afternoon walk.

The **Ochil Hills** form an area of grassy, rounded summits about 28 miles from east to west, and 8 miles from north to south at their broadest point. The range is divided in two by Glen Devon and Glen Eagles, and the highest hills (all those over 2000 ft.) are in the western portion.

On their south side these hills form a steep and imposing front overlooking the wide valley of the River Forth, and the name Ochil is derived from the Celtic word 'uchil' meaning high. On the north the hills fall away gently in long, even slopes towards Strath Allan and Strath Earn. From most viewpoints the Ochils appear as a continuous range of gently undulating hills rather than well-defined separate tops, and this impression is quite correct. The main range of 2000 ft. hills is 7 miles long (as the crow flies), reaches its highest point at Bencleuch, 2363 ft., and never drops below 1750 ft.

With the exception of Dumyat, the small hill at the western end of the Ochils, the rest of the range is grassy and smooth. There is very little heather, only a few areas of rough, eroded peat occur, and there are practically no crags or areas of scree. One can therefore wander more or less at will over these hills, and there are comparatively few well-defined walkers' paths. Sheep tracks abound, but they do not always lead the walker in the direction in which he wants to go. In very thick weather the featureless nature of these hills may make route finding difficult; however, the existence of fences on most of the ridges and summits makes the task of navigation through clouds much easier.

Access to the main tops of the Ochils is particularly easy from the south, and Menstrie, Alva, Tillicoultry and Dollar are the usual starting points. The hills rise steeply above these towns, and there are several glens cutting deeply into the hillsides. Some of these glens are so steep-sided as to form narrow gorges which, although they are spectacular in scenery, do not give easy walking. From the north-east there is easy access up Glensherup, Glen Quey and the head of Glen Devon, but these approaches to the tops are generally longer than those from the south. At the north-west corner of the Ochils there is a minor road from Dunblane over Sheriff Muir, and this makes a convenient starting point for walks in that part of the hills.

North-east of Glen Devon, the hills are lower, through still of the same rounded, grassy character. Several roads cross this area; the B934 from Muckhart to Dunning is the highest of these, and most of the hills in the area can be climbed easily from it. In addition, there are a few pleasant and easy cross-country walks; for example, a track leaves Glen Devon near the Youth Hostel, crosses a pass about a mile north and descends the Coul Burn to Auchterarder, a distance of 10 miles.

Bencleuch, 2363 ft., (named Glenwhappen Rig on some older maps) is the highest, and in many ways the most attractive of the Ochils. Its summit is well-defined and more distinctive than most of its neighbours, and commands an extensive and unrestricted view in all directions. The ascent can be made from several points. From Alva a path climbs across the south face of The Nebit and continues up the Silver Glen to the col between The Nebit and Ben Ever. From there it is probably best to climb northwards to **Ben Ever,** 2010 ft., and then descend slightly before making the final ascent to Bencleuch along the line of a fence. There is an indicator on the summit. From Tillicoultry one can climb north-westwards up the grassy ridge on the west side of the Daiglen Burn to join the preceding route at Ben Ever. Alternatively, one can climb the grassy ridge between the Daiglen and Gannel burns to **The Law**, 2094 ft. From there the continuation to Bencleuch involves hardly any descent, and a fence can be followed past a rather unsightly radio beacon.

The ascent of Bencleuch from Dollar is rather longer. The road on the west side of the Dollar Burn is followed and then a path beside the golf course leads to the open hillside opposite the magnificently situated Castle Campbell. A grassy path up the south-west side of the Burn of Sorrow is followed and eventually the source of the burn is reached at Maddy Moss. (This point can also be reached by a path from Tillicoultry.) Easy walking leads to **Andrew Gannel Hill**, 2195 ft., whose summit is marked by a very small cairn a hundred yards south of the fence. (This hill is not named on the One-inch Map, but is marked by the 2150 ft. contour.) A short descent across a peaty hollow leads to the easy ridge of Bencleuch.

An alternative route from Dollar to Bencleuch is over **King's Seat Hill**, 2111 ft. The grassy ridge dropping towards Castle Campbell makes an easy line of ascent or descent. There is a large cairn overlooking Dollar, but the highest point appears to be about two hundred yards north-west, and is marked by a smaller cairn.

North-west of Bencleuch a grassy ridge leads out to Ben Buck, a flat-topped and uninteresting spur. From there to **Blairdenon Hill**, 2073 ft., (the westernmost of the 2000 ft. hills) there is a wide expanse of rough and boggy ground which is likely to be very confusing in thick weather. However, three fences meet at the summit of Blairdenon Hill, and so route-finding is made easier. A few hundred yards west of this top a wooden cross marks the remains of a crashed aircraft. The shortest ascent of Blairdenon Hill can be made from the road over Sheriff Muir, either up Glen Tye or along the tops on the north side of this glen.

There is a good cross-country walk from Tillicoultry (or Dollar) to Blackford. A path climbs steeply from Tillicoultry up the east side of the Mill Glen and continues along the slopes on the east side of the Gannel Burn. At the head of the burn this path (which becomes rather indistinct) turns north, crosses the open pass between Andrew Gannel Hill and Skythorn Hill, and descends the east side of the Broich Burn to the Upper Glendevon Reservoir. The way to Blackford continues northwards by Glen Bee, over the low pass west of Craigentaggart Hill and down to Kinpaunch and Blackford (10 miles). Alternatively, from the reservoir one can descend by the Lower Reservoir to the main road in Glen Devon. A shorter walk takes one from Dollar northwards by a right-of-way over the narrow pass leading to Glen Quey, which is followed past a reservoir to Glen Devon.

Tarmangie Hill, 2117 ft., and **Whitewisp Hill,** 2110 ft., lie to the north of Dollar and can be easily climbed from there. From Glen Devon the round of Glen Sherup can be made over **Innerdownie,** 2004 ft., Whitewisp, Tarmangie, Scad Hill and Ben Shee. These summits are broad and grassy, and a dry-stone dyke runs along the crest of Tarmangie Hill and out towards Innerdownie.

In winter a modest covering of snow is enough to give excellent ski-touring over the Ochils; the smooth contours of the hills make ideal terrain, although some of the southern glens are rather steep-sided. Unfortunately it is unusual for a lot of snow to lie on the Ochils for long periods, and good skiing days are probably few in an average winter.

Before leaving the area around Dollar, there are a few more points of interest that may be mentioned. Castle Campbell is magnificently situated above Dollar on a promontory between the Burn of Sorrow and the Burn of Care. It is now owned by the National Trust for Scotland, and is well worth a visit. A quarry on the right of the road leading from Dollar up to the castle might give a little rock-climbing. At Rumbling Bridge, 3 miles east of Dollar, the River Devon rushes through a deep gorge, and a mile downstream at Cauldron Linn the river plunges from one cauldron to another down a chasm 80 ft. deep.

Turning now to the western end of the Ochil Hills, **Dumyat,** 1376 ft., is the very prominent little hill which despite its modest height is much more easily recognised than its higher neighbours. Its summit is a little cone, and a level shoulder forming the smaller west top projects out towards Stirling. The south side of the hill drops steeply in a series of crags and little cliffs to the road between Menstrie and Blairlogie. The most prominent feature of the south side of the hill is the big gully – the Warlock Glen – which separates the summit from the west top.

The hill can be easily climbed from Menstrie by a path up its south-east shoulder. A more interesting route starts at Blairlogie, and taking the lane eastwards through the village, climbs gradually across

1. Langlauf on the Campsies, looking towards Ben Lomond.

2. Strath Blane and Dumgoyne.

3. Jenny's Lum Arête, the hardest climb on the Campsies.

4. Backstep Chimney, a classic problem at the Whangie.

5. Looking west from Benarty to the Ochils.

6. West Lomond from the north.

the south face to reach the foot of the Warlock Glen. The glen is followed upwards through an impressive little gorge until it is possible to turn right and climb easy grass slopes to the summit.

Rock-climbing in the Ochils is for all practical purposes confined to Dumyat as the only other big crag, Craig Leith above Alva, is not at all pleasant. The topography of the rocks on Dumyat is more or less as follows: Warlock Glen divides the hill in two, and the main rock-climbing area is on the east side of the glen at an altitude of 800 to 1000 ft. The west side of the glen has some rounded buttresses high up, but they are very vegetatious. To the east of the glen there is a line of cliffs high up extending towards the corner of the hill overlooking Menstrie, and to the west of the glen there are two lines of cliffs, the higher one extending round into Warlock Glen to join the buttresses there. In addition there are several small outcrops and buttresses at a lower level than the main cliffs.

Nearly everywhere the rock is of a very unreliable nature, being a conglomerate of a rather 'plum pudding' character. The 'plums' are rounded stones (from the size of marbles to oranges) which serve as holds, and they must be handled with care, being gently pressed inwards rather than pulled outwards; Dumyat resents rough handling. Nevertheless, a number of sound climbs have been discovered among the many whin and grass covered crags, and these climbs give some very good sport.

The most pleasant way to combine the rock-climbs with an ascent of Dumyat is to start at Blairlogie and proceed upwards from crag to crag. Take the lane eastwards through the village and beyond the iron gate turn uphill along a path climbing leftwards. The lowest crag is only 50 yards ahead behind a big tree, and it overhangs its base except at the right end where there is a slab in a corner. This is the start of the first climb.

1. *Prelim* (70 ft., V.D.). Climb the slab for 30 ft. to a tree, and then a crack behind the tree. Traverse left to a ledge, climb some detached blocks, traverse to another tree and climb the wall above.

One can continue directly upwards through whin bushes for about 300 ft. to a little crag with two stunted trees growing on it. To the right of the right-hand tree there is a short Moderate slab in a corner. To the left and slightly higher there is another steep little crag with two prominent parallel cracks. The right-hand one is Difficult, the other one is much harder. One now traverses for some distance eastwards across a grassy depression, climbing slightly to the lowest point of a continuous line of crags. The next climb starts just to the right of this lowest point.

2. *Maureen* (60 ft., M.). Climb a pleasant slab onto an easy-angled rock rib which is followed over a short wall to a grass ledge.

Traverse downwards to the right along this ledge to the start of the next climb.

3. *Murphy's Crack* (30 ft., V.D.). Climb the obvious crack and exit right at the top.

About 60 yards to the right of these climbs, and only slightly higher, there is a steep wall with an open groove on its left. This groove is the next climb.

4. *Communion Wall* (50 ft., V.D.). Climb to a ledge at the foot of the groove and continue straight up.

Continue walking uphill and rather towards the right for about 100 yards to the foot of a continuous line of crags. Look for a narrow grass gully with a pillar projecting from the crag on its right. To the right of the pillar is a curving crack, and a few feet further right, in the middle of the wall, there is a small circular cave. The next three routes are here.

5. *Pillar Crack* (40 ft., V.D.). Climb the crack which is undercut at one point, but provided with good holds.

6. *Logie Buttress* (50 ft., D.). Climb up to the cave, step left and continue parallel to the crack.

7. *Nameless* (60 ft., V.D.). 20 ft. left of the previous route one can climb the wall by the line of least resistance.

Continue eastwards by a narrow path along the foot of this line of crags. As one approaches the Warlock Glen a steep wall with a prominent crack at its right edge is reached. The left side of the wall has been climbed with a top rope up a slab and heathery groove. The crack is a more feasible route.

8. *The Black Crack* (60 ft., D.). Climb the crack by wedging tactics to an excellent belay.

The path continues round the hillside into the Warlock Glen, but the next climbs are at a lower level so one must descend a short distance towards two prominent little gullies on the opposite side of the glen. The lower (right-hand) of these gullies is Raeburn's Gully, and it gives the best climb on the hill.

9. *Raeburn's Gully* (150 ft., V.D.). Scramble up the narrow entrance to the start of the difficulties, and climb three chimney pitches to a large chockstone. Traverse across a slab on the left of

the gully and finish up the outside on easier rock and steep grass. The gully on the left of Raeburn's is Cirque Gully, and it is an easy scramble. On its left wall is Raeburn's Pinnacle which can be reached by a Moderate chimney on the left wall of Cirque Gully. The direct ascent of the Pinnacle from the foot of the gully has been done with a top rope, but the rock is bad. A few yards left of Cirque Gully, a short grassy gully ends below two cracks. The right-hand crack is easy and ends on a ledge from which a scramble leftwards across an easy-angled slab leads to the Pinnacle.

A few yards further left another short grassy gully ends at a ledge under an ivy-covered overhang.

10. *Ivy Slab* (50 ft., S.). Scramble up the gully to the ledge and traverse right to reach a smooth slab which is climbed direct. The route ends just above Raeburn's Pinnacle.

A few yards further left there is an obvious crack facing down the glen. It ends on a ledge half way up the cliff.

11. *Bell's Crack* (20 ft., S.). Climb the crack (watch for crows in the nesting season) and traverse left along the ledge to an easy descent in a gully.

Continuing up the glen for a few yards, one comes to a prominent chimney formed by two diverging cracks separated at the top by an overhang.

12. *Fork Chimney* (30 ft., S.). Climb the chimney taking the left-hand crack at the top.

13. *Knife Chimney* (20 ft., V.D.). This short and strenuous chimney is a few yards beyond and above Fork Chimney.

Beyond this climb Warlock Glen opens out as the flat col at its head is approached, and one can turn eastwards to the summit of Dumyat, passing a small crag en route. By continuing over the col at the head of the glen and descending towards Sheriff Muir one reaches a line of crags on the right of the burn. These crags have been climbed at almost every point, and the climbs are easily found.

Below Raeburn's Gully, on the east side of Warlock Glen, there is an area of vegetatious crags with a few trees and many whin bushes. There is some indeterminate climbing in this area, including Hornbeam Gully which the author has failed to identify from among several possible grassy gullies. Traversing eastwards at a high level, a very narrow path crosses the steep hillside below a line of crags, and beyond a grassy gully one comes to a little pinnacle jutting out from the cliff. The crack behind the pinnacle is *Lizard Chimney* (35 ft.,

V.D.); the rock is sound. Further east the path, which is very narrow in places, passes below a steep wall with bulging overhangs at its top. Attempts to climb this part of the crag seem (not surprisingly) to have been unsuccessful, but a short distance further east, near the corner overlooking Menstrie, two short, difficult climbs have been done on unreliable rock.

Low down in Warlock Glen there is a crag on the east bank of the burn (which is barely a trickle in dry weather). The south face of this crag is whin-covered, but the west face is clean and gives a good short route on excellent rock, *Scott's Corner* (30 ft., S.). The problem is to reach the niche high up on the right edge of the face. About 50 yards east and down from this climb, there is another whin-covered crag. At its right side a clean slab in a corner provides the start of *Slab and Groove* (60 ft., V.D.). On the west side of the burn, and at the same level, there is a small isolated buttress which gives two or three climbs – easy on the right, harder in the centre.

Credit for the climbs on Dumyat goes to H. Raeburn, J. H. B. Bell and (more recently) members of the Ochils Mountaineering Club.

Finally, on the south side of the hill under the Wallace Monument, R. N. Campbell and his associates have unearthed (the word is used advisedly) a few interesting climbs on Abbey Craig. There are two crags, the upper one on which no routes have yet been completed, and the lower one which is just above the River Forth. This lower crag forms a rounded buttress; two routes have been done. The better route is on the left of the buttress. Start 20 ft. up from and left of the lowest rocks, go up and then right into a groove which is climbed to an overhang. Traverse 10 ft. left to a niche, pull out on the right and climb a 40 ft. wall to the top. The difficulty is sustained (100 ft., S.). The other route starts 20 ft. to the right of the foot of the buttress; climb leftwards to the crest of the buttress and follow a groove up its front (100 ft., V.S.).

Transport and Accommodation
The area covered in this chapter has many bus services, and it would be superfluous to list them. All the hills described can be easily reached from bus routes.

Similarly, there are numerous hotels in the towns and villages near these hills, and a list is unnecessary. There are Youth Hostels at Falkland, Glendevon, Stirling and (rather further from the hills) at Perth.

3

The Luss Hills

Maps: Ordnance Survey One-inch Series, Sheet 53, and Loch Lomond and the Trossachs Tourist Map.
Bartholomew's Half-inch Series, Sheet 44.

This group of hills is situated between Loch Lomond and Loch Long, and is bounded on the south by Glen Fruin. The group is roughly ten miles in extent from north to south, and seven miles from east to west at its widest point.

The highest point in this group, Doune Hill, is 2409 ft. high, and there are about a dozen distinct hills over 2000 ft. Generally speaking they are smooth and grassy in character, particularly in the southern half of the group; however, the hills have a certain amount of individuality as they are separated from each other by low cols and glens. Because of their very grassy character these hills have nothing to offer the rock-climber, and it is even doubtful if any interesting winter climbing could be found. On the other hand, the very smooth grassy ridges of the southern hills make them suitable for ski-touring with only a comparatively thin covering of snow.

The main attraction of the Luss Hills is the pleasant hill-walking that they offer within easy reach of Glasgow and its neighbouring towns, and their position between the Firth of Clyde, Loch Lomond and the Arrochar Alps gives some grand views from their tops.

The A82 road from Balloch to Tarbet along the east side of Loch Lomond gives easy access to the Luss Hills by roads up Glen Fruin, Glen Luss and Glen Douglas. There is a good road through Glen Fruin from Loch Lomond to Garelochhead. In Glen Luss the road goes about two miles from Luss village to Edentaggart Farm, beyond which a rough track leads a further two miles up the glen to the shepherd's cottage at Gleann ma Caoruinn. A few miles further north a narrow road levels from Inverbeg on Loch Lomond through Glen Douglas to Loch Long. Thus all the hills described in this chapter are within very easy reach of the nearest road. Access from the west is less easy, and is restricted in some areas by military installations and firing ranges.

The hills between Glen Fruin and Glen Luss are smooth and grassy, with broad ridges, and they are probably the best of the Luss Hills for skiing. The southern slopes above Glen Fruin are very gentle, but the northern sides drop steeply into the head of Glen Luss. The highest of this group is **Beinn Chaorach**, 2338 ft., and this hill can be most easily climbed from Auchengaich Farm near the head of Glen Fruin. Alternatively it can be climbed from Glen Luss by continuing beyond Edentaggart Farm for a mile, crossing the Luss Water, and climbing the east ridge of the hill. The view from Beinn Chaorach south-westwards down the Firth of Clyde towards Arran is very fine.

From Beinn Chaorach a broad ridge leads south-east for half a mile to **Beinn Tharsuinn**, 2149 ft., (marked by a very small cairn), and then eastwards to the flat grassy top of Pt. 2275 ft. Here the ridge divides, the southern branch dropping gradually over Balcnock, 2092 ft., to the moors above Glen Fruin. The eastern continuation from Pt. 2275 ft. goes to **Creag an Leinibh,** 2158 ft., where the ridge divides again and one can descend to Loch Lomondside either eastwards by Coille-eughain Hill to Luss village, or south-eastwards by Beinn Ruisg and Creachan Hill. The lower slopes of these hills above Loch Lomond are beautifully wooded.

Beinn a' Mhanaich, 2328 ft., is a more isolated hill. It lies about two miles north-north-west of Beinn Chaorach, and is separated from it by a low col about 1150 ft. The long, gradually rising south ridge gives an easy ascent from Strone at the head of Glen Fruin. The north side of Beinn a' Mhanaich is one of the few places in the Luss Hills that is distinctly steep and rocky.

The central group of the Luss Hills is best approached from Edentaggart Farm. **Beinn Eich,** 2302 ft., (the prominent conical hill seen from Luss or from the east side of Loch Lomond near Balmaha) is easily climbed from the farm in just over an hour. From the summit, which is marked by a small cairn of quartzite stones, a well-defined grassy ridge leads north-west and drops to a broad, peaty col. The ascent to **Doune Hill** along the broad grassy ridge from this col takes one over Beinn Lochain, and there is a slight dip between these two hills which is not shown on the One-inch Map. Doune Hill itself has two tops, the lower one, 2298 ft., being separated from the higher one, 2409 ft., by half a mile and a steep descent and reascent. A shorter approach to Doune Hill can be made from Doune Farm in Glen Douglas. The north-east side of the hill is seamed by several tree-filled gullies.

Cruach an t-Sithein, 2244 ft., a mile south-west of Doune Hill, is a fine little peak, possibly the shapeliest of all the Luss Hills, with steep sides all round and a small, grassy summit table. The shortest approach is from Glenmallan on Loch Long, ascending by the birch-wooded Allt Derigan. The approach by Glen Luss is longer, but very pleasant, the track up the glen being followed to the cottage at Gleann ma Caoruinn. From there the walk continues along the grassy flats by the river to the foot of Cruach an t-Sithein which is easily climbed up its south-east side. The walk up Glen Luss to its head, and down the Allt Derigan to Loch Long is the best low-level route through the Luss Hills.

There is also an easy pass from Glen Luss to Glen Douglas. Starting near Glenmallochan Farm two miles up Glen Luss, a good track leads for a mile or so up Glen Mallochan, but in due course the path deteriorates and the glen becomes trackless and boggy. At the foot of Doune Hill the way turns north-east, crosses a low grassy pass at about 750 ft. and descends to Glen Douglas at Inveruchitan cottage. To the east of this pass are **Mid Hill,** 2149 ft., and **Beinn Dubh,** 2108 ft., the latter being easily climbed from Luss village by its long south-east ridge. The south side of these two hills is steep and grassy, but the north side is more rugged, with several tree-filled gullies dropping to the wooded lower reaches of Glen Douglas.

The upper part of Glen Douglas and the Cona Ghleann below Doune Hill are rather desecrated by military installations, most of them fortunately underground. The northern side of Doune Hill resembles a large-scale concrete rabbit warren. On the north side of Glen Douglas are the last three hills of this chapter, **Beinn Bhreac,** 2233 ft.; **Ben Reoch,** 2168 ft., and **Tullich Hill,** 2075 ft. All three can be easily climbed in a short round starting and finishing at Invergroin Farm in Glen Douglas. They have no special features, however Ben Reoch (which can also be easily climbed from Arrochar or Tarbet) commands a very fine view of the Arrochar Alps across the head of Loch Long and the Crianlarich mountains beyond the narrow, northern end of Loch Lomond.

Although the Luss Hills have been described in small groups suitable for short days' walking, it is of course possible to make much longer expeditions through the hills. For example, one could go from Garelochhead Station to Arrochar and Tarbet Station between trains, and include three or four summits en route.

Transport and Accommodation

There is a frequent bus service between Glasgow and Luss, and the Glasgow to Fort William bus service passes along the A82 road on the west side of Loch Lomond. The Glasgow to Oban bus service goes by Helensburgh, Garelochhead and the A814 road along the east side of Loch Long.

There is a frequent train service between Glasgow and Helensburgh every day. The West Highland Line from Glasgow to Oban and Fort William has four or five trains per day (no Sunday service); there are stations at Helensburgh (Upper), Garelochhead and Arrochar and Tarbet.

There are hotels at Helensburgh, Garelochhead, Luss, Inverbeg, Arrochar and Tarbet.

Youth Hostels at Loch Lomond (Auchendennan House near Alexandria), Inverbeg and Ardgartan (near Arrochar).

4

Ben Lomond and Surroundings

Maps: Ordnance Survey One-inch Series, Sheet 53 and the Loch Lomond and the Trossachs Tourist Map.
Bartholomew's Half-inch Series, Sheets 45 and 48.

Ben Lomond, 3192 ft., is the most southerly of Scotland's 3000 ft. mountains, and with the possible exception of Ben Nevis and Cairngorm it is the most popular and frequently ascended of all the major Scottish peaks. No doubt this popularity is in part due to the accessibility of the mountain from Glasgow and mid-Scotland; it is quite possible to leave Glasgow by car after lunch, climb Ben Lomond and be back in time for supper. In addition, however, the dominating position of the mountain on the edge of the Highlands and the wonderful views from its summit (on a clear day) contribute to its popularity.

The references to Ben Lomond in literature show that its fascination is not only of recent date, but that the mountain exercised its spell on many who passed along the shores of Loch Lomond in the years gone by. One of the earliest narrated attempts to ascend Ben Lomond appeared in a poem, dated 1785, inscribed on a pane of glass in the old inn at Tarbet. Unfortunately the pane is no longer there.

In most of the early references to Ben Lomond there is a tendency to magnify the difficulties of the ascent, due no doubt to the air of mystery and lurking danger that surrounded the mountains two hundred years ago. Thus John Stoddart in 1799 wrote of the ascent: 'That which you look toward as an unbroken surface, upon your approach becomes divided by impassable valleys: an unheard rill becomes a roaring torrent, and a gentle slope is found to be an unscalable cliff.' He went on to describe the north side of Ben Lomond as 'exciting a degree of surprise, arising almost to terror: this mighty mass which hitherto had appeared to be an irregular cone placed on a spreading base, suddenly presents itself as an imperfect crater, with one side forcibly torn off, leaving a stupendous precipice of two thousand feet to the bottom.' One may question the accuracy of Stoddart's estimate of the height of the northern cliffs, but no one would quarrel with his feelings on reaching the summit: 'far above the clouds of the vale ... it seemed as if I had been suddenly transported into a new state of existence, cut off from every meaner association and invisibly united with the surrounding purity and brightness.'

There is a good account in *S.M.C.J.* Vol. 1 of an early ascent of Ben Lomond in 1822 by William and Mary Howitt, and they too were mightily impressed by the dangers – trembling bogs and impetuous torrents. However, as far as the usual route from Rowardennan is concerned, John MacCulloch very truly described it in 1811 as 'an ascent without toil or difficulty: a mere walk of pleasure.'

Ben Lomond completely dominates the surrounding hills, moorland and forests on the east side of Loch Lomond. To the south-east an extensive, undulating moor stretches towards Drymen. There is little of interest for the climber or walker in this area except possibly the picturesque little Conic Hill, 1175 ft., which lies on the Highland Boundary Fault near Balmaha and repays the short ascent with a fine view over the south end of Loch Lomond. North-east of this rather uninteresting moorland is the extensive Loch Ard Forest on the south side of Loch Ard. This is part of the Queen Elizabeth Forest Park, and in fact most of the area described in this chapter, including Ben Lomond, lies within this Park. North of Ben Lomond there is a stretch of rough hill country extending to Loch Arklet, and on the north side of this loch there is a small group of hills, of which Beinn a' Choin, 2524 ft., is the highest, in the area bounded by Glen Gyle and Loch Lomond.

No description of Ben Lomond and its surroundings would be complete without a mention of Loch Lomond which is without doubt the best known of Scotland's lochs, and also one of the most beautiful. The entire twenty-two miles of the loch encompasses some grand and contrasting scenery; the southern end is broad and open, dotted with islands and backed by low hills and parkland, but the north end is narrow, steep-sided and enclosed by mountains. Almost the entire shoreline is beautifully wooded with oak, birch, rowan, hazel and alder, as well as more recent coniferous plantations. These woods fortunately screen the main road which passes along the west side of the loch; however, the volume of traffic along this road during the summer greatly detracts from its peace and charm. The east side of the loch is more tranquil; there is a narrow road from Drymen to Rowardennan, but beyond this point the forest road is not accessible for cars and walkers can enjoy this side of the loch in comparative peace (disturbed only by the distant rumble of traffic on the west side of the loch).

Two minor roads give access to the area described in this chapter. The road to Rowardennan has just been mentioned, and on the north-east side of the area there is a road from Aberfoyle to Inversnaid. Both these roads end on the east shore of Loch Lomond and, except at the height of the tourist season, they are fairly quiet. The hills in the extreme north of the area can be reached from the north end of Loch Lomond. In addition there are ferries for foot passengers across the loch to Inversnaid and Rowardennan.

The name Lomond may well be derived from an old British word 'Llumnan', meaning beacon, and this would certainly be an apt description of the mountain. It is interesting to note that the Lomond Hills of Fife are of the same shape and there again the name 'beacon hill' seems applicable. It is probably also significant that Loch Leven lies at the foot of the West Lomond in Fife, and that Loch Lomond was once called Loch Leven and the River Leven flows from its south end. It seems likely that the name of the hill has been applied to the loch.

Geologically, Ben Lomond consists of a hard mass of mica-schist dipping steeply to the south-east. The summit appears from many viewpoints to be a conical peak set on a broadly spreading base, but it is in fact a short, level ridge enclosing a north-facing corrie, the actual summit being at the north-west end of this ridge. The corrie is ringed by crags, below which scree and grass slopes drop steeply towards Comer Farm at the head of Gleann Dubh.

The mountain has three principal spurs or ridges. The long and broad south ridge rises on the east side of Loch Lomond above Rowardennan and leads gradually upwards over Sron Aonaich to its final steepening just below the summit. On the other side of the mountain a well-defined ridge drops north-west from the summit for half a mile and then, turning northwards, it becomes broad and grassy. At the point where this ridge turns north, a third ridge runs out south-west to the subsidiary top called Ptarmigan, 2398 ft. This hill stands out prominently in views of Ben Lomond from the south.

There are three main routes for the ascent of Ben Lomond, starting at Rowardennan, Inversnaid and a point west of Loch Ard. The Rowardennan route is the most popular, and a few thousand walkers annually make the pilgrimage up the four-mile path to the summit. The path starts at Rowardennan Hotel and climbs north-east beside the forest for half a mile or so before turning northwards to Sron Aonaich and so along the crest of the broad south ridge. As the final slopes steepen, the path zigzags up to the summit ridge which is followed for a quarter of a mile round the corrie to the top. In good weather this route presents absolutely no difficulties, and two and a half hours should be sufficient time for the ascent. For climbers starting from Rowardennan Youth Hostel (which is half a mile north of the hotel) a shorter route can be made by climbing beside the wooded ravine north-east of the hostel. There are paths up the grassy hillside on both sides of the ravine, although the one on the south-east side crosses the stream above the falls at about 1000 ft. Beyond that point there is no clearly defined path, but the going is perfectly easy and by heading north-east the main path is soon reached. This route is also very convenient if one is including Ptarmigan in the ascent; the north-west side of the ravine is taken, and one diverges northwards at about 1250 ft. up the south ridge of the hill.

From Inversnaid follow the path along the east side of Loch Lomond as far as the Cailness Burn whose south bank is then ascended and a way made across flatter grassy ground to the 1500 ft. col between Ben Lomond and Cruinn a' Bheinn. From the col the north ridge is followed to the summit, there being a faint path for part of the way. Most of the west side of Ptarmigan between Rowardennan and the Cailness Burn is forested; any ascent of this side of the mountain involves making a way through young trees and over fences, and is best avoided.

From the east the approach to Ben Lomond is very attractive and leads naturally into the main corrie. The nearest starting point is at Loch Dhu, six miles along the road from Aberfoyle to Inversnaid. A forest road leads over a low ridge to Gleann Dubh and Ben Lomond rises grandly ahead, its north face coming into view as one walks up the glen towards Comer Farm. From there one can follow the stream into the main corrie and up to the summit ridge just south-east of the top; alternatively, one can keep to the south of this stream and so reach the ridge which leads round the top of the corrie to the summit. The ascent from Comer by either of the two routes just mentioned is steeper than the other routes on Ben Lomond, but it takes one up the grandest side of the mountain; it is a good approach to the cliffs, and the route up the corrie is particularly fine in winter – easy step-cutting or cramponing with the possibility of a good glissade on the descent.

The view from the summit is very extensive, and gives a grand contrast between the low lands to the south and the mountains to the north. The view towards the south end of Loch Lomond and its many wooded islands is very attractive; westwards the Cowal and Ardgoil hills stand out, but the Arrochar Alps dominate the view in this direction and Ben Lomond is possibly the best viewpoint for them. North-westwards Bens Cruachan and Lui are very prominent, then Nevis appears above the Blackmount hills. The Crianlarich mountains form a grand array to the north, and the north-eastern skyline is dominated by Ben Lawers. Further round to the east, Stuc a' Chroin and Ben Vorlich are the main features of the view, and then one comes to the Ochils beyond the nearer wooded hills around Loch Ard and the Lake of Menteith. Altogether it is a wonderful panorama, one that is not surpassed in the Southern Highlands.

Serious climbing on Ben Lomond is confined to the main north-facing corrie which is ringed by cliffs up to almost three hundred feet high. The rocks are not suited for summer rock-climbing as they are extremely vegetatious; however, there are some very pleasant, short winter climbs, and some of the routes which were pioneered in summer are probably much more interesting in winter conditions, but records of such ascents are surprisingly scarce. The small top nearest to the summit of Ben Lomond is the highest point of a broken and fairly easy crag on which no definite routes have been recorded. A short distance south-east of this top there is a col from which it is usually easy to descend into the corrie, and this is probably the best approach from Rowardennan to the foot of the cliffs. Descending from this col in an easterly direction below the cliffs, the first section is rather broken, but climbs have been done on this part of the cliff which is only about a hundred and fifty feet high. Continuing the descending traverse, the main features of the corrie are reached – three parallel narrow gullies separated by ribs. The easternmost gully is very narrow at its foot, and quite easy (Grade I); the central gully has a small chockstone pitch which may be difficult, but it is possible to traverse out of this gully across the rib on the right and into the western gully which is easier (Grade II). The lower half of the western gully is not well defined. The ribs between these gullies have been climbed in summer conditions, and winter ascents would doubtless be more interesting.

Beyond these three gullies there is a steep groove of which there is no recorded ascent. The cliff to the left of the groove has been climbed in summer and named *Pinnacle Route* by virtue of some prominent pointed rocks near the top of the climb. To the north-east the cliff becomes larger and is crossed diagonally by a grass ledge. Two gullies split this part of the cliff, the left-hand one has been climbed in summer, but again there is no record of any winter ascent. North-east of these gullies the cliff becomes progressively smaller as it drops towards Comer.

Apart from Ben Lomond, there is very little hill-walking or climbing in the area covered by this chapter. The low hills around Ben Lomond are, with the exception of Ptarmigan, all rather uninteresting. North of Loch Arklet there are three hills – Stob-an Fhainne, Beinn a' Choin and Maol Mor – which can be climbed in an easy round from Corriearklet, but they have no features of particular interest. North of them, Ben Ducteach at the head of Glen Gyle is an impressive little peak when seen from the south-east, and there are some fair-sized crags on that side of the hill which might well repay investigation.

There is plenty of good walking to be had in the forests and glens west of Aberfoyle. As a glance at the One-inch Map will show, the Loch Ard Forest has many tracks through it which give delightful walks, but detailed descriptions are unnecessary. Suffice to say that one can leave Aberfoyle and walk westwards by any one of several tracks through the forest which lead along the south side of Loch Ard or up the Duchray Water, and continue as far as Loch Chon or up Gleann Dubh towards the foot of Ben Lomond.

One cross-country route does deserve mention because of its popularity as a direct route between Rowardennan and Loch Ard Youth Hostels. From Rowardennan Hotel the Ben Lomond path is followed to about 1250 ft., and then one heads east by north to cross the Moin Eich pass and descend to the Bruach Caoruinn Burn and so to the Duchray Water. Once in the forest one can either follow a track round the west end of Loch Ard to reach Kinlochard and Loch Ard Youth Hostel (9 miles), or one can continue eastwards along the Duchray Water to Aberfoyle (12 miles).

Finally, mention must be made of the walk along the east side of

Loch Lomond. From Rowardennan a forest road continues northwards past Ptarmigan Lodge to Rowchoish; the bothy at Rowchoish has been repaired for use by walkers, and is some distance below the road, which ends a short distance further north. A footpath continues past Cailness to Inversnaid, and from there onwards there is a choice of route. One may either continue along the lochside, but the going is very rough and there is no path; alternatively, one can walk up the road to Garrison of Inversnaid and continue northwards by the Snaid Burn to a pass overlooking steep slopes above Loch Lomond from where a descending path leads to the lochside near Doune. North of Doune there is a path past Ardleish, over the little col east of Cnap Mor and so to Beinglas Farm (14 miles).

Transport and Accommodation
There is a bus service to Balmaha from Balloch and Drymen (both these points are connected with Glasgow by regular bus and train services). There is a weekend bus service to Kinlochard from Aberfoyle which is reached from Glasgow by a regular bus service.

The steamer 'Maid of the Loch' sails on Loch Lomond in the summer months between Balloch, Balmaha, Rowardennan, Tarbet, Inversnaid and Ardlui. There are two public ferries across Loch Lomond for foot passengers, one from Inverbeg to Rowardennan and the other to Inversnaid from a point on the A82 road a mile south of Inveruglas. Both ferries operate on request, weather permitting, during daylight hours.

There are hotels at the following places around the perimeter of the area described in this chapter: Drymen, Rowardennan, Inversnaid, Ardlui, Inverarnan, Aberfoyle and Gartmore. There are Youth Hostels at Rowardennan and Loch Ard, and a bothy at Rowchoish.

BIBLIOGRAPHY

An Ascent of Ben Lomond by William and Mary Howitt in 1822, S.M.C.J., Vol. 1, p. 123.
Ben Lomond, A. E. Maylard, S.M.C.J., Vol. 3, p. 140.
The Cliffs of Ben Lomond, (Note), J. Maclay, S.M.C.J., Vol. 3, p. 343.
Ben Lomond by the Cliffs, W. I. Clark, S.M.C.J., Vol. 4, p. 331.
Ben Lomond, Guide Book Article, S.M.C.J., Vol. 6, p. 112.
Ben Lomond, (Note), W. C. Newbigging, S.M.C.J., Vol. 8, p. 87.
Queen Elizabeth Forest Park Guide, (H. M. Stationery Office), 1954.

5

The Trossachs Hills

The principal hills in the area are:
(1) **Ben Venue,** 2393 ft., 1½ miles S.W. of the east end of Loch Katrine.
(2) **Ben A'n,** 1520 ft., 1 mile N.E. of the east end of Loch Katrine.
(3) **Ben Ledi,** 2873 ft., 4¼ miles W.N.W. of Callander.
(4) **Benvane,** 2685 ft., 2½ miles S.W. of Strathyre.
(5) **Point** 2526 ft., 2 miles S. of Monachylemore at the west end of Loch Voil.
(6) **Stob a' Choin,** 2839 ft., 2 miles S.W. of Inverlochlarig beyond the west end of Loch Doine.

Maps: Ordnance Survey One-inch Series, Sheets 53 and 54 and Loch Lomond and the Trossachs Tourist Map.
Bartholomew's Half-inch Series, Sheet 48.

This chapter includes not only the Trossachs, but also the surrounding hills and lochs. The area occupies a strategic position in the centre of Scotland between the low-lying valley of the River Forth and the mountains of the Highlands, and there is a wonderful gradation of scenery as one goes north from the parkland and cultivation around the Lake of Menteith to the mountains on the north side of Loch Voil. The area described in this chapter is bounded on the south by Glen Gyle, the west end of Loch Katrine and the roads from Stronachlachar to Aberfoyle (B829) and from Aberfoyle to Callander (A81). The northern and eastern boundaries are formed by the River Lochlarig which flows eastwards from its source near the head of Glen Gyle, through Lochs Doine and Voil and then turns south through Loch Lubnaig to become the River Leny.

The name Trossachs applies, strictly speaking, only to the short, wooded glen between Loch Katrine and Loch Achray, an area of no more than a square mile. However, by common use the name has come to be applied to a much larger area embracing the country from Loch Ard and Aberfoyle northwards to Lochs Katrine, Achray and Venachar.

7. Carlin Maggie, a pinnacle in the Lomond Hills.

8. Beinn Eich in the Luss Hills.

9. At the head of Glen Luss, looking towards Cruach an t-Sithein.

10. Skiing on Beinn Eich in the Luss Hills.

The Trossachs have for many years been one of the most popular areas in Scotland for the traveller and tourist. At the beginning of the nineteenth century William and Dorothy Wordsworth travelled on foot through Glen Gyle, along Loch Katrine and over the hills from there to Loch Voil and Strathyre. Their journey was recorded by Dorothy in her *Recollections of a Tour Made in Scotland*, and William was inspired to write several poems. A few years later Sir Walter Scott published his poem *The Lady of the Lake*, followed shortly afterwards by the novel *Rob Roy*, and the fame of the Trossachs was established in literature. Since then no traveller's tour of Scotland has been complete without a visit to the Trossachs.

The whole area embraces a great variety of scenery from the pastoral to the very wild and rugged. Ben Venue and its neighbouring tops occupy the south-west corner between Loch Ard and Loch Katrine, and the Menteith Mills in the south-east corner overlook the Lake of Menteith and the flat expanse of Flanders Moss through which winds the River Forth. The road from Aberfoyle to the Trossachs crosses the Duke's Pass between Ben Venue and the Menteith Hills, and from the top of the pass the traveller gets a grand impression of the Trossachs as a whole – a region of forests, lochs and rugged hills.

The Trossachs, and in particular the glen between Loch Katrine and Loch Achray which is the true heart of the Trossachs, is a fine example of Highland scenery in miniature. The glen and the steep hillside of Ben A'n above it are beautifully wooded with birch and oak, with darker and more regimented plantings of spruce and larch on the slopes of Ben Venue to the south. On both sides of the glen the hills have a steepness and craggy character which belie their modest height. Loch Katrine is the reservoir for Glasgow's water supply and has remained largely unspoiled. The road along the north shore is private and the loch is free from motor traffic and its attendant crowds and noise. The east end of the loch with its wooded crags and tiny islands is particularly beautiful. Loch Achray is very much at the centre of tourist traffic in the Trossachs; however, in winter when the crowds and the cars have departed it regains its natural peace and beauty.

North of the Trossachs the country as far as Loch Voil is hilly, and the interior is wild and uninhabited. The two highest mountains of this area are Ben Ledi in the south-east corner and Stob a' Choin in the north-west. Between them there is a rather desolate stretch of

E

featureless hills which are seldom visited by the climber or walker. A recently created reservoir in Glen Finglas supplies additional water to Loch Katrine through a pipeline under Ben A'n. (This reservoir is shown on Bartholomew's Half-inch Map, but not on the Ordnance Survey One-inch Map. It is about 500 ft. above sea level, and the dam at its south end is about three-quarters of a mile north of Brig o' Turk.) In the north-east corner of this area there is some beautiful country round Loch Voil, Balquhidder, Strathyre and Loch Lubnaig, but the landscape of this corner, with the big mountains such as Stobinian and Ben Vorlich showing their peaks above the lower hills, is more akin to the Highlands than to the Trossachs.

If the hills of the Trossachs, with the exception of those already mentioned, lack outstanding character or interest, the same cannot be said of the lochs. There are, if one includes those just outside the perimeter of our area, twelve lochs (or to be more precise, eleven lochs and a lake). Each one has its own particular beauty and character, from the placid expanse of the Lake of Menteith to the narrow, mountain-girt Lochs Voil and Lubnaig.

The Trossachs are approached from the south-east either by road through Callander and along Loch Venachar or alternatively by the road from Stirling through Thornhill to Aberfoyle. From the south-west the approach from Glasgow leads to Aberfoyle. The road westwards from Aberfoyle up Loch Ard ends at Inversnaid on the east side of Loch Lomond, and there is a ferry across the loch for pedestrians only. The steamer service on Loch Katrine carries pedestrians between the east end of the loch and Stronachlachar. On the north and east of the area the road from Callander to Kingshouse Hotel (just north of Strathyre) and from there westwards through Balquhidder to the road end at Inverlochlarig gives access to the hills in that region.

The Trossachs hills have more to offer the hill-walker than the rock-climber, for whom there are only the small, but very pleasant, crags on Ben A'n and some boulders and pinnacles on Ben Ledi. For the winter climber there is practically nothing at all, although in a hard winter it might be possible to find some interesting climbing on the east side of Ben Ledi or the north face of Stob a' Choin. There are many good walks in the area through the hills and forests and along the lochsides, and it is worth emphasising that of the four seasons autumn is undoubtedly the best for the Trossachs. Then the summer crowds have dwindled, and the colours on the hillsides and in the woods add an extra dimension to the beauty of the region.

Part of the Queen Elizabeth Forest Park lies within the area covered by this chapter, and the Park Guide published by H.M. Stationery Office, Edinburgh is a good source of information about the district. **Ben Venue** is a rugged hill, very much more of a mountain than its height would suggest. Its finest aspect is the north-east face as seen from Loch Achray, and this is one of the best known views of the Trossachs. From the south the hill is not well seen, and the twin summits just appear over the long flat ridge of Beinn an Fhogharaidh. The two tops are less than a quarter of a mile apart, the north-west one being 2393 ft., and the south-east one 2386 ft.

Low down on the north side of the hill the Bealach nam Bo (Pass of the Cattle) is a little notch in the hillside through which the highlanders from Glen Gyle drove the stolen cattle on their return from plundering raids on the lowlands. Just below the pass, in the crags above Loch Katrine, is the Goblin's Cave (Corrie na Urisgean) which may give the mountain its name.

The shortest and most scenic ascent of Ben Venue is from the north-east, starting at the Loch Achray Hotel. Behind the hotel a forest road leads westward beside the Achray Water. Just beyond the edge of the forest, near the Loch Katrine sluices, a steep path climbs uphill and is followed beside the stream which comes down from near the south-east top. A less steep route can be made by continuing beyond the sluices along the path which climbs gradually to the Bealach nam Bo. From the pass the north ridge of Ben Venue can be climbed directly to the summit.

From the south the normal route of ascent starts at Ledard Farm near the west end of Loch Ard. The way follows a good path which starts on the west side of the Ledard Burn, and after about a mile crosses to the east side and continues to the pass between two of Ben Venue's outliers, Beinn Bhreac and Creag Tharsuinn. The path contours across the north side of the latter hill and reaches the col between it and Ben Venue, whose summit is reached by the south-west ridge. The last few hundred yards of the path are not too well defined as it twists and turns between little crags. The view from the summit gives a beautiful contrast between the forests and low hills to the south-east and the high mountains to the north-west, but its greatest charm is the nearer view of lochs and wooded shores on the north side of the hill.

The east side of Ben Venue is extensively forested and there are no very good routes from this side except possibly the long traverse from the Aberfoyle Quarries (near the Duke's Pass) over Beinn an Fhogharaidh and Creag Tharsuinn. Beinn Bhreac, 2295 ft., a mile and a quarter west-south-west of Ben Venue, can be easily climbed from the Ledard Burn path on the way to or from Ben Venue.

Ben A'n, 1520 ft., is the conspicuous little hill which is seen across Loch Achray from the north side of the Duke's Pass. Its sharp pointed summit and rocky front rise grandly above the birch woods of the Trossachs, and it is difficult from some view points to realise that it is just a spur of the rather featureless hill Meall Gainmheich. However, it has such individuality and character that it is always regarded among climbers as being a distinct hill in its own right, and it is probably the most popular hill in the Trossachs with both walkers and rock-climbers.

The best approach is by the path which climbs steeply uphill at the edge of the woods a few hundred yards west of the Trossachs Hotel. Recent plantings by the Forestry Commission have rather spoiled this path in places, but it is nevertheless a very beautiful and easy climb with some lovely glimpses of Ben A'n as one approaches the hill. Just beyond the last trees the path divides and the walkers' route to the summit takes the right-hand path by a little stream, goes through a notch on the north-east side of the hill and reaches the summit from the north.

An alternative ascent can be made from the south-west, but the going is much rougher. A few hundred yards beyond the pier at the east end of Loch Katrine a stream comes down from Ben A'n. A path is followed up this stream, but the going becomes boggy and the path disappears. One then must avoid the steep rocks of the south face of the hill by keeping either to the west or the east, (in the latter case the route just described is joined).

The panorama from the summit is out of all proportion to the height of the hill, and is a delightful reward for a very enjoyable little climb. Ben Venue in particular looks very impressive on the south side of the wooded Trossachs glen, and the view westwards up Loch Katrine is also very fine. It is quite possible on a fine summer evening to leave Glasgow after work, drive to Ben A'n, enjoy a leisurely stroll uphill, a few rock-climbs and sunset on the summit, and be home before midnight.

The south face of Ben A'n above the trees is very steep, with many rock outcrops and small cliffs. There is a grand variety of short climbs of all sorts – walls, slabs, cracks and chimneys. The rock is very sound and because of its southerly exposure it dries quickly after rain. Although only one of the climbs exceeds 100 ft. in length and some are not much more than boulder problems, it is possible by linking routes (with a bit of walking between them) to get 500 ft. of excellent climbing of Difficult to Severe standard. The wonderful outlook from the hill combined with the many comfortable heather ledges promotes a feeling of carefree relaxation as one progresses from one climb to the next.

The best approach to the rocks is by the 'tourist' route from the Trossachs Hotel. Just above the tree-line, where the path divides, the left-hand branch leads directly to the lowest rocks where an ash tree at the foot of the cliff is a good landmark. Several yards right of this tree there is a little shallow gully bounded on its right by a steep rock bluff on which the first two climbs are found.

1. *The First Thirty* (30 ft., D.). A straightforward climb on good, small holds on the right wall of the gully.
2. *Preamble* (40 ft., S.). Start just right of the foot of the rock bluff. The initial overhang is followed by an easier section, then traverse left towards the edge of the bluff where a few hard moves finish the climb. An easier finish can be made by trending right in the upper half of the pitch.
3. *Ash Wall* (60 ft., M.S.). Start behind the ash tree and step up from a narrow flake into a steep little groove. A few feet higher the route bears right then left on open rock, and the finish on small polished holds leads to a broad ledge with a birch tree.
4. *Birch Wall* (30 ft., S.). The route starts just to the left of the finish of (3) and follows an open corner in the steep wall. The first few moves are on very sloping footholds, but higher up, as the corner steepens, the holds improve.
5. *The Hook* (30 ft., V.S.). A steep and almost holdless wall just left of (4).
6. *Rowan Rib* (35 ft., V.D.). This route is directly above (4), but the tree after which it is named has long since disappeared. A steel spike now provides a belay. The first few overhanging feet are awkward, but thereafter the route is easier.
7. *Jughandle Wall* (30 ft., D. to V.D.). Above and slightly left of the finish of (1) there is a steep wall with excellent holds. There is some scope for variation, the easier climbing being on the left.
8. *Diagonal Groove* (30 ft., S.). Left of (7) there is another very steep

wall with a rightward sloping groove leading to a small rowan tree just below the top. Climb the groove on small holds (more awkward than it looks) and then go straight up past the rowan tree.

9. *Hawthorn Rib* (130 ft., D.). This rather indefinite route lies above and to the left of (6). The lower part is a fairly well-defined rib and higher up, where the climb steepens, there is some scope for variation.

10. *Right-Hand Gully* (100 ft., V.D.). This gully is very much overgrown by briars and brambles and is seldom climbed. The hardest section is a chimney in the upper half.

11. *Left-Hand Gully* (100 ft., V.D.). Another rather overgrown gully with some good little chimney pitches.

12. *Atom Slab* (15 ft., S.). Some distance directly above (6) there is an outcrop of rock with some very short routes. Atom Slab is the polished wall at the top of this outcrop.

The final tier of rock is immediately below the summit and reaches its greatest height at the corner between its south and east faces.

13. *The Last Eighty* (80 ft., M.S.). This climb goes directly up the corner between the south and east faces. The ordinary start is a

BEN A'N

few feet right of the corner and the overhanging direct start (H.S.) is a few feet left of the corner. The route is the best on Ben A'n and has a fine sense of exposure. Running belays available.

14. *The Rent* (30 ft., S.). This is the obvious crack a few yards right of (13) which gives an excellent little climb.

15. *Oblique Crack* (70 ft., V.D.). The deep slanting chimney left of (13) is climbed to a ledge on the left, above which the finish is on steep grass.

16. *Nameless* (70 ft., S.). Two fine routes have been done on the wall immediately left of (15). The starts overhang, but good flakes are available for pulling up. After about 40 ft. the climbs become grassy, but it is possible to keep to a rock rib and avoid the grass.

Left of (16) the final tier is much more broken, and grass and heather predominate. For those who enjoy such things, there are one or two steep, vegetatious climbs.

17. *McLay's Chimney* (100 ft., V.D.). This climb, which is identified by a jammed block forming an arch in the chimney half way up, is very grassy and apparently seldom climbed.

18. *Record Slab* (20 ft., M.). This easy angled slab lies immediately below the summit (the western knob of rock). The fastest time for the ascent is reputed to be eight seconds.

Ben Ledi, 2873 ft., is the highest of the Trossachs Hills and occupies a very commanding position on the southern edge of the Highlands between Lochs Venechar and Lubnaig. It is prominently seen from Stirling and many other points in Central Scotland, and from Callander it completely dominates the view up the River Leny.

The main spine of the hill rises as a broad, grassy ridge above the east end of Loch Venachar. The ridge narrows at the summit and then turns north to a broad, peaty col in which is situated Lochan nan Corp, (so named after a funeral party which, on its way to St. Bride's Chapel, disappeared through the ice one winter's day). North of the Lochan there is a nameless top (ca. 2450 ft.) and there the main ridge divides, the north-east branch going out over several knolls to Ardnandave Hill, and the north-west branch dropping to the col (ca. 2000 ft.) which separates Ben Ledi from Benvane.

The western and southern slopes of Ben Ledi are for the most part rather featureless and uninteresting, but the east face overlooking the Pass of Leny and the south end of Loch Lubnaig is much grander, and in places is quite craggy. The east face of Ardnandave Hill is a very steep buttress overlooking Loch Lubnaig, but it is vegetatious and tree-clad, and although impressive to look at it is not likely to entice the climber. The whole hillside overlooking Loch Lubnaig is forested and access is only possible in a few places. The Stank Glen is a pleasant forested corrie between Ben Ledi and Ardnandave Hill. High up above the tree-line on the Ben Ledi side of the corrie there is a group of pinnacles and boulders which give the only rock-climbing that the hill has to offer.

The easiest route up Ben Ledi is probably the long south-east ridge, starting at Coilantogle near the east end of Loch Venachar. This ridge is however rather uninteresting, and is best used for the descent or as a ski route in winter. A much finer route can be made up the Stank Glen and the north-east face of the hill. The forest road on the south side of the Stank Burn is followed for a short distance to a point fifty yards past the first bend where a path climbs upwards through the forest parallel to the burn. Some care is needed to avoid losing this path, but it eventually rejoins the end of the forest road and thereafter it is easily followed up the glen. Once clear of the forest one turns left and climbs south-westwards beside a small stream directly towards the summit of Ben Ledi. The boulders and pinnacles previously mentioned are passed, a little hanging corrie just below the summit is reached and one of its bounding ridges is climbed. The south bounding ridge ends near the cairn, and the north bounding ridge ends about a quarter of a mile north of the cairn.

The traverse northwards and then north-east from Ben Ledi towards Ardnandave Hill involves some fairly rough going over peat bogs and hummocks. The most direct route to Ardnandave Hill is by the path up the Stank Glen just described. At the point where the Ben Ledi route turns south-west the Ardnandave Hill route turns right, crosses the burn and goes north-eastwards up a break in the trees to the south-east ridge which is followed over a few knolls to the top. There are three little boulder strewn corries on the north side of Ardnandave Hill, and in the middle one there is a small pinnacle (rather like the Cioch in Skye) which can be seen on the skyline from the road near the north end of Loch Lubnaig.

The only recorded rock-climbing on Ben Ledi is on the pinnacles and boulders in the upper part of the Stank Glen. The pinnacles, which are at a height of just over 2000 ft., can be seen from the south end of Loch Lubnaig from where they have a serrated outline.

The boulders are several hundred feet below them. The climbs are all (with one exception) very short, but some are very sporting and there is enough to keep one busy for two or three hours.

The approach is by the previously described Stank Glen route to Ben Ledi. The first boulder to be reached (just above the boundary fence of the forest) is the Cottage Boulder (No. 1). This is really three boulders close together, the lowest one being separated from the middle one by a narrow cleft. There are several routes, the longest being the traverse of the three boulders. The ascent of the north-east face of the lowest boulder is a pleasant pitch just left of the cleft and a short descent leads to the narrowest part of the gap between it and the middle boulder. A stride across the gap followed by an easy slab leads to the top of the middle boulder from which an easy descent on the other side leads to ground level. The highest boulder is then traversed by a sloping ledge on its east face followed by a steeper descent with good holds on the west face. There are several other routes on these boulders, including two on the middle one from the cleft between it and the lowest one.

The other three boulders on which short routes have been recorded all lie to the north-west and north of the Cottage Boulder. Only one of these boulders has an easy route, so an abseil rope is useful.

No. 2 Boulder is the nearest one to the Cottage. An upward traverse across the south-east face on sloping holds is the most obvious route. A few feet left of this, on the south side, there is a steep climb on tiny holds. On the north face, which overhangs somewhat, there is a thin crack and two routes have been made on this side. *Sunset Wall* (30 ft., V.D.) starts on the right of the crack; climb the overhang and go slightly leftward up the steep wall on good holds. *Watkins Overhang* (30 ft., S.) is on the left of the crack; climb the overhang strenuously to a little heather ledge and continue by easier rock to the top.

No. 3 Boulder is south-west of No. 2. Its north-east face is very steep and the south-west face is continuously overhanging. There are three routes on this boulder. On the right side of the north-east face mantelshelf onto a little ledge 7 ft. above ground level and continue up the steep wall on good holds. At the left end of this face there is a slightly overhanging crack with good holds. On the overhanging south-west side there is a strenuous climb up the middle of the face.

No. 4 Boulder is downhill from Nos. 2 and 3, and is much smaller than them. It is the only one with an easy route to the top. The vertical north corner of the boulder is *Burnie's Climb,* and a few feet to the left of it is an easier groove. At the west corner of the boulder *Piker* consists of awkward balance moves on a steep wall.

Continuing uphill, one comes to a broken and vegetatious cliff below the main line of pinnacles. There is a 70 ft. Severe route up a slab (climbed by a crack) followed by a groove.

On the main pinnacles there is less climbing than appears likely from below. The right-hand rocks are rather vegetatious, and the left-hand rocks are little more than large pointed boulders. The only good climbing is on the Ben Ledi Pinnacle in the centre. It is not strictly speaking a pinnacle but rather a group of boulders of which the largest is a tall pillar leaning against the steep hillside. There are three or four routes which are all rather artificial but nevertheless give some pleasant climbing.

Ordinary Route (100 ft., S.). At the bottom of the Pinnacle there is a narrow crack between the main wall and a slab at right-angles to it. Climb the slab, crawl upwards through a tunnel and move left onto a boulder whose narrow crest is climbed à cheval. Traverse right along an overhung ledge to the crest of the Pinnacle and climb directly up a slab to the top.

Cavern Route (100 ft., S.). This is a variation of the previous route. From the top of the initial slab descend through a hole into a cavern. Climb the wall at the back of the cavern (usually wet and slimy), and join the previous route at the start of the right traverse. The cavern can also be reached through a narrow slit a short distance up the right-hand side of the Pinnacle.

Direct Start (25 ft., S.). Start just round the corner to the left of the initial slab of the Ordinary Route and climb directly up the wall on small holds.

It is also possible that a direct ascent of the middle part of the Pinnacle might be made from the top of the jammed block above the tunnel of the Ordinary Route. This part of the Pinnacle is a smooth slab, and the ascent would lead to the end of the right traverse of the Ordinary Route.

The top of the Pinnacle is very small and the drop on the uphill side is only 20 ft. A small rock spike just below the top safeguards the descent with a rope.

To the east of and lower than the Ben Ledi Pinnacle there is a smaller, isolated pinnacle which looks very impressive from below.

The ascent of its narrow north-east ridge is Severe. Start a few feet up a little gully on the left and traverse onto the ridge above the initial overhang (rock spikes for running belays or pendulum). Once on the ridge the route goes up a shallow groove just right of the crest. The pinnacle can be reached by a short, easy scramble on the south-west side.

The cliff on the north of the spur above the pinnacles is loose and, apart from some scree gullies which might be interesting in winter, there is no hope of any climbing.

Benvane, 2685 ft., is 3 miles north-west of Ben Ledi, and is a rather featureless, grassy hill. The main backbone is a long ridge running from south to north and the shorter south-east ridge leads to Ben Ledi. The west side of the hill falls quite steeply into the desolate Gleann nam Meann, while the east side drops more gradually towards the north end of Loch Lubnaig, the lower slopes being extensively forested.

A good route of ascent starts at Strathyre. Follow the road southwards along the west side of the River Balvag and after about a mile and a quarter take the right fork into the forest (the left fork descends to Laggan). A few hundred yards further on take another right turn and follow the forest road westwards towards the col leading to Glen Buckie. Near the upper limit of the trees the road turns north, but a path through the trees leads to open country beyond the forest and from there a course south-westwards leads directly to Benvane or (more easily) to the ridge just north of the top.

The hill can be traversed in a pleasant expedition from Brig o' Turk to Strathyre or Balquhidder, and the ascent of Creag na h-Airigh above the Glen Finglas Reservoir gives the opportunity for scrambling on scattered outcrops.

Beinn an t-Sithein, 1871 ft., is a craggy little hill between Strathyre and Glen Buckie. The east side of the hill is forested, and from Strathyre the best route of ascent is by the path which climbs through the forest opposite the village and then circles round the south side of the hill. From the highest point of the path one can climb northwards for three-quarters of a mile over a few knolls to the summit. The hill can also be climbed from the north or west without difficulty. The view from the summit north-westwards to the mountains beyond Loch Voil is very fine.

The hills between Loch Voil and Loch Katrine are not often

climbed. They are featureless, trackless and very boggy in places. The highest hill in this area is **Point 2526 ft.**, and it can be climbed in a circular tour from Balquhidder. Take the very pleasant road along the south side of Loch Voil and half a mile beyond Muirlaggan follow the path which climbs diagonally towards the Bealach Driseach. From the top of the pass climb the north-east ridge of Ceann na Baintighearna and continue southwards along a gradually rising ridge to Point 2526 ft. The descent is made eastwards to Gleann Dubh and a road on the north side of the Calair Burn leads back to Balquhidder.

Stob a' Choin, 2839 ft., is the dominating hill in the north-west corner of the area covered by this chapter, but in height, character and position it is as much a part of the Crianlarich hills as the Trossachs hills. Its north side overlooking the Lochlarig River is continuously steep for 2000 ft., while the south side of the hill drops gradually in a long, broad ridge to Loch Katrine. The view from the summit towards the Crianlarich hills, particularly Beinn Chabhair, is very fine.

The shortest ascent of Stob a' Choin is from Inverlochlarig at the end of the road from Balquhidder along Loch Voil. From the cottage continue west for a mile or so, cross the river and climb directly up the steep hillside north-east of the summit. A more gradual but slightly longer route is the north-east ridge leading from Blaircreich to the subsidiary 2700 ft. top three-quarters of a mile south-east of Stob a' Choin.

From the south Stob a' Choin can be climbed from Loch Katrine either by the Allt a' Choin or by the long south-south-east ridge, both routes being rather uninteresting. The approach along the north side of Loch Katrine is very pleasant but long, and bicycles could be used to advantage.

Inverlochlarig is the site of the farmhouse where Rob Roy MacGregor lived for the last years of his life, and he was buried in the churchyard at Balquhidder.

To the west of Stob a' Choin a rather featureless ridge separates Glen Gyle from the Lochlarig Glen. At the west end of this ridge the Bealach nan Corp (Pass of the Corpses) is the pass between these two glens that was once used by funeral parties travelling from Loch Voil to Glen Gyle, and it is still possible to see cairns marking the route. Glen Gyle itself is on the line of an old drove road from Dalmally to the head of Loch Lomond, then south-east through the glen to the Trossachs and Falkirk. There was once a village near the head of Glen Gyle, but it is now quite uninhabited and desolate beyond the west end of Loch Katrine.

There are many good walks in the Trossachs area which are listed below. Most of them follow forest roads, tracks or paths, and detailed descriptions are unnecessary.

1. Aberfoyle to Callander by the Menteith Hills, (9 miles). Go east from Aberfoyle and take the forest road which starts a quarter of a mile east of the golf course and leads north-east over the hills to Loch Venachar. The road along the south side of the loch leads to Callander.

2. Aberfoyle to Brig o' Turk by the Menteith Hills, (10 miles). Follow route (1) to Loch Venachar, then turn west past Invertrossachs House and follow forest tracks to Brig o' Turk or Loch Achray.

3. Trossachs Pier to Stronachlachar, (13 miles). The walk along the road on the north side of Loch Katrine to the west end and back along the south side to Stronachlachar is very pleasant, and might be combined with steamer sailings on the loch. The complete circuit of Loch Katrine is about 20 miles, of which 5 are trackless.

4. Brig o' Turk to Balquhidder, (10 miles). Take the road north from Brig o' Turk by the Glen Finglas Reservoir to Duart Farm. Continue northwards by the boggy and trackless Gleann nam Meann over the pass at its head and down to Gleann Dubh. Once in this glen the road on the north side of the river leads to Balquhidder.

5. Circuit of Beinn an t-Sithein from Strathyre, (7 miles). Take the forest path which climbs the east side of Beinn an t-Sithein and then circles round its south side. Descend towards Glen Buckie and keep to the east side of the Calair Burn where pleasant paths lead through trees by the stream. The circuit is completed by returning along the road on the south-west side of the River Balvag. This walk can be lengthened (and the amount of climbing reduced) by taking the route from Strathyre to Benvane (q.v.). At the edge of the forest (MR 546150) descend north-west and then north to Glen Buckie.

6. Stronachlachar to Inverarnan, (9 miles). Take the road to the west end of Loch Katrine and continue by a track up Glen Gyle to the pass on the north side of Ben Ducteach. From there the way continues across boggy ground to the Ben Glas Burn and down the path to Inverarnan. Electricity transmission lines along most of this route detract from its scenic value.

Transport and Accommodation

There are frequent bus services from Glasgow to Aberfoyle and a very infrequent service from Aberfoyle to Kinlochard. There is also an infrequent service between Stirling and Aberfoyle by Thornhill and the Lake of Menteith.

There is a regular service from Stirling to Callander with a less frequent continuation by Loch Lubnaig to Kingshouse Hotel (Balquhidder). A once daily service (except Sundays, summer only) operates between Callander and the Trossachs (Loch Katrine) in conjunction with steamer sailings (British Rail tour).

In summer there are frequent bus tours to the Trossachs from Glasgow, Edinburgh and Stirling.

The best situated hotels for the climber and walker are at Aberfoyle, Loch Ard, Lake of Menteith, Loch Achray, Callander, Strathyre and Kingshouse (Balquhidder).

There are Youth Hostels at Loch Ard, Trossachs and Balquhidder.

BIBLIOGRAPHY

Ben A'n, H. C. Boyd, *S.M.C.J.*, Vol. 4, p. 155.
Stob a' Choin, A. Frazer, *S.M.C.J.*, Vol. 4, p. 247.
Ben Venue, A. W. Russell, *S.M.C.J.*, Vol. 4, p. 298.
Cliffs of Ben A'n, W. W. Naismith, *S.M.C.J.*, Vol. 5, p. 52.
Glen Finlas to Glen Falloch, J. Maclay, *S.M.C.J.*, Vol. 5, p. 58.
Guide Book Article, *S.M.C.J.*, Vol. 6, p. 238.
Ben A'n, J. B. Nimlin, *S.M.C.J.*, Vol. 23, p. 134.
The Trossachs, Campbell Nairne, (Oliver and Boyd), 1961.
Queen Elizabeth Forest Park Guide, (H.M. Stationery Office), 1954.

The Loch Earn Group

The principal hills in this area are:
(1) **Ben Vorlich,** 3224 ft., 4 miles S.E. of Lochearnhead.
(2) **Stuc a' Chroin,** 3189 ft., 1¼ miles S.W. of (1).
(3) **Beinn Each,** 2660 ft., 1⅓ miles S.W. of (2).
(4) **Meall na Fearna,** 2479 ft., 1¼ miles E. of (1).
(5) **Uamh Bheag,** 2181 ft., 4½ miles N.E. of Callander.
(6) **Am Bioran,** 2011 ft., 1½ miles S. of St. Fillans.
Maps: Ordnance Survey One-inch Series, Sheet 54 and Loch Lomond and the
    Trossachs Tourist Map.
    Bartholomew's Half-inch Series, Sheet 48.

The area covered by this chapter is enclosed by the ring of roads
through Dunblane, Comrie, Lochearnhead, Callander and back to
Dunblane. More than half the area, namely that part south of the
line from Comrie to Callander, is high moorland and nearly all the
climbing interest is concentrated in two mountains, Ben Vorlich and
Stuc a' Chroin, in the north-west corner of the area. The hills in the
north-east corner, between Glen Artney and St. Fillans, have
recently been planted by the Forestry Commission, and they are not
of much interest to climbers.

Ben Vorlich and Stuc a' Chroin are two of Scotland's best known
and most popular mountains. They are prominently seen from many
viewpoints in Central Scotland; from Stirling and other points to the
south-east the two mountains, particularly Ben Vorlich, appear as
well defined peaks, however from the south-west (for example from
the Queen's View on the Glasgow to Drymen road) they appear more
as long, hump-backed ridges. The two mountains have always been
popular by virtue of their accessibility, and in the days when trains
and not cars were the standard form of transport, the traverse of the
two peaks between Callander and Lochearnhead stations was one of
the few expeditions that could be done in a day from Edinburgh.

The roads which encircle this area give access to most of the hills. In addition there is a public road for five and a half miles up Glen Artney and another narrow road from Callander northwards up the Keltie Water which is passable for cars for two miles as far as Braeleny Farm.

In common with most of the Southern Highlands, the rock of this group is mica-schist, and the hills are characterised by the usual grassy slopes with rock outcrops and some larger vegetatious cliffs. The Ordnance Survey One-inch map is rather optimistic in its indication of cliffs and crags on Ben Vorlich and Stuc a' Chroin, and in reality there are no continuous cliffs of any height, and no summer rock climbs have been recorded. In winter, however, under suitable conditions the east face of Stuc a' Chroin may give some good climbing.

The main ridge of **Ben Vorlich**, 3224 ft., runs from south-east to north-west, the actual summit being a level ridge about a hundred yards long with a large cairn at the south-east end and an Ordnance Survey trig. point at the north-west end. A short distance down the north-west ridge two more ridges branch off to the north and south-west, so that the plan of the mountain is rather X-shaped. The south-west ridge drops to the Bealach an Dubh Choirein (ca. 2400 ft.) and from this pass the north-east buttress of Stuc a' Chroin rises very steeply.

The main features of **Stuc a' Chroin**, 3189 ft., are its rocky north-east buttress just mentioned, the long, grassy south-east ridge and the twisting and hummocky south-west ridge which drops south-west from the summit for half a mile, turns north-west for a third of a mile and then continues south-west again for another half mile to the Bealach nan Cabar (ca. 2200 ft.). South of this pass the ridge continues to Beinn Each.

Ben Vorlich has a very steep north-east face which is mostly grass, scree and broken rock. Its south face is also steep and there are two or three rock ribs just below the summit. On Stuc a' Chroin the north-east buttress is the most prominent feature of the mountain and gives it a characteristic appearance when seen from the south-east or north-west. The east face of the mountain is also steep with some vegetatious cliffs and scree gullies dropping from the ridge between the summit and the top of the north-east buttress.

Ben Vorlich and Stuc a' Chroin are usually climbed together and there are five points at which the traverse of the two mountains can

12. Ben Lomond from the north end of Loch Lomond.

13. Ben Lomond from Ben Vorlich.

14. The Arrochar Alps from Ben Lomond.

15. The summit ridge of Ben Lomond.

16. Loch Lomond from Duncryne. The Cobbler, Ben Vorlich and Ben Lomond are all prominent beyond the wooded islands at the south end of the loch.

17. Ben Lomond from the west.

18. Ben A'n and a glimpse of Loch Katrine.

start or finish, so several combinations of routes are possible. The five starting or finishing points are: Ardchullarie More on the side of Loch Lubnaig, Edinample at the foot of Glen Ample and Ardvorlich at the foot of Glen Vorlich (both on the south side of Loch Earn), the head of Glen Artney where the public road ends near Auchinner, and finally Callander from where the approach may be shortened by driving two miles up the Keltie Water to Braeleny Farm.

The approach from Ardvorlich is the easiest route to Ben Vorlich. Behind the big house a good track climbs up the west side of the burn. After about three-quarters of a mile this track divides and the higher (west) branch is followed for some distance further into Coire Buidhe. Crossing the corrie towards the south, the north ridge of Ben Vorlich is reached and a well-defined path leads to the summit. The last few hundred feet of this path is steep and calls for care in winter.

The approach from Edinample is only slightly longer, and is equally suitable for both Ben Vorlich and Stuc a' Chroin. A good track leads up the west side of the Burn of Ample and in due course crosses the burn to reach the house at Glenample. Beyond the house the glen and hillsides are forested, and one can either follow the Allt a' Choire Fhuadaraich to reach the Bealach an Dubh Choirein, or climb directly to Stuc a' Chroin by its north-west ridge whose steep lower part is called Creag Dhubh. From the Bealach an Dubh Choirein, Ben Vorlich is easily reached by its short south-west ridge which is marked by a broken fence. The ascent of Stuc a' Chroin is slightly more difficult as the north-east buttress is quite steep, although the rock is very broken. The direct ascent of the buttress involves a little scrambling, but an easier way can be found by keeping to the north-west of the crest of the buttress.

The route to Stuc a' Chroin from Ardchullaric More follows the right-of-way which climbs steeply through the trees behind the house and joins a forest road leading northwards. Once beyond the trees there is a choice of route. Beinn Each may be included by climbing north-eastwards beside the stream which comes down in a series of small waterfalls from near its summit, and from there a steep but not difficult descent northwards leads to the Bealach nan Cabar. Alternatively the bealach can be reached directly by climbing diagonally upwards from the highest point of the right-of-way at the head of Glen Ample. From the Bealach nan Cabar the route to Stuc a' Chroin follows the knobbly and tortuous south-west ridge, which is marked by a broken fence. There is plenty of scope for scrambling on the many little outcrops on this ridge which would be a very confusing place in misty weather were it not for the old fence.

The approach to Ben Vorlich and Stuc a' Chroin from Callander is a good deal longer and less interesting than the routes already described. One can drive up the Keltie Water to Braeleny Farm, beyond which the road becomes rough. The way continues to the end of this road at Arivurichardich and a path climbs diagonally across the hillside to reach Stuc a' Chroin's broad and grassy south-east ridge. If this hill is the objective the ridge is followed to the summit in a further two miles of easy ascent. If one is heading for Ben Vorlich it is necessary to descend three-quarters of a mile (and 500 ft.) north-eastwards to a ruined shieling in Gleann an Dubh Choirein, and then climb the south-east ridge of Ben Vorlich which is broad and grassy at first, but becomes narrower and stony as one nears the top.

From Glen Artney the approach to the mountains follows the well marked track (right-of-way) beyond the end of the public road. This track crosses the moor between Glenartney Lodge and the Water of Ruchill and descends to the Allt an Dubh Choirein. The path up the north-east side of this burn is followed to the ruined shieling just mentioned from where Ben Vorlich and Stuc a' Chroin can be climbed by the routes described in the preceding paragraph. It is probably advisable not to follow the Allt an Dubh Choirein to its source in the corrie between the two mountains as this corrie is a rough and trackless expanse of eroded peat bog.

Of the several routes described the best in the author's opinion is the Ardvorlich–Ben Vorlich–Stuc a' Chroin–Beinn Each–Ardchullarie More traverse. This route gives the climber a constantly changing impression of these mountains, and on the final descent there is a beautiful view across Loch Lubnaig to Ben Ledi.

The east face of Stuc a' Chroin has always attracted climbers in search of winter routes, but the climbs on this face have seldom quite lived up to expectations. There is a terrace across this face at a height of about 2600 ft. from which the climbs start. Below, and slightly to the north of the summit there are two narrow gullies, both quite easy. North of them there is a broken face of rock which gave W. Garden and party a good climb in 1911; the middle part of the climb followed a prominent rib on the face. Between this face and the flank of the north-east buttress is the wide north gully which is also quite easy. (All the routes just mentioned are essentially winter climbs and are not worth doing in summer.) The direct ascent of the north-east buttress is a good climb in hard winter conditions, possibly the best on the mountain, and north-west of the buttress, on the hillside overlooking the head of Choire Fhuadaraich, at least one other easy gully has been climbed in winter. The only climbing on Ben Vorlich is on the south-facing rock ribs just below the summit. The foot of these climbs can be reached by a traverse across the steep hillside from the south-east ridge. Because of their southern exposure the rocks are cleaner and drier than the Stuc a' Chroin cliffs, and there is some very pleasant scrambling (with the possibility of some hard pitches) on these ribs.

Beinn Each, 2660 ft., has a very steep face overlooking the head of Gleann a' Chroin, and exploration there might produce some good rock climbs. The broad grassy south-east ridge of the hill drops towards the Keltic Water, but the cliffs marked on the One-inch Map on the side of this ridge are non-existent.

The hills east of Ben Vorlich between Glen Artney and Strath Earn are not of great interest to the climber. For the most part they are grassy, with heather and peat bog, and are the home of many deer and grouse. Gleann Ghoinean and the eastern hills Mor Bheinn and Ben Halton have recently been planted by the Forestry Commission and their present bare appearance will in due course be changed.

The highest hill in this area is **Meall na Fearna**, 2479 ft., just over a mile east of Ben Vorlich. It is most easily accessible from Ardvorlich by the path that leads southwards towards Glen Artney. From the highest point of the path at the head of Glen Vorlich, Meall na Fearna is about half a mile distant. Coire na Cloiche, which is a mile north-east of this top, does not appear to offer any climbing; however, there is a lower crag at the head of Srath a' Ghlinne which might give some climbing. The easiest approach to this crag is by a private road from Auchinner in Glen Artney.

The finest, though far from the highest hill in this area is **Am Bioran**, 2011 ft., a mile and a half south of St. Fillans. The feature of this little hill as seen from Strath Earn is the north-east ridge which drops sharply down to the valley, giving the impression of a narrow, rocky ridge. The ascent of this ridge is a very pleasant short climb with the possibility of a little scrambling on the many rock outcrops on the way up. The climb may be started from the old church near Wester Dundurn Farm. From Am Bioran a broad, undulating ridge of heathery hills extends westwards for about four miles and gives a good high-level walk which can be completed by descending to Glen Vorlich.

A mile and a half south-east of St. Fillans (near Dundurn Farm) a delightful forest road leads up into Gleann Ghoinean to the foot of Mor Bheinn, Ben Halton and the nameless 2317 ft. hill on the north side of Glen Artney. Access to these hills may became more difficult as the area has recently been planted by the Forestry Commission.

South of Glen Artney there is a large area of very rough moorland, culminating in **Uamh Bheag,** 2181 ft., and Beinn Odhar. The former commands a very fine view of Ben Vorlich and Stuc a' Chroin, and has in addition some interesting caves in its slightly lower shoulder called Uamh Mhor. From Burn of Cambus, one and a half miles along the Callander road from Doune, a rough road leads to Loch Mahaick and Severie from where a gradual rise over thick heather leads to Uamh Mhor. The caves are to be found on the western shoulder at the prominent scarp of rock, and close to a tiny rift valley known locally as 'Rob Roy's Cattle Fank'. From there it is only a short climb north-east to the top of Uamh Bheagh.

There are three good cross-country routes in the area covered by this chapter, two of which are rights-of-way. The shortest is the right-of-way from Ardchullarie More on Loch Lubnaig to Edinample on Loch Earn by way of Glen Ample, a distance of 6 miles. The route is easy to follow although the head of Glen Ample is boggy and the path is in places hard to follow. Forestation in the upper reaches of Glen Ample will in due course alter the character of this walk.

The second right-of-way goes from Callander to Comrie by the Keltie Water and Glen Artney. From Callander the road to Arivurich-ardich is followed to the bridge over the Keltie Water, and a few yards further on the right-of-way branches off to the east to cross a low col and descend to the Allt an Dubh Choirein. There one joins the track leading over the Monadh Odhar into Glen Artney, and the public road is soon reached. The total distance from Callander to Comrie is 16 miles, this but can be shortened to less than 6 miles by driving as far as possible at both ends.

The third route is from Callander to Ardvorlich. From Callander it follows the road to Arivurichardich and then the path over Stuc a' Chroin's south-east ridge to the old shieling at Dubh Choirein. From there the route climbs alongside the stream under Ben Vorlich's east face to the pass at the head of Glen Vorlich. The pass is rather boggy and trackless, and on the Glen Vorlich side one should keep to the east side of the burn where the path eventually reappears. and leads down the beautifully wooded glen to Ardvorlich. The total distance is about 10 miles.

Transport and Accommodation

Dunblane, on the extreme southern edge of the area covered by this chapter, can be reached by train. Apart from this there are only bus services on the roads which encircle the area. The most useful services for climbers and walkers are those between Callander, Lochearnhead St. Fillans (along the north side of Loch Earn), and Comrie. This service is operated by W. Alexander and Sons (Midland) Ltd.

There are hotels at Callander, Strathyre, Kingshouse (Balquhidder), Lochearnhead, St. Fillans and Comrie.

There is a Youth Hostel at Balquhidder.

BIBLIOGRAPHY

Stuc a' Chroin's East Face, W. Brown, *S.M.C.J.*, Vol. 3, p. 19.
Ben Vorlich and Stuc a' Chroin, G. Thomson, *S.M.C.J.*, Vol. 3, p. 107.
A Saturday Afternoon on the Face of Stuc a' Chroin, J. Gall Inglis, *S.M.C.J.*, Vol. 6, p. 102.
Ben Vorlich (Perthshire) Group, (Guide Book Article), *S.M.C.J.*, Vol. 6, p. 200.
The North-east Face of Stuc a' Chroin, W. Garden, *S.M.C.J.*, Vol. 11, p. 278.
Ben Vorlich and Stuc a' Chroin, (Note), H. J. A. McIntyre, *S.M.C.J.*, Vol. 14, p. 92.

7

Ben Chonzie and Glen Almond

The principal mountain in this area, and the only one over 3000 ft., is:
Ben Chonzie, 3048 ft., 5½ miles N. of Comrie in Strath Earn.
Maps: Ordnance Survey One-inch Series, Sheets 48, 54 and 55.
Bartholomew's Half-inch Series, Sheet 48.

The region described in this chapter lies between Loch Tay and Strath Earn; it is bounded on the east by the road from Crieff to Aberfeldy, and extends as far west as Glen Ogle. It is an area composed almost entirely of rolling, heather-clad hills and high moorland with no outstanding features of a mountainous nature.

This expanse of hills and moorland is intersected by several glens, of which Glen Almond is the longest and probably the finest as far as its scenery is concerned. It runs from west to east through the centre of the area, and there are some attractive corries in the hills on the south side of the glen. Glen Quaich lies to the north-east of Glen Almond, and a minor road leads up the glen from Amulree and over the moors to Kenmore. (At the time of writing the higher parts of this road are very rough.) South and south-east of Glen Almond two more glens lead into the hills from Strath Earn – Glen Turret and Glen Lednock.

There is a public road up Glen Lednock for 6 miles to the dam on Loch Lednock, and a right-of-way (which is in places submerged under the waters of the loch) continues north-west to Ardeonaig on Loch Tay. In Glen Turret a private road leads for 5 miles to the dam at the foot of Loch Turret. In Glen Almond there is a private road which becomes rather rough beyond Auchnafree, but it is passable for cars almost to the head of the glen, a distance of 9 miles. This road is a right-of-way for walkers which continues north-westwards from the head of the glen to Ardtalnaig on Loch Tay.

This area is mostly given over to sheep farming and grouse moors with a few deer in the high corries, and it should certainly be avoided in the shooting and stalking season. A feature of interest is the very large number of mountain hares on Ben Chonzie and its neighbouring hills; no other area in Scotland seems to support such a large population.

These hills and glens are essentially hill-walkers' country, and there is a solitude among them that is not found in more popular parts of the Highlands. In winter there is some excellent and easy ski-touring along the smooth, broad ridges; unfortunately, however, the hills are too low to carry much snow in springtime. The rock-climber will not find much to interest him in this area. There are some low-lying crags on the west side of Glen Lednock which have not yet been thoroughly explored, and a fair-sized buttress on Meall Dubh (on the south side of Glen Almond) once enjoyed some popularity with local climbers, but is seldom climbed nowadays. Elsewhere, as for instance on the Glen Turret side of Ben Chonzie and on the Blue Craigs just east of Loch Turret, there are some steep and craggy hillsides, but the crags are too broken and vegetatious to afford any rock-climbing, and the best that they might offer are some short and probably easy winter climbs.

The main hills can be subdivided into two groups, one to the north of Glen Almond, and the other to the south. The former group is a long, broad and undulating ridge which culminates at its western end in Creagan na Beinne, 2909 ft. On the south side of Glen Almond, Ben Chonzie is the dominant hill, and it is situated centrally between glens Almond, Lednock and Turret. To its east a broad ridge extends from Auchnafree Hill, 2565 ft., towards the Sma' Glen, and to its west Greag Uchdag, 2887 ft., is the highest of a group of hills between Loch Lednock and the head of Glen Almond. Elsewhere, namely to the north-east of Glen Quaich and to the west of Glen Lednock, the hills are much lower, more in the nature of high, undulating moorland, and they are of no interest to the climber.

Ben Chonzie (or Ben y Hone), 3048 ft., is the highest hill in this part of Perthshire, and it is the only one that is much visited by hill-walkers. Although the hill itself has no features of interest (except its large population of mountain hares), its position midway between the Highlands and Lowlands makes it a conspicuous feature on the north side of Strath Earn, and it is also a fine viewpoint for the surrounding country. The crest of the hill is a rather flat and broad ridge running roughly from south to north, with the summit at the north end. It is a featureless top, and the summit might be difficult to find in thick weather; however, three fences converge beside the cairn and route finding difficulties are thus eliminated, (unless the depth of snow in winter is sufficient to cover these fences).

Ben Chonzie may be climbed equally well from any one of the three glens which surround it The shortest approach is probably from Glen Lednock, starting at Invergeldie Farm. A well made track leads up the west side of the Invergeldie Burn for almost a mile and then crosses the stream and continues up the south-west side of Ben Chonzie to shooting butts. This track ends just below Point 2759 ft., from where a fence leads along the very broad ridge to the summit. Although not very exciting as a walking route in summer, this makes a good ski-route in winter; there is plenty of scope for easy skiing on the upper part of the hill, and lower down the track is likely to be the best route of ascent and descent, particularly if it has a good covering of snow.

From the dam at the south end of Loch Turret the route is slightly longer. One can follow the east side of the loch past the remains of Glenturret Lodge and continue up the Turret Burn to its source just beyond Lochan Uaine. A fence and path then lead steeply up to the north-east shoulder of Ben Chonzie, and so to the top. Alternatively, a slightly more direct approach to the summit can be made by striking uphill from the Turret Burn just before reaching Lochan Uaine. The craggy hillside immediately west of the lochan might give an interesting ascent in winter.

From Glen Almond there is a variety of easy routes to Ben Chonzie. A mile and a half west of Auchnafree a track leads uphill from a deserted cottage towards the Moine Bheag – the flat col between Ben Chonzie and Auchnafree Hill. This gives a quick approach to the north-east shoulder of Ben Chonzie.

Carn Chois, 2571 ft., is two miles south-east of Ben Chonzie, and its steep east face overlooks Loch Turret. This face consists of broken rocks and steep grass, and there are some scrambles, especially towards the north on Creag nan Uan. Further south, and high up on the hillside, there is a small buttress of rough schist which has given a difficult but incomplete climb for half its height.

Auchnafree Hill, 2565 ft., is the highest of the hills extending eastwards from Ben Chonzie towards the Sma' Glen. It can be very easily climbed from the head of Loch Turret or from Glen Almond.

The top is very flat, and the large summit cairn is about a hundred yards south of the fence which crosses the top from north-west to south-east. The continuation of the broad, grassy ridge south-eastwards leads to a peaty col just north of the Blue Craigs; at this point the ridge turns slightly north of east and continues (with a faint path for most of the way) over Point 2498 ft. and several small humps and hollows to Meall Dubh. It is worth keeping to the north edge of this ridge to get some pleasing views downwards into the corries above Glen Almond. In one of these corries – Coire Chultrain – the Kirk of the Grove was once a meeting place of the Covenanters.

Some distance to the west of Ben Chonzie, and separated from it by the headwaters of the Invergeldie Burn, there is a group of three hills of which Creag Uchdag, 2887 ft., is the highest and most interesting. (It is named Creag Uigeach on the Half-inch map.) This hill has rather a craggy south-west side, and it is easily climbed either from Glen Lednock or from Ardeonaig by the right-of-way which crosses the south-west shoulder of the hill at about 1850 ft. The ascent up this shoulder can be enlivened by some scrambling on boulders and small outcrops.

The hills to the north of Glen Almond form a broad and undulating ridge of little interest to the climber, although there is some very good terrain for the mountain skier. The highest point, Creagan na Beinne, 2909 ft., is at the west end of the ridge and is most easily approached from Ardtalnaig on Loch Tay by the right-of-way which leads round the west side of the hill to Glen Almond. At the other end of the ridge Meall nam Fuaran, 2631 ft., has a steep face overlooking Glen Lochan, but it is mostly scree and broken crags. On the south side of Glen Lochan, Beinn na Gainimh, 2382 ft., also has a craggy face overlooking the glen, but it is of a similar character and does not offer any climbing.

Glen Lochan itself is a fine little pass between Loch Freuchie in Glen Quaich and Auchnafree in Glen Almond. From Loch Freuchie a good track leads to Lochan a' Mhuilinn, the noisy breeding place for hundreds of gulls, and a path continues into the narrow glen between Meall nam Fuaran and Beinn na Gainimh. Just below the pass one reaches the Lochan Uaine, a very shallow, reedy loch which almost disappears in dry weather. On the south side of the lochan there is a fair path which continues through the pass and down to Auchnafree.

There are several other good walks in these hills, of which the longest is the right-of-way from Newton Bridge in Glen Almond to Ardtalnaig. The walk up the glen is very pleasant, characteristic of the tranquillity and beauty of the Perthshire glens. Five miles beyond Auchnafree the road fades out, and a track continues to the deserted cottage at Dunan. The right-of-way turns north, crosses a flat, grassy pass and descends almost imperceptibly towards Loch Tay along the Allt a' Chilleine. Below Tullichglass a road is joined for the last mile and a half to Ardtalnaig, a distance of 14 miles from Newton Bridge.

Another right-of-way leads from Glen Lednock to Loch Tay. Just below Loch Lednock (which is a new loch created by the North of Scotland Hydro-Electric Board) one passes the cascades of Sput Rollo, but these falls have lost much of their character since the building of the dam. It is probably best to keep on the north-east side of the loch, although there is a road on the south-west side leading to a little power station at its west end. There is no continuous path as the right-of-way has been submerged, but near the head of the loch the track appears and climbs quite high over the south-west shoulder of Creag Uchdag before dropping to the pass at the head of the Fin Glen. There is a grand view of Ben Lawers as one descends the path down this glen towards Ardeonaig, (6 miles).

Yet another cross-country route can be made from Glen Lednock to Ardtalnaig. From Invergeldie the track up the Invergeldie Burn is followed, keeping to the west of the burn to cross the hills to Dunan in Glen Almond. From there the previously described route is followed to Loch Tay, (9 miles).

In Glen Almond the corrie on the north-east side of Meall Dubh contains a big, but rather broken buttress on which several climbs have been recorded by M. B. Nettleton. This corrie is best approached by crossing the River Almond at an island a mile and a quarter above Newton Bridge and climbing up the west side of the stream flowing from the corrie. The buttress is on the west side of the corrie and faces north-east. It is quite steep and consists of short rock pitches separated by grass ledges, so that no well-defined route exists; however, the ascent can be started at the lowest rocks and continues by a series of zigzags up short pitches and along ledges, (350 ft., D.).

Near the south side of the buttress there is a straight-cut gully leading to the top of the cliff; this is *Pinnacle Gully*. In summer it is likely to be a wet scramble with a cave pitch near the top, (200 ft.). The gully gives a much better climb in winter conditions. On the south (left) side of the gully, and just above the cave pitch, there is on the face of the buttress a small pinnacle which gives the gully its name. This pinnacle can be reached from the gully by a traverse along a narrow ledge, and from its top, which is sensational perch, one can lean across the gap and swarm up a steep arête to a good stance, (35 ft., V.D.). Scrambling follows to the top of the buttress.

Central Gully lies between Pinnacle Gully and the centre of the buttress, and is rather indeterminate. The top pitch is slippery and wet, and it is preferable in summer to climb the upper half of the gully by a branch on the south (left) which gives three good chimney pitches (300 ft., D.). In winter the main line of the gully has been followed and can give a good climb.

Elsewhere in Glen Almond there are some easy scrambles in the corrie to the west of Meall Dubh. In the Sma' Glen, a mile below Newton Bridge and quite low down on the east side of the river, there is a considerable rock face which gives a good 200 ft. climb up its left edge.

In Glen Lednock there are some small cliffs on the south-west side of the road on Crappich Hill. Two miles further up the glen there is a big cliff on the hill called Balnacoul Castle. This cliff is low down, little more than half a mile from the road and very steep; it is divided into two big buttresses and several smaller ones. R. N. Campbell has reported a route on the left-hand large buttress as follows: *Carcase Wall.* Start just left of the lowest point of the buttress at a crack. Climb crack to trees, then step left and follow steeper crack to reach grassy terrace. Move up this to tree belay (100 ft.). From top of grass climb cracked bulging wall by a series of layback moves, then trend right to grass ledge below obvious cracked overhang on crest of buttress. Piton belay (100 ft.). Move right, then up wall right of overhang to gain slab. Move up slab and round nose on right to easier ground and go up to tree belays, (70 ft.). (270 ft., S., R. N. Campbell, J. Moran and P. M. Rust.) There are likely to be other hard routes on this crag that will repay investigation.

Transport and Accommodation

There are hotels at Crieff, Comrie, St. Fillans, Amulree, Kenmore and Ardeonaig.

The area is not well served by buses. There is a service from Crieff up Strath Earn and along Loch Earn to Lochearnhead, and Crieff itself can be reached by bus from Edinburgh, Glasgow and Perth.

There are no bus services through the Sma' Glen and Glen Cochill to Aberfeldy, nor along the south side of Loch Tay.

BIBLIOGRAPHY

Ben-y-Hone, (Note), *S.M.C.J.*, Vol. 4, p. 179.
Ben Chonzie, (Guide Book Article), *S.M.C.J.*, Vol. 6, p. 244.
Ben Chonzie on Ski, J. H. Wigner, *S.M.C.J.*, Vol. 8, p. 133.
Some Hill Roads in Scotland, W. A. Smith, *S.M.C.J.*, Vol. 14, p. 95.
Some Glen Almond Climbs, M. B. Nettleton, *S.M.C.J.*, Vol. 23, p. 90.
Skis in Scottish Mountaineering, G. J. F. Dutton, *S.M.C.J.*, Vol. 26, p. 121.

8

Cowal and Ardgoil

Maps: Ordnance Survey One-inch Series, Sheets 52, 53 and 59 and Loch Lomond
and the Trossachs Tourist Map.
Bartholomew's Half-inch Series, Sheet 44.

The area covered by this chapter is the large peninsula between Loch
Long and the Firth of Clyde on the east, and Loch Fyne on the west.
The peninsula is about thirty five miles long from north to south, and
sixteen miles from east to west at its widest point; and its southern
tip, facing the Island of Bute, is divided into three prongs by Loch
Riddon and Loch Striven.

Ardgoil is the district at the northern end of the peninsula, and is
enclosed by Glen Kinglas, Glen Croe, Loch Long, Loch Goil,
Hell's Glen and Loch Fyne. It is rugged and entirely mountainous,
and includes the three highest peaks in the area covered by this chapter, namely Ben Donich, The Brack and Beinn an Lochain, of which
only the last-named exceeds 3000 ft.

Cowal is much more extensive. In its northern part adjacent to
Ardgoil it is also mountainous, but gradually as one goes south the
hills become lower and the western and south-western parts of Cowal
are mainly moorland with farms on the lower ground by Loch Fyne.
Cowal is also extensively forested, and Glenbranter is an example of
a fair-sized village that has grown up around the forest industry.

Cowal was at one time part of the Kingdom of Dalriada which was
colonised by the Irish Gaels between the third and sixth centuries
A.D., and the name Cowal is derived from Comghall, one of the Irish
chieftains of that time. Following the arrival of St. Columba at Iona
in 563, Celtic priests established Christian outposts at several places
in Cowal including St. Catherine's, Strachur and Strathlachlan on the

93

shores of Loch Fyne. The Norsemen were not attracted to Cowal which was much less fertile than the neighbouring lands, and only at the end of their occupation of the western coast did they sail up Loch Long. After the departure of the Norsemen, Cowal and Ardgoil came under the power of the leading clans of the area, and gradually the Campbells gained control of the whole area.

Ardgoil and Cowal are the only parts of the Southern Highlands in which the sea and sea-lochs form a significant part of the scenery, and the combination of mountain, loch and forest makes this area one of great beauty, embodying in miniature many of the finest features of Highland scenery. Despite this, the area is surprisingly neglected by the hill-walker (possibly because of the more obvious attractions of the neighbouring Arrochar Alps) and it deserves to be better known for it has many fine and rugged little mountains.

Ardgoil and Cowal are reached by road along the A83 from Arrochar to Inveraray through Glen Croe and Glen Kinglas. The pass between these glens is known as the Rest and be Thankful. At the foot of Glen Kinglas the A815 road branches south along the side of Loch Fyne to Strachur and then passes through the heart of the Cowal hills by Lock Eck to Dunoon, the capital of Cowal. Dunoon can also be reached by steamer from Gourock, there being several sailings every day. In addition to the main access routes just mentioned, there are also steamer services to Blairmore and Kilmun, and many minor roads and forest roads give access to all parts of Ardgoil and Cowal.

The Argyll National Forest Park lies within Ardgoil and the north-eastern part of Cowal, and includes most of the mountains of these areas. The Park is administered by the Forestry Commission, and the Forest Park Guide (published by H.M. Stationery Office) is invaluable for the visitor wishing to gain a complete understanding of the district. In addition to the extensive forests of larch and spruce, there are some fine groups of Scots pines near Loch Eck and the Holy Loch, and in the same area the Younger Botanic Garden, the Benmore Pinetum, the Kilmun Arboretum and Puck's Glen should all be visited. The Younger Botanic Garden is said to have the largest collection of rhododendrons in the country.

The principal hills of Ardgoil are:
(1) **Beinn an Lochain,** 3021 ft., 1¼ miles S.W. of Butterbridge in Glen Kinglas.
(2) **Beinn an t-Seilich,** 2359, 1 mile W. of (1).

(3)   **Stob an Eas,** 2400 ft., 1 mile W.S.W. of (2).
(4)   **Ben Donich,** 2774 ft., 2¼ miles N.E. of Lochgoilhead.
(5)   **The Brack,** 2580 ft., 1¾ miles W. of Ardgartan at the foot of Glen Croe.
(6)   **Cnoc Coinnich,** 2497 ft., 2 miles, E.S.E. of Lochgoilhead.
(7)   **Beinn Reithe,** 2141 ft., 1½ miles S. of (6).

Ardgoil is divided into two unequal parts by the road from the Rest and be Thankful to Lochgoilhead through Gleann Mor (B828). The first three hills in the list above are on the north side of this road, and the others are on the south. Access to all the hills in Ardgoil is easy from the roads already mentioned, and also from the Forestry Commission road along the west side of Loch Long from Ardgartan to Corran Lochan near the southern tip of the Ardgoil peninsula. (This is a private road, and the gates on it are sometimes locked.) Lochgoilhead is probably the best centre for the Ardgoil hills, all of which are within easy walking distance of the village.

Beinn an Lochain, 3021 ft., is the highest peak in Ardgoil. The height given on the One-inch Map, 2992 ft., refers to the lower top which is about 150 yards south-west of the summit. The east face of the mountain is its finest feature; it plunges very steeply for 1200 ft. from the twin summits to the dark waters of Loch Restil, and is seamed with crags and small gullies. Unfortunately none of these crags or gullies are long enough or sufficiently well-defined to give distinct climbing routes. The north face of Beinn an Lochain has a fine little corrie high up under the summit. These two faces are separated by the north-east ridge of the mountain which rises from Butterbridge directly to the summit. The south and west sides of Beinn an Lochain are less interesting, being mainly grass slopes, steep in places.

For the hill-walker the best route up the mountain is probably the north-east ridge, and near its top the ridge becomes quite narrow and steep with a fine view of the crags of the north corrie. A slightly shorter, but less interesting ascent can be made from the road a short distance south of the Rest and be Thankful. The climb westwards is continuously steep, but not difficult, and leads to the summit ridge of Beinn an Lochain a quarter of a mile south of the top. The walker coming from Lochgoilhead must follow the Gleann Mor road for almost four miles to the bridge over the Allt Glinne Mhoir, and then follow the smaller side stream northwards for half a mile before heading north-east to the top of Beinn an Lochain.

A few hundred feet below the summit of the mountain the

north-east ridge forms the east wall of the north corrie. The west wall is a steep and vegetatious rock face sloping up from west to east. Near the centre of this face there is a remarkable pinnacle which juts out from the cliff and looks very unstable. *Raeburn's Route* (600 ft., M., H. Raeburn, Dr. and Mrs. Inglis Clark) takes a rather indeterminate route from the bottom to the top of the cliff, visiting the pinnacle en route. There is scope for a good deal of variation as grass ledges abound, but there are also some short difficult sections. *Saxifrage Gully* (250 ft., M., J. B. Nimlin and B. H. Humble) is about 400 ft. below the summit of the mountain on the last steep rise of the north-east ridge. The gully is open in its lower part, but higher up is closed by a rock mass which is climbed on the left. In summer the gully abounds in mountain plants and loose rubble.

There is a slope of fallen boulders below the corrie, and at a height of about 1450 ft. (M.R. 214087) two huge boulders leaning against each other form a howff which is known among cave-dwellers as 'Sunset Arch'. A large sheet of polythene and some ingenuity are needed to make this howff waterproof.

Beinn an t-Seilich and **Stob an Eas** are seldom visited although both hills are easily climbed either from Hell's Glen or from Glen Kinglas. There is a footbridge over the Kinglas Water at the foot of the grassy corrie between the two hills, and this makes the best starting point on the north side.

On the south side of Gleann Mor the Ardgoil peninsula (marked on some maps as Ardgoil Estate) is entirely within the Argyll National Forest Park. The peninsula south of The Brack is marked on some maps as Argyll's Bowling Green, a surprising name for an area of rough and knobbly hills. It appears that the name originated in the days (before the building of the road through Glen Croe) when the Dukes of Argyll travelled south from Inveraray by Lochgoilhead and the pass over the hills between the Saddle and Tom Molach to Mark and the ferry to Portincaple. The Bowling Green was a pasture at the top of the pass where the horses were rested after the ascent from the lochside, but the name has now been extended to include the whole peninsula.

Ben Donich, 2774 ft., is the highest hill south of Gleann Mor. It is grassy on most sides, with an extensive area of small crags and fallen boulders just north of the summit. The mountain has three principal ridges which give the three usual routes of ascent. The shortest and most interesting route starts just south of the Rest and be Thankful

19. Climbing on Ben A'n.

20. Ben Lomond from Loch Ard.

21. Cruach Ardrain and Beinn Tulaichean from Stob a' Choin.

22. Ben Vorlich and Stuc a' Chroin from Meall an t-Seallaidh.

23. Loch Lubnaig.

24. Carrick Castle and Cruach nam Miseag, Loch Goil.

25. Beinn an Lochain from Glen Croe.

and after going through the forest follows the north ridge of Ben Donich. Towards the top of the ridge the path (which is not very distinct) twists and turns through fallen boulders just below the crest of the ridge. The ridge itself ends at a false summit, and there is a walk of several hundred yards south-westwards over a few knolls to reach the true summit which overlooks Lochgoilhead.

The ascent from Lochgoilhead is perfectly straightforward, but rather less interesting than the previous route as the southern slopes are featureless. The gradually unfolding view southwards is probably the best reward of an ascent of this side of the mountain. The north-south traverse of Ben Donich from the Rest and be Thankful to Lochgoilhead is the best combination of these two routes.

The east ridge of Ben Donich is broad and grassy, and drops to the col separating the mountain from The Brack. The route from Ardgartan to Ben Donich follows the Forestry Commission road on the south side of Glen Croe past the cottage at Creagdhu to a point half a mile north-east of this col. A marked path through the trees leads out above the forest and so to the col from which the east ridge is followed to the top.

The Brack, 2580 ft., is a grand mountain, steep and rugged on all sides, particularly the north where there is a fine corrie backed by vertical cliffs. A long, level shoulder extends eastwards from the summit towards Ardgartan, and the entire northern, eastern and southern slopes of the mountain are forested up to about the 1000 ft. contour.

The Brack is usually climbed from Ardgartan, and there are three possible routes. The most direct one goes steeply up through the forest due west of Ardgartan and along the east shoulder to the final steep climb to the summit. The second route follows the Forestry Commission road southwards from Ardgartan for a mile and a half and then takes the branch road up the Coilessan Glen. A mile further on this road doubles back, but a path continues up the glen and is followed over a stile on the forest boundary fence. One can then turn north to reach The Brack's south-west ridge which is followed to the summit.

The third route is up the steep north-east side of The Brack and is scenically the best of the three. The forest road on the south side of the Croe Water is followed past Creagdhu cottage and then uphill. Just beyond a double bend the road crosses a little stream coming down from The Brack. The east bank of this stream is followed through the

G

forest (faint track) and onto the open hillside. The direct route to the summit continues straight ahead up the stream, but a short diversion to the west leads to 'Cobbler View', one of the best howffs in the area (M.R. 250036). The howff is under one of several huge boulders which have rolled down the hillside from the cliffs above. The walking route to the summit continues directly uphill, passing to the left (east) of the cliffs. A small upper corrie is reached and a faint track threads upwards between boulders and little pinnacles to the summit.

The Brack can also be climbed easily from Lochgoilhead by the track on the south side of the Donich Water which leads to the south-west ridge. The traverse of this hill and Ben Donich is a good round, starting and finishing at Lochgoilhead, or traversing from Ardgartan to Lochgoilhead.

There are several rock-climbs on The Brack which are described in detail in the S.M.C.'s Climber's Guide to *Arrochar* by J. R. Houston. The three best climbs are all of Very Severe standard, and there are several short and vegetatious climbs of Moderate and Difficult standard. Unfortunately there is nothing between these two extremes, and The Brack has little to offer the average rock-climber.

The longest climbs are all on the main cliff several hundred feet directly above 'Cobbler View' howff. The features of the cliff are the big dark gully at its right-hand end, the prominent groove in the centre and the easy angled ridge forming its left-hand edge. The big gully is *Elephant Gully* (300 ft., D., A. C. McLaren, S. G. Shadbolt and C. P. Shadbolt). It is a very vegetatious climb, likely to appeal more to the botanist than the climber, but it is in a very impressive situation. The first section is climbed on the right wall by grassy ledges and the gully is regained above the first big cave. One then scrambles up under a huge chockstone and the right wall is again climbed to reach the top of this chockstone (on which one could almost pitch a small tent). An upward traverse (still on the right wall) leads back to the bed of the gully. There is an easy exit at this point, but the gully narrows and disappears under some huge boulders; one can crawl easily up the tunnel and finally emerge through a small hole in the hillside. Entertaining, but hardly rock-climbing. The winter ascent (J. B. Nimlin and R. Grieve) follows the summer route, but is a much more serious proposition. If the top of the final tunnel is blocked by snow, an exit half way up the pitch may be possible.

The prominent groove is *Great Central Groove* (300 ft., V.S.,

P. Mitchell and J. Morrison). The first ascent in 1958 was the culmination of many unsuccessful attempts. The rock is none too good and the groove is rather muddy; however, it is a grand climb if these features are ignored. The winter ascent (W. Skidmore and R. Richardson) is the hardest winter route done in the Arrochar area to date. *Mammoth* (280 ft., V.S. and A.3., W. Skidmore, R. Richardson and J. Crawford) follows the crack in the left wall of Great Central Groove, and *Mainline* (400 ft., V.S., W. Skidmore and J. Crawford) follows an obvious line in the face between Elephant Gully and Great Central Groove. *Sideline* (150 ft., A.3, R. Richardson and W. Skidmore) is a one-pitch artificial route on the overhanging left wall of Elephant Gully which finishes on the ledge at the same level as the big chockstone in the gully.

The left-hand edge of the cliff is a series of steps formed by short pitches and grass ledges. Below this edge there is a huge pointed boulder with a good cave under it, (an excellent, but seemingly unfrequented howff). *Inglis Clark Arête* (300 ft., M., W. Inglis Clark, C. Inglis Clark and M. Inglis Clark) starts just above the boulder and keeps close to the north-eastern edge of the cliff in a succession of short pitches, most of them avoidable on the left. Above and to the right of this climb there is another rather indeterminate climb, *May Route* (350 ft., D., J. B. Nimlin and R. Peel) which consists of a series of steep, vegetatious crags and slabs.

The upper north-east corrie of The Brack contains numerous small crags and pinnacles. Split Pinnacle is in the southern side of the corrie and can be seen in profile as one walks up into the corrie by the route already described. Its eastern edge and the crack which splits the pinnacle both give short Moderate climbs. A few yards north of Split Pinnacle the crack in a small, steep crag is *Bobcrack* (50 ft., D.). A few yards further north there is a series of four rock steps, one above the other; this is *Four Step Ridge* (150 ft., D., J. B. Nimlin and R. Peel). The first two steps involve straightforward chimneys, the third step is a difficult crack and the final step is easy.

Moving south from The Brack to Argyll's Bowling Green, the walk along the crest of this peninsula is a fine expedition with magnificent views of mountain and loch. It is probably best done from north to south. From Ardgartan the Coilessan Glen road is taken, followed by the path to the pass at the head of the glen. Then, turning south, one climbs easy slopes to the grassy summit of Cnoc Coinnich, marked by a small cairn. The ridge to Beinn Reithe follows a semi-circular detour to the west along a broad and rather rough ridge, but there are sheep tracks here and there along the way. The south side of Beinn Reithe drops steeply, and it is probably best to keep to the west side of the ridge dropping to the heathery hollow below the Saddle which is next reached by a short, steep climb. Once again a steep descent south-westwards leads to rough, boggy ground near the original Bowling Green, and on to the last two hills in the peninsula, Tom Molach and Clach Bheinn. The return can be made by descending to the lonely Corran Lochan and walking along the Forestry Commission road back to Ardgartan.

On the east side of Cnoc Coinnich, well above the tree-line, there is an area (marked Garbh on the One-inch Map) of huge fallen boulders and small crags. Although nothing has been recorded on these boulders, there is probably sufficient scope for short climbs to justify a visit.

There are three good cross-country walks in Ardgoil between Ardgartan and Lochgoilhead. One follows the Coilessan Glen route to the Brack–Cnoc Coinnich col, and then descends westwards to Lochgoilhead along the south side of the Donich Water. Another follows the Forestry Commission road on the south side of Glen Croe (q.v.) to reach the Brack–Ben Donich col and then descends by the Allt Coire Odhair and the Donich Water to Lochgoilhead. Both these routes follow forest roads and well-defined paths for most of their lengths, but in places where they are indistinct they are marked by posts. There is no coastal path round the Ardgoil peninsula, and the southern tip near the isolated cottage at Corran is trackless and extremely rough. However a third route from Ardgartan to Lochgoilhead can be made by taking the forest road to Corran Lochan, crossing the pass northwards and descending towards Beach on Loch Goil (the old route of the Dukes of Argyll) and so along another forest road to Lochgoilhead.

The Cowal hills are subdivided naturally into several groups, and the principal hills over 2000 ft. are listed from north to south. The first group lies west and north-west of Lochgoilhead, and includes –

(1) **Cruach nam Mult,** 2001 ft., 3 miles N.W. of Lochgoilhead.
(2) **Mullach Coire a' Chuir,** 2098 ft., 2¼ miles N.W. of Lochgoilhead.
(3) **Point 2159 ft.,** ½ mile S. of (2).
(4) **Beinn Tharsuinn,** 2037 ft., ½ mile S.S.W. of (3).
(5) **Beinn Lochain,** 2306 ft., ¾ mile S.S.W. of (4).

The second group, separated from the first by the Bealach an Lochain, lies south-west of Lochgoilhead between the heads of Loch Goil and Loch Eck.

(6) **Beinn Bheula**, 2556 ft., 3½ miles S.W. of Lochgoilhead.
(7) **Carnach Mor**, 2074 ft., 1 mile N.W. of (6).
(8) **Beinn Dubhain**, 2114 ft., 1 mile S.W. of (6).

The third group lies south of the preceding one, and forms a long, nearly level ridge between Loch Goil and Glen Finart.

(9) **Sgurr a' Choinnich**, 2148 ft., 1¾ miles S.S.E. of (6).
(10) **Beinn Bhreac**, 2043 ft., 1 mile S. of (9).
(11) **Cruach a' Bhuic**, 2084 ft., ½ mile S.E. of (10).
(12) **Cruach Eighrach**, 2100 ft. contour, 1 mile S.E. of (11).
(13) **Creachan Mor**, 2156 ft., ½ mile S.E. of (12).
(14) **Cruach a' Chaise**, 2069 ft., ½ mile S.S.E. of (13).

South of the preceding group, and standing by itself near the south end of Loch Eck is

(15) **Beinn Ruadh**, 2179 ft., 1¼ miles N.E. of the south end of Loch Eck.

The next group is on the west side of Loch Eck.

(16) **Beinn Bheag**, 2029 ft., 2¾ miles S.S.E. of Glenbranter village.
(17) **Beinn Mhor**, 2433 ft., 1¾ miles S.W. of (16).
(18) **Clach Bheinn**, 2109 ft., 1¾ miles S.E. of (17).

Separated from this group by Garrachra Glen is

(19) **Creag Tharsuinn**, 2103 ft., 1¼ miles W.N.W. of (17).

Finally, on the south side of Glen Lean, the highest point of a ridge of low hills is

(20) **Cruach nan Capull**, 2005 ft., 5½ miles W.N.W. of Dunoon.

The first group of hills listed above forms a continuous ridge over-looking Lochgoilhead and the River Goil. The eastern slopes are steep, rugged and forested up to about 1000 ft., but the western slopes are broad, grassy ridges dropping towards the River Cur and its tributaries. These slopes have also been recently planted with trees and their present bare appearance will in due course be completely altered. The backbone of each of the hills is an east–west running ridge, and the drops between them are 400 ft. or more, so that the complete traverse involves a fair amount of up and downhill work. However, this is a fine expedition and the hills will be described from the point of view of the climber traversing them from south to north.

Access through the forest on the east side of these hills is rough and difficult unless a path is followed. The recognised access route starts at Lettermay Farm (1 mile S.W. of Lochgoilhead) and follows a forest road high up on the south side of the Lettermay Burn for a mile. Just before the end of this road is reached one strikes west and, crossing the Lettermay Burn, climbs up beside the steep stream which descends in a series of waterfalls from the Curra Lochain. Above the falls flatter ground is reached and a path on the south side of the burn leads to the lochan, a beautiful and lonely spot in the narrow pass between Beinn Bheula and Beinn Lochain.

From the east end of the Curra Lochain the ascent of **Beinn Lochain** is steep but straightforward. There is a jumble of fallen boulders on the south face of the hill, but there does not seem to be any scope for rock-climbing. It is probably best to aim for the summit ridge a few hundred yards east of the top and then climb the last bit of this ridge. The traverse northwards calls for little special mention; **Beinn Tharsuinn** is a grassy summit with no cairn, but its south-east face overlooking Gleann Beg is very steep and rocky. The next top, 2159 ft., is crossed and one comes to **Mullach Coire a'Chuir** whose summit ridge is cut away very sharply on its north side to leave a large, partially detached flake of rock which gives this summit a characteristic cleft appearance when seen from the east. The traverse can be ended at this point by descending the east ridge and the Eas a'Chruisgein to Drimsynie. The continuation to **Cruach nam Mult** involves a descent northwards of a thousand feet and a reascent of almost as much. Cruach nam Mult has a grassy top with no cairn, and its north face is steep. The descent can be made either north-west then north down easy grass slopes to the summit of the Hell's Glen road, or alternatively south-east to Drimsyniebeg.

The walk from Lochgoilhead to Strachur on Loch Fyne is one of the best cross-country routes in Cowal. The way as far as the Curra Lochain has just been described, and it continues westwards over the grassy Bealach an Lochain and down to the Glenbranter Forest where the forest road which encircles Beinn Lagan is joined and followed north-west to the River Cur and Strachur.

Beinn Bheula is the highest hill in Cowal. Its east face is steep and forms a fine corrie at the head of the Lettermay Burn. There is a possibility of some interesting climbing in this corrie, particularly in winter, but it seems to have suffered the same neglect as most of the Cowal hills. The other sides of Beinn Bheula are much less interesting, and **Carnach Mor** and **Beinn Dubhain** are little more than spurs enclosing Coire Aodainn. There are some caves on the north-west end of Carnach Mor, and some south-facing outcrops near the summit of Beinn Dubhain might offer a little scrambling.

The most interesting route to Beinn Bheula is probably the north-east ridge which is reached from Lettermay by the Curra Lochain path (q.v.). By keeping rather on the east side of the ridge one gets a good impression of the east corrie. The return can be varied by descending south from Beinn Bheula over the 2507 ft. top and swinging eastwards to Lochain nan Cnaimh. From the lochan one can either descend northwards by a path which joins the forest road above Lettermay, or descend eastwards to Loch Goil by rough ground on the south side of Cruach nam Miseag.

From Invernoaden near the head of Loch Eck one can make an easy round of Beinn Bheula and its two spurs. A forest road leaves the Strachur–Dunoon road about half a mile south of Invernoaden and climbs through the forest on the south-west side of Beinn Dubhain to end near the tree-line in Coire Ealt. There is also a steep path from Craigbrack on Loch Eck up the Coire Ealt burn which leads to the same point. These routes give access to Beinn Dubhain and the hills south of Beinn Bheula, and they also provide the start of another good cross-country route between Loch Eck and Loch Goil by Coire Ealt, the bealach at its head leading to Lochain nan Cnaimh and the path down to Lettermay.

The next group of hills is a four-mile long ridge between Glen Finart and Loch Goil. Access to these hills from the Glen Finart side is complicated by the forest, but possible routes include the Coire Ealt path already mentioned, another path that crosses the ridge from Sligrachan in Glen Finart to Carrick on Loch Goil, and the southern end of the ridge which drops from Am Binnein towards Shepherd's Point on the north-side of Finart Bay. The Carrick Burn on the Loch Goil side of the ridge gives access to its northern end. The ridge itself is a pleasant, easy walk in either direction with only slight drops between the several tops and intermediate knolls.

There is a good coastal walk from Ardentinny to Carrick. From Glenfinart House a forest road goes north through the trees above Loch Long. Beyond Knap a path continues up the Knap Burn and crosses the Rubha nan Eoin high above the loch before descending to the shore a mile south-east of Carrick.

Beinn Ruadh on the opposite side of Glen Finart is probably best climbed from the south end of Loch Eck by the Inverchapel Burn. There is a path up this burn and once flatter ground is reached at about 1250 ft. one can either turn north to Beinn Ruadh, south-east to Stronchullin Hill, or continue north-eastwards over the col between these hills and descend to Barnacabber Farm in Glen Finart.

The west side of Loch Eck is an almost continuous line of steep, wooded crags with three corries penetrating into the higher hills beyond. The loch itself is long and narrow, and the perfect combination of forest, crag and water makes Loch Eck the jewel of Cowal and one of the most beautiful lochs in the Southern Highlands.

The walk along the forest road on the west side of the loch from Benmore Farm to Glenbranter is very fine. The hills on this side of the loch form a more or less continuous range from Glenbranter to the foot of Glen Massan. The highest hill, **Beinn Mhor,** is at the centre of the group. Beinn Bheag lies to the north across the deep pass at the head of the Bernice Glen, and Clach Bheinn stands out from the main ridge overlooking the south end of Loch Eck.

The shortest approach to Beinn Mhor starts just west of Glen-massan Farm and goes up the south-south-west ridge over Sron Mhor; however, this route is featureless and completely misses the interesting side of the hill. The corries on the west side of Loch Eck give much more interesting, though longer, routes to Beinn Mhor, and a bicycle can be used to reach Bernice. There is a forest road for a short distance up the north side of the Bernice Glen, and beyond it an ill-defined path continues to the narrow defile at the top of the glen. Both Beinn Mhor and Beinn Bheag can be reached easily from this pass. The first few hundred feet of the climb to Beinn Mhor is steep, but thereafter one can follow the north-east ridge along the edge of the corrie above Bernice which has some small crags and pinnacles. The summit is a flattish plateau and the highest point is at the southern end overlooking Glen Massan.

Clach Bheinn is most easily climbed from the south-east. The north side of the hill overlooking Coire an t-Sith has some remarkable pinnacles and boulders at about 1400 ft. which can easily be seen from the road on the opposite side of Loch Eck. The most prominent pinnacle is called The Bishop on account of its resemblance to a bishop's mitre, and there are two smaller pinnacles to its west. The west ridge of Clach Bheinn drops almost 500 ft. from the summit and leads to the long and broad south-south-east ridge of Beinn Mhor.

Creag Tharsuinn is separated from the Beinn Mhor group by the Garrachra Glen. The east face of the hill is steep and has many rock outcrops, but the west side drops more gradually to the forest at the head of Glen Daruel. The easiest approach is from Glen Massan by the track to Garrachra. From there a diagonal ascent of the hillside leads to the Bealach nan Sac and so to the summit of Creag Tharsuinn by the south-west ridge.

Cruach nan Capull is the highest point of the ridge which extends north-west from Dunoon along the south side of Glen Lean, and a very pleasant expedition may be made from Dunoon by climbing Bishop's Seat behind the town and continuing north-west to Cruach

26. Lochgoilhead, looking towards Ben Donich (left), The Cobbler and The Brack (right).

27. Loch Eck and Clach Bheinn.

28. *Opposite:* The Cobbler from the Narnain Boulder.

29. *Above:* The North Peak of The Cobbler.

30. NORTH PEAK OF THE COBBLER

1. Chimney Arête
2. Right-angled Chimney
3. Cat Crawl
4. Direct Direct
5. Punster's Crack
6. Right-angled Gully
7. Club Crack
8. Right-angled Groove
9. Ramshead Ridge
10. Wether Wall
11. Ramshead Gully
12. Whither Wether
13. Ramshead Wall
14. Incubator
15. Recess Route
16. Fold Direct
17. N'Gombi
18. Gangway
19. Maclay's Crack
20. North Rib

31. THE COBBLER, S.W. FACE OF THE SOUTH PEAK

1. Original Route
2. North-west Crack
3. Porcupine Wall

4. Dicer's Groove
5. Glueless Groove
6. Ithuriel's Wall

7. Gladiator's Groove
8. „ Direct Start
9. Ardgartan Arête

32. THE COBBLER, N.E. FACE OF THE SOUTH PEAK

1. Jughandle
2. Bow Crack
3. S Crack
4. Aeon
5. Grassy Traverse
6. Sesame Groove
7. Deadman's Groove
8. Grossen Zinnen
9. McLean's Folly
10. North Wall Groove
11. North Wall Traverse
12. Slack's Route (joining Direct Route)

33. CREAG THARSUINN

1. Sugach Buttress, Direct Route
2. Sugach Buttress, Original Route
3. Slab and Groove
4. Maclay's Gully
5. McLaren's Chimney
6. Curving Gully

7. Eighty Foot Gully
8. Face Route
9. V Groove
10. Hangover
11. Solo Buttress
12. Alfresco

34. The last pitch of Punster's Crack on the North Peak of The Cobbler.

nan Capull and Cruach Neuran. These hills command grand views of the Firth of Clyde and the Cowal hills to the north. There are some pleasant low-level walks in this area, one of which goes from Glen Kin (a mile west of the head of the Holy Loch) southwards over the Bealach na Sreine to Inverchaolain on Loch Striven. There are also good walks on the east and west sides of Loch Striven where footpaths exist on the roadless sections of the lochside.

There is not much of interest for the rock-climber in Cowal. Creag Liath on the lower slopes of Beinn Ruadh above the south end of Loch Eck is the best crag to have been explored to date, but it is lichenous and becomes very slippery when wet. Six routes on this crag of Severe and Very Severe standard have been recorded in the S.M.C.'s Climbers' Guide to *Arrochar*. The pinnacles on Clach Bheinn have been explored and many short routes discovered. On The Bishop the west ridge and the chimney on the east face have been climbed, and on one of the smaller pinnacles called The Pawn there is a cave route. The head of Coire an t-Sith under Beinn Mhor has some gullies which might give good climbs in winter. There are some steep crags just below the summit of Clach Bheinn on its south-west side which might give hard routes, and at the head of the Allt Corrach (about half a mile south-west of Clach Bheinn) there are some bigger cliffs that might repay exploration. There are some short, hard routes on the north-east face of An Creachan opposite Stonefield in Glen Massan. Apart from these possible rock-climbing areas there are some low-level crags and boulders near Coylet (Loch Eck), Stonefield (Glen Massan) and the quarry north of Benmore Farm at the south end of Loch Eck.

The Paper Cave above Lock Eck is worth a visit with a torch and rope. The cave is in the forest on the north-east side of Clach Bheinn, below the highest point of the upper forest road just south of Coirantee. According to tradition, the deeds and documents of the Campbell family were hidden in the cave during troubled times at the end of the seventeenth century when Cowal was plundered by Highlanders from Atholl.

Transport and Accommodation

MacBrayne's bus service from Glasgow to Inveraray, Ardrishaig and Campbelltown passes Ardgartan and goes through Glen Croe and Glen Kinglas.

Cowal Motor Services (Dunoon) operate local buses between

Dunoon and Kilmun, Strone, Blairmore, Benmore (Younger Botanic Garden), and Ardentinny. There is an infrequent service between Dunoon and Strachur.

Steamer services operate between Gourock and Dunoon (regular sailings seven days a week). There are less frequent sailings from Gourock and Craigendoran to Blairmore and Kilmun.

There are many hotels in the Dunoon area and round the Holy Loch as far as Blairmore. Other hotels in the mountainous parts of Cowal and Ardgoil are at Coylet, Whistlefield, (both by Loch Eck), Ardentinny, Strachur, St. Catherine's, Lochgoilhead, Carrick and Arrochar.

There is a Youth Hostel at Ardgartan, and just outside the area covered by this chapter there are also Youth Hostels at Inveraray and Tighnabruaich.

BIBLIOGRAPHY

Cowal, Guide Book Article, *S.M.C.J.*, Vol. 6, p. 172.

Beinn an Lochain, H. Raeburn, *S.M.C.J.*, Vol. 7, p. 242.

The Brack, W. Inglis Clark, *S.M.C.J.*, Vol. 9, p. 19.

Cowal and its Hills, S. M. Penney, *S.M.C.J.*, Vol. 11, p. 313.

The Brack. The Elephant Gully, H. Raeburn, *S.M.C.J.*, Vol. 12, p. 209.

Clach Bheinn, (note on the pinnacles), A. Arthur, *S.M.C.J.*, Vol. 12, p. 235.

The Brack: Elephant Gully, (note), J. M. Wordie, *S.M.C.J.*, Vol. 12, p. 294.

Argyll's Bowling Green, F. S. Goggs, *S.M.C.J.*, Vol. 12, p. 323.

Rest and be Thankful Stone, Glencroe, (note), F. S. Goggs, *S.M.C.J.*, Vol. 12, p. 344.

Coast and Hill Paths Around the Firth of Clyde, B. H. Humble, *S.M.C.J.*, Vol. 23, p. 68.

Great Central Groove, The Brack, P. Mitchell, *S.M.C.J.*, Vol. 26, p. 356.

The Brack, New Routes on an Old Mountain, R. Richardson, *S.M.C.J.*, Vol. 29, p. 227.

Argyll Forest Park Guide, published by H.M. Stationery Office, (1967).

9

Beinn Bhuidhe and South-West Argyll

The only noteworthy mountain in this area is:
(1) **Beinn Bhuidhe,** 3106 ft., 4 miles N. of the head of Loch Fyne.
Maps : Ordnance Survey One-inch Series, Sheets 52, 53, 58 and 65.
Bartholomew's Half-inch Series, Sheets 43, 44, 47 and 48.

Beinn Bhuidhe is one of the most isolated mountains in the Southern Highlands, being six miles from its nearest neighbour Ben Lui and slightly more from the Arrochar Alps. It is the only mountain over 3000 ft. in the area covered by this chapter which includes that part of Argyll to the west of Loch Fyne and Glen Fyne, and south of the River Orchy, the Pass of Brander and Loch Etive. This area includes the districts of Kintyre, Knapdale and part of Lorne.

The western coast of Argyll is very indented by sea-lochs, of which Loch Fyne is by far the longest. It is a coast of sandy bays, rocky headlands and little islands, and the views from the mainland across firth and sound to Arran, Jura and Mull are among the most beautiful sea and mountainscapes in Scotland. Unfortunately, from the climber's point of view, Kintyre, Knapdale and the part of Lorne south of Loch Etive are non-mountainous, and although he may be attracted to these regions for the beauty and tranquillity of this part of Scotland, he will not be attracted by the mountains because there are none. The best that this region has to offer are a few low, rocky hills, some sea cliffs, one fine granite crag and many coastal and cross-country walks.

The A83 road from Arrochar to Inveraray, Lochgilphead, Tarbert and Campbelltown passes through the area covered by this chapter from north to south and gives access to most of the country except the Lorne coast which is reached by the A816 road from Lochgilphead to Oban, and the area around Loch Awe which is reached by the B840 road. There are in addition many minor roads penetrating to the remote corners of the west coast.

Beinn Bhuidhe is a massive and isolated mountain situated a few miles north of the head of Loch Fyne. Although it has only a single top over 3000 ft., the mountain is a long and well-defined ridge with three tops running from south-west to north-east between the upper reaches of glens Shira and Fyne. The highest point is near the middle of this ridge.

North-east of the summit the main ridge is well-defined for a short distance and drops to a broad col before rising to the north-east top, 2950 ft. Beyond this point the ridge continues to Ceann Garbh, 2635 ft., and as the name implies this end of the mountain is quite rough. By contrast the south-west ridge which runs out between Glen Shira and the Brannie Burn is smooth and grassy, and the upper part of this ridge is a haunt of golden plovers in summer. The sides of Beinn Bhuidhe overlooking glens Shira and Fyne are steep in places with rock outcrops, but there does not seem to be scope for any climbing.

It is not easy to get a good impression of Beinn Bhuidhe from the south as the foothills such as Clachan Hill tend to obstruct the view. The best views of the mountain are probably to be had from the east and north-east. From Ben Oss, for example, the long ridge of Beinn Bhuidhe is seen end-on, and its isolated position is apparent.

The best approaches to Beinn Bhuidhe are by Glen Fyne and Glen Shira, and there are private roads up both glens. In Glen Fyne it is possible with permission to drive as far as the cottage at Inverchorachan and this provides the shortest approach to the mountain. The last mile and a half of the road is rather rough and it might be considered preferable to walk, however the glen at this point is beautifully wooded and the River Fyne cascades down a series of little falls, so the walk is well worth while. From Inverchorachan the direct route to Beinn Bhuidhe is up the side of the stream which comes down behind the cottage. In dry weather the direct ascent of the stream itself is very pleasant, leading up a tree-filled ravine with several short, easy pitches. At about 1500 ft. a grassy corrie is reached and the route can be varied either by bearing right to reach the 2950 ft. top, or by keeping straight ahead to reach the main summit. There are many rock outcrops below the main ridge, but it is easy to find a route between them. To include Ceann Garbh in the traverse, the path beyond Inverchorachan is followed for half a mile and then a steady climb north-westwards leads to that top.

The approach by Glen Shira is rather longer. It may be possible to drive about four and a half miles up the glen to the last inhabited cottage, and one continues on foot up the hydro-electric road that leads up the glen to the new Lochan Shira on the north-west side of Beinn Bhuidhe. The Brannie Burn is crossed about half a mile above Rob Roy's house and the south-west ridge of the mountain is reached. The going up this ridge is very easy, possibly rather dull, and it is probably better as a route of descent. The traverse of Beinn Bhuidhe from Inverchorachan to Glen Shira is the best route over the mountain.

There are two much longer cross-country routes to Beinn Bhuidhe. From Succoth Lodge, three miles east of Dalmally, a way can be made by the Allt Coire Lair and the Allt an Taillir to the headwaters of the River Fyne. From there the north side of Ceann Garbh is climbed and the ridge followed to the summit. The second route starts at Inverarnan at the head of Loch Lomond and goes westwards up the Allt Arnan. A desolate and trackless pass, the Lairig Arnan, is crossed and on the west side a hydro-electric reservoir (not marked on the One-inch Map) is reached. The descent to Glen Fyne follows a road for almost a mile and then bears north-west towards Inverchorachan where there is a footbridge over the river. Thereafter the ascent of Beinn Bhuidhe follows the route already described.

Because of its isolated position Beinn Bhuidhe commands a very fine view. South-westwards the distant islands and coastline of Lorne and Knapdale spread out beyond the low intervening hills. In all other directions are mountains: Ben Cruachan to the north-west, the Black Mount to the north, Ben Lui close at hand to the north-east Ben More and Stobinian to the east and so round to the Arrochar Alps with a glimpse of the Ochils beyond.

Glen Fyne and Glen Shira are both worth visiting for their own sakes, the lower half of Glen Shira in particular being beautifully wooded. A fine long walk can be made up one of these glens, round the north side of Beinn Bhuidhe and down the other. Starting for example in Glen Fyne, the route to Inverchorachan has already been described and one continues beyond the cottage along a good track beside the river. The track deteriorates as one approaches the ruins of a shieling (M.R. 245206), beyond which one bears westwards up the main stream. A trackless section leads towards the col between the heads of glens Fyne and Shira, and a hydro-electric road is joined. This road is followed along the north side of Lochan Shira and then down the length of Glen Shira.

A number of cross-country walks can also be done in this area. Starting in Glen Fyne, one can take the route just described to the ruined shieling at which point the glen opens out into rather feature-less moorland on the south side of Ben Lui. The walker can continue north-west by the col between Beinn a' Chleibh and Meall nan Tighearn to Succoth Lodge and Glen Orchy, or eastwards to reach the hydro road in Gleann nan Caorrunn and so down to Glen Falloch. From Glen Shira the walker can continue due north from the Lochan Shira dam across four miles of rough and desolate moorland to Dalmally.

Low down in Glen Fyne on its east side there is a remarkable wooded gorge below Cruach Tuirc. Near the head of this gorge is the Eagle's Fall which in dry weather may be approached by a pleasant scramble up the bed of the stream among pools and waterworn rocks. The steep sides of the gorge may be climbed in places, but they are damp, grassy and unpleasant. The volume of water flowing down the falls has been greatly reduced since the headwaters of the stream were diverted into Loch Sloy.

Lorne
The district between Loch Awe and the Firth of Lorne is not of great interest to the climber. The coastline from Loch Etive down to Crinan is much indented by sea lochs, and this is the most interesting and beautiful part of the district, and the only part of the Southern Highlands to have the flavour of Scotland's north-west coast. How-ever, exploration of the many delightful sea lochs and little islands is better done by small boat or canoe than on foot, and so it is rather outside the scope of this book. The interior, between the coast and Loch Awe, is for the most part heathery moorland and low hills which are forested in Glen Lonan, Glen Nant and along the north-west shore of Loch Awe.

In addition to the main coast road (A816) along the west side of the district, there are roads suitable for cars from Oban to Taynuilt through Glen Lonan; and from Taynuilt through Glen Nant to Kilchrenan, along Loch Awe to Loch Avich and west to Kilmelfort. Although there is little of interest in this district for the climber, there are some good long walks through a part of the country that is completely unspoiled and seldom visited:

1. Kilninver to Loch Awe (Barnaline Lodge), (10 miles). Two miles south of Kilninver take the road up Glen Euchar. Beyond Loch Scamadale bear south-east up the Allt Braglenmore, over the pass near Loch na Speinge and down to Loch Avich. Barnaline Lodge is reached in a further two and a half miles along the road.

2. Kilninver to Kilchrenan, (16 miles). Follow the preceding route beyond Loch Scamadale to Braglenbeg and then take the path on the south side of the Allt a' Choromaig to Musdale. Continue north-eastwards up the Allt an Loin Mhoir to join a path which leads east to Midmuir, Sior Loch and down the Amhainn Cam Linne. The path crosses to the south side of this stream and bears south-east past Loch Nant and over a low ridge to Kilchrenan.

3. Kilmore to Kilchrenan, (11 miles). From Kilmore (3 miles south of Oban) take the road eastwards up Glen Feochan. This road leads eventually to Musdale, but one leaves it at the Eas nan Seileacha and follows a footpath eastwards to Midmuir from where the preceding route is followed to Kilchrenan.

4. Kilmore to Loch Awe (Barnaline Lodge), (11 miles). From the foot of Glen Feochan take a path south-eastwards over the hills to Loch Scamadale and join route (1).

Loch Awe is one of Scotland's largest lochs, and like many of the greater lochs of the Highlands it is dotted here and there with little wooded islands. Of these Inishail – 'green Inishail' – at the north end of the loch is the most interesting. It was at one time the site of a Cistercian nunnery, as well as being the burial place for the clans who lived on the shores of the loch. (Refer to the bibliography for authoritative articles on this and other islands in Loch Awe.)

Argyll

The district between Loch Awe and Loch Fyne is known as Argyll, but should not be confused with the county of Argyll of which it is a small part. Like Lorne, Argyll is an area of moorland and low hills with some extensive forests in its southern part. It is not climbers' country, but there are many cross-country walking routes by paths and forest roads. A study of the One-inch Map (Sheet 52) will suggest many possibilities, of which the following are but a few:

1. Furnace (Loch Fyne) to Durran (Loch Awe), (8 miles). From Furnace take the main road northwards for a mile and then the side

road to Brenachoille. Follow a path on the west side of the Leacann Water, past Loch Leacann and over the flat ridge to the north-west. The descent is along the Amhainn a' Bhealaich.

2. Furnace to Kilmichael, (15 miles). Go from Furnace to Brenachoille as in the previous route and then take the track which goes west-south-west over moorland to reach the Abhainn Bhuidhe. The path follows this stream for a few miles and then in the Kilmichael Forest it diverges, passing to the north of Dun Alva and Dun Dubh, and then descends towards Kilmichael.

3. Furnace to Ford, (14 miles). Take the preceding route to the Abhainn Bhuidhe and at Carron (M.R. 945996) follow a path north-westwards over undulating moorland studded with lochans to Ford at the south-west end of Loch Awe.

On the south face of Dun Leacainn, a little hill just north-east of Furnace, there is a very fine cliff known as Dunleachan Crag. At its centre the crag is about 250 ft. high, and two pillars of excellent granite enclose a shallow groove. All the main climbs done so far are on this central part of the crag, and the east and west wings are rather vegetatious. Of the six distinct climbs recorded so far, five are Very Severe and one is Severe, so this is not a crag for the novice. All these climbs are described in the Scottish Mountaineering Club's Climbers' Guide to *Arrochar* by J. R. Houston.

Knapdale

The district of Knapdale lies between Loch Fyne and the Sound of Jura, and is bounded on the north by the Crinan Canal and on the south by the narrow neck of land at Tarbert. The north part of Knapdale consists of parallel rocky ridges, glens and narrow lochans lying south-west to north-east. This very pronounced characteristic of the landscape is well illustrated by Loch Sween and the forested promontories at its head.

The highest hill in north Knapdale is Cruach Lusach, 1530 ft., and despite its modest height it commands a grand view, particularly westwards across the Sound of Jura. It is probably best climbed from Kilmichael (Loch Sween) by the Lussa Water. The lower hills north of Cruach Lusach can be climbed from Ardrishaig.

The parallel ridges are often rocky along their sides, and some scrambling can be found on them. The west face of Cruach Lusach is mostly rock, and a section 300 ft. below the summit has three steep cracks separated by rocky ribs, which provide climbing of almost any standard required. Further west is Creag nan Iallaig, a steep stretch of good rock. Scrambling can be discovered on Cruach nan Chilean, on An Stuchd and on the 610 ft. top above Loch na Bric. Best of all is Creag nam Fitheach, 1 mile up the Lussa Water. On its 100 ft. face there are some very steep and difficult cracks, an exposed arête and an easier slab and crack climb. (Information from A. C. D. Small.)

The hills of south Knapdale are higher but less interesting than those immediately to the north. There is a single ridge of six tops running along the centre of the peninsula, and the highest is Sliabh Gaoil, 1840 ft., near the north-east end of the ridge. Lying as they do in the centre of the peninsula, there is little to choose between ascents from west or east, but a good start in terms of height can be had by starting at the highest point of the road which bisects Knapdale. The tops command good views of Jura, Arran and the Cowal hills.

Kintyre

There is little of interest for the climber in Kintyre. The backbone of the peninsula is a range of low hills whose highest point is Beinn an Tuirc, 1491 ft., but they are little more than high moorland. There is some pleasant walking in the Barr Glen and also in the glens above Carradale Bay and Saddell from which Beinn an Tuirc can be climbed. The view across the Kilbrennan Sound to the Arran hills is magnificent.

In the extreme south-west tip of Kintyre, Beinn na Lice, 1405 ft., can almost be climbed by the road to South Point lighthouse, and it is a good viewpoint for the Atlantic Ocean. The entire south-west tip of Kintyre consists of low hills dropping steeply into the ocean, and there is some grand scenery along this quite uninhabited part of the coast.

Transport and Accommodation

MacBrayne's bus service from Glasgow to Inveraray, Ardrishaig, Tarbert and Campbetown is the life-line of south-west Argyll.

There are many hotels in the extensive area covered by this chapter, but the only ones of interest to the climber and walker are at Dalmally, Inveraray, Ford, Kilchrenan, Oban, Kilmelfort, Crinan, Lochgilphead, Ardrishaig and Tarbert.

There are Youth Hostels at Cruachan (Loch Awe), Oban and Inveraray.

BIBLIOGRAPHY

Ben Bhuidhe, S. M. Penney, *S.M.C.J.*, Vol. 7, p. 124.
The Islands of Loch Awe, W. Douglas, *S.M.C.J.*, Vol. 12, pp. 65, 137, 189, Vol. 13, p. 73.

10

The Arrochar Alps

The principal peaks of the Arrochar Alps are:
  (1) **Beinn Ime,** 3318 ft., 3¾ miles N.W. of Arrochar.
  (2) **Beinn Narnain,** 3036 ft., 2¼ miles N.W. of Arrochar.
  (3) **The Cobbler (Ben Arthur),** 2891 ft., 1 mile S.W. of (2).
  (4) **A'Chrois,** 2785 ft., 1¼ miles N.E. of (2).
  (5) **Ben Vane,** 3004 ft., 1⅝ miles N.E. of (1).
  (6) **Ben Vorlich** (South Top), 3092 ft., 2¼ miles N.W. of Inveruglas.
  (7) **Ben Vorlich** (North Top), 3055 ft., ⅜ mile N. of (6).
The highest peaks in the area north and west of Glen Kinglas are:
  (8) **Binnein an Fhidhleir,** 2658 ft., 2 miles E. of Cairndow on Loch Fyne.
  (9) **Point** 2680 ft., 1 mile E. of (8).
  (10) **Meall an Fhudair,** 2508 ft., 3 miles W. of Inverarnan in Glen Falloch.
Maps: Ordnance Survey One-inch Series, Sheet 53 and Loch Lomond and the
          Trossachs Tourist Map.
          Bartholomew's Half-inch Series, Sheet 48.

The mountains to the north and west of Arrochar at the head of Loch Long are among the best known and most popular not only in the Southern Highlands, but in the whole of Scotland. They are usually called the Arrochar Alps, and the six principal peaks are Beinn Ime (the highest), Beinn Narnain, The Cobbler, A'Chrois, Ben Vane and Ben Vorlich.

Of these six peaks The Cobbler is undoubtedly the finest, although not by any means the highest, and the extraordinary outline of its three rocky summits is only equalled in Scotland by the Torridonian mountains and the Cuillins of Skye. The names Cobbler and Arrochar are almost synonymous, signifying the best rock-climbing centre in the Southern Highlands. The Cobbler has at three times in the history of Scottish mountaineering been a focal point in the development of rock-climbing. In the early days (at the end of the last century) when trains and not cars were the standard form of transport to the mountains, Arrochar on the West Highland Line was probably the most accessible rock-climbing centre in Scotland, and much exploration was done in the eighteen-nineties. Almost forty years later, in the days of the depression on Clydeside, young climbers from Glasgow under the leadership of J. B. Nimlin carried out the second wave of climbing exploration on The Cobbler, and some classic little routes were discovered. Finally, in the late nineteen-forties and early fifties the third wave of climbers, mainly from the Creag Dhu Mountaineering Club, pioneered many new routes which were at that time and still are among the hardest rock-climbs in Scotland.

The other mountains of the Arrochar Alps may suffer somewhat by comparison with The Cobbler (few mountains in Scotland don't), but they are all fine peaks in their own right. They are a good deal steeper and rockier than most other peaks of the Southern Highlands, and although none of them can offer rock-climbing to compare with The Cobbler, there are fair sized buttresses on Beinn Ime and Creag Tharsuinn (between Beinn Narnain and A'Chrois), and some smaller crags elsewhere. These mountains certainly have an individuality and boldness of outline which, together with their accessibility, account for their popularity.

The Arrochar Alps are enclosed by Loch Lomond and the head of Loch Long on the east, Glen Croe on the south, and Glen Kinglas and the Srath Dubh-uisge on the west and north. The area described in this chapter also includes the rather featureless expanse of hills and moorland to the west and north of Glen Kinglas. This area has nothing in common with the Arrochar Alps from the point of view of mountain character, but it falls more logically into this chapter than any other; it is bounded on the west by Glen Fyne and on the north by Gleann nan Caorrunn, and is seldom visited by climbers.

Arrochar has the reputation, probably deservedly, of a rather wet climate, and climbers are warned that Arrochar rock, which is mainly mica-schist with a coating of lichen, becomes as slippery as soap when wet. For this reason The Cobbler and its neighbours tend to be out of condition for serious rock-climbing during the all too frequent spells of wet weather. However, the good weather and dry rock are worth waiting for.

Although the Arrochar Alps are not noted as a winter climbing centre, there is no doubt that in the right conditions there are some excellent snow and ice routes of all standards of difficulty. Unfortunately, because of the proximity to the west coast and the modest height of the mountains, the right conditions for winter climbing tend to be rather rare, and not infrequently the winter passes with little build up of snow or ice.

The Scottish Mountaineering Club's *Climbers' Guide to Arrochar* by J. R. Houston (published in 1970) contains descriptions of all rock-climbs and winter routes in the Arrochar Alps, and it is not intended to repeat these descriptions in this guide book. A shortened selection of routes will be given, but the author does not claim that this selection represents all that is best in Arrochar climbing – it is just his choice.

The Arrochar Alps lie partly within the Argyll National Forest Park, and the Forestry Commission has extensive forests along the lower slopes of the hills above Glen Croe, Loch Long, Glen Loin and Coiregrogain, as well as on the low hill Cruach Tairbeirt between Glen Loin and Loch Lomond. Coiregrogain is a fine, wild glen enclosed by the steep crags of Ben Vane, A'Chrois and Beinn Ime; it is the true heart of the Arrochar Alps, but its lower reaches are rather spoiled by electricity transmission pylons and a switching station. North of Coiregrogain, Loch Sloy lies in the deep glen between Ben Vane and Ben Vorlich, and is the reservoir for the North of Scotland Hydro-Electric Board's generating station at Inveruglas by Loch Lomond. Much of the area described in this chapter is within the catchment area of this scheme, and many of the mountain streams are dammed just above the 1000 ft. contour to provide their share of water for Loch Sloy.

Access to the hills is very easy. Arrochar, which is the main centre, is little more than an hour's drive from Glasgow and is also reached by bus and train. All the main peaks are within easy walking distance of the village. Inveruglas, three miles north of Arrochar, is another good starting point for the hills and there is a private 'hydro' road up Coiregrogain. (At the time of writing it is possible to obtain permission at Inveruglas Power Station to drive up this road to the Loch Sloy dam.) In addition to these two starting points there are several others including Ardlui (four miles north of Inveruglas) and two or three places on the road from Arrochar through Glen Croe and Glen Kinglas to Loch Fyne.

Beinn Ime, 3318 ft., is the highest of the Arrochar Alps. Its summit ridge encloses a north-east facing corrie, and there are two tops, the higher one (crowned by a large cairn) being at the north-west end of this ridge. The east and west faces of the mountain are fairly rugged, particularly the east face which has some steep buttresses and gullies overlooking the head of Coiregrogain. The north-east ridge is well-defined and fairly narrow near its top where there is a steep step just before the ridge merges with flatter ground near the summit. The only really easy side of the mountain is the south side where broad, grassy slopes drop towards the Bealach a' Mhaim.

From Glen Kinglas the mountain appears as a symmetrical cone rising steeply above Butterbridge, and from Coiregrogain the more rugged north-east side is well seen. From several points to the north Beinn Ime shows up well above its neighbouring mountains, but it cannot be seen from Arrochar and presents its rather dull south side to The Cobbler.

There are four noteworthy routes to Beinn Ime of varying length and interest. From Arrochar the usual approach is by the Allt a' Bhalachain (Buttermilk Burn) which is also the normal route to The Cobbler. One can start at the Torpedo Station on the west side of Loch Long opposite Arrochar and climb up the right bank of the stream by a steep path along the edge of the forest; alternatively, one can start near the head of Loch Long and climb steeply by an obvious path (in places almost a staircase of concrete blocks) to reach an old track which is followed horizontally south-westwards to the Allt a' Bhalachain. The two routes converge at a dam just above 1000 ft., and the path continues up the left bank of the stream. Half a mile further on the path (which is very muddy in places) passes the two large Narnain Boulders. The lower boulder provides a rather squalid shelter under an overhang and the upper one gives some short climbs on well polished holds. A short distance beyond the boulders the main path crosses the stream and heads towards The Cobbler, but the route to Beinn Ime continues alongside the stream to reach the flat, grassy Bealach a' Mhaim. The final thousand feet to the summit up grassy slopes is easy and rather uninteresting.

There is a fine route from Inveruglas which follows the 'hydro' road on the north side of the Allt Coiregrogain as far as the stream coming down from the north side of Beinn Ime. This stream is followed uphill for a short distance to the foot of the north-east ridge which gives a pleasant ascent with the possibility of a little scrambling on the rocky steps. At its top the ridge merges with flatter, grassy slopes just below the lower top, beyond which the summit is reached.

The ascent from Butterbridge in Glen Kinglas is the shortest route to Beinn Ime. From a ruined cottage near the roadside one climbs alongside the stream which flows down from the west side of the mountain, and where the stream divides one can follow either the north branch to the Glas Bhealach or the south branch to the broad col south-west of Beinn Ime. The final ascent from either of these cols is easy. The direct ascent of the west face is perfectly feasible, but rather steep.

There is an easy but rather featureless route of ascent from Glen Croe, following the headwaters of the Croe Water up the grassy southern side of the mountain.

Beinn Chorranach, 2903 ft., and Beinn Luibhean, 2811 ft., are both outliers of Beinn Ime which can be easily climbed from Butterbridge.

Rock-climbing on Beinn Ime is concentrated on the east face overlooking Coiregrogain. Fan Gully Buttress is a big, but rather vegetatious buttress about 400 ft. high. On its left there is an easy scree gully and on its right Fan Gully ends near the top of the north-east ridge. The foot of Fan Gully Buttress can be reached from Coiregrogain by following the 'hydro' road to its end and then climbing directly uphill, or from the Allt a' Bhalachain by climbing a short distance beyond the Bealach a' Mhaim towards Beinn Ime and then following a sheep-track horizontally across the east face. The rock routes on Fan Gully Buttress are very vegetatious, and cannot be recommended in wet weather; however, the crag is worth a visit if one is looking for solitude.

The original route on the buttress is *Ben's Fault* (400 ft., D., J. B. Nimlin and D. Easson). It follows a grassy recess in the centre of the buttress for 200 ft. and then a line of short, deep chimneys to the top of the crag. As an alternative to the grassy recess one can climb directly up the rocks on the left of the recess starting at their lowest point (cairn); after three pitches one arrives at the same level as the start of the chimneys (200 ft., V.D., J. Snowdon and D. J. Bennet). The left-hand edge of the buttress overlooking the easy gully gives a Moderate scramble. *Airy Ridge* (300 ft., V.D., R. D. Stewart and R. R. Shaw) goes up the front of the buttress just right of Ben's Fault, and the *Buttress Route* (400 ft., D., P. Mitchell and D. McLuckie) is an indeterminate route on the right-hand side of the buttress.

In winter *Fan Gully* (300 ft., Grade II to III, J. B. Nimlin and R. Peel) gives a good climb with some variation possible at the only ice-pitch. Ben's Fault has also been climbed in winter conditions

(W. Skidmore and R. Richardson) and gave a very fine and difficult climb, one of the best winter routes in the Arrochar Alps.

Beinn Narnain, 3006 ft., is one of the most prominent mountains of the Arrochar Alps, and its characteristic flat summit is easily recognised. The mountain is rather T-shaped with ridges dropping north-west, north-east and south-east from the summit. The south-east ridge is the most prominent feature of the mountain; it rises above the head of Loch Long to the subsidiary top of Cruach nam Miseag and after a slight drop continues towards Beinn Narnain. The final rise of the ridge is a fine, narrow buttress of rock – the Spearhead Ridge – which abuts onto the summit plateau. The north-west ridge drops to the Bealach a' Mhaim and is quite broad. The third ridge runs north-eastwards over Creag Tharsuinn towards A'Chrois and encloses the beautiful Coire Sugach.

Apart from the Spearhead Ridge, there are no notable rock features on Beinn Narnain, although the upper slopes of the mountain overlooking the Allt a' Bhalachain and Coire Sugach have innumerable rock outcrops, some as much as 150 ft. high.

The usual approach to Beinn Narnain is from Arrochar, and there are three variations. One can follow the Allt a' Bhalachain (as already described for Beinn Ime) as far as the Narnain Boulders and then climb northwards beside a little stream directly towards the summit; the upper part of this route is quite steep as it threads a way between rock outcrops towards the base of the Spearhead Ridge. Secondly, one can start near the head of Loch Long and climb (by the concrete staircase) towards the south-east ridge of Narnain; once on the ridge a fairly well-defined path leads over Cruach nam Miseag and so to the foot of the Spearhead Ridge which can be avoided by a gully on its north-east. Thirdly, one can approach the mountain by the Coire Sugach. There is a good path up the left bank of the Allt Sugach, but beyond the trees the path disappears and the going up the corrie tends to be rather boggy, but perfectly easy. From the upper part of the corrie one can either climb to the col between Beinn Narnain and Creag Tharsuinn and turn left up the north-east ridge, or head westwards directly for the summit through broken rocks and outcrops.

There are other possible approaches to Beinn Narnain from Glen Croe and Coiregrogain, but they ascend the least interesting side of the mountain and cannot be particularly recommended.

Rock-climbing on Beinn Narnain is nearly all to be found on the

35. The Spearhead Buttress, Beinn Narnain. The climber is on the Arête, the dark chimney in the centre is Jamblock Chimney.

36. The North Peak of The Cobbler, the climber is on Chimney Arête.

37. Chimney Arête, North Peak of The Cobbler.

38. The Summit of The Cobbler.

39. *Below :* The South and Centre peaks of The Cobbler from the corrie.

40. Nimlin's Direct Route on the South Peak of The Cobbler.

41. *Below:* The South Peak of The Cobbler, with the Luss Hills beyond.

42. The South-west face of the South Peak of The Cobbler. The leader is on the crux of Gladiator's Groove.

43. Ben Lomond from Beinn Narnain.

44. The North Peak of The Cobbler.

45. The Cobbler.

Spearhead Ridge. The *Spearhead Arête* (150 ft., V.D., J. Maclay and W. Naismith) is a classic little route up the nose of the ridge; the rock is excellent and variation is possible. Just to the left of the Arête on the south face of Spearhead Ridge is a prominent groove – *Spearhead Chimney* (40 ft., D.). A few yards left of this the prominent deep chimney is *Jamblock Chimney* (120 ft., V.D., J. Maclay and Workman). This climb gives excellent practice in various techniques, including strenuous wriggling if one chooses to climb through the small hole in the roof of the upper cave. To the left of Jamblock Chimney the much narrower chimney is *Restricted Crack*, and it gives a Moderate climb up its outer edge. It is possible, however, to penetrate into the bowels of the rock from Restricted Crack and then struggle upwards by back and knee towards daylight and the top of the Spearhead Ridge; this sporting subterranean route is *Engine Room Crack* (70 ft., D.), and a torch is useful. On the north side of Spearhead Ridge there are Difficult crack climbs on the opposite sides of Jamblock Chimney and Restricted Crack, but, facing north as they do, they are more vegetatious and generally damper than the routes already mentioned.

Yawning Crag is a large outcrop a quarter of a mile south of the summit of Beinn Narnain at 2700 ft. The crag is identified by a deep chimney, the *Muckle Mou'*, which gives a 110 ft. Very Difficult climb. There are two other routes, *Lip Route* (70 ft., V.D.) on the left edge of Muckle Mou', and *Cicatrice* (110 ft., D.) on the right; all were first climbed by P. Mitchell and J. R. Ewing.

Creag Tharsuinn is a large crag at the head of Coire Sugach, and its top forms a minor summit on the ridge midway between Beinn Narnain and A'Chrois. The crag itself is one of the largest in the Arrochar Alps; however, it is rather broken up by grassy ledges and gullies. The main feature is the Sugach Buttress, the prominent rock mass on the left (south-west) of the crag. Separated from it by a steep gully (Maclay's Gully) is the Central Buttress whose left-hand half is a vertical, unclimbed wall. Above the buttress there is a broad grass ledge, The Rake, rising from right to left across the crag, and above The Rake the Upper Tier is rather vegetatious. To the right of the main crag there are several smaller crags and outcrops.

The *Direct Route* on Sugach Buttress (400 ft., V.D., J. A. Garrick and D. Biggart) is the longest route on Creag Tharsuinn, the rock is good and the climb can be recommended. Start at the lowest rocks (cairn) and climb to a sentry box (belay). A short right traverse followed by a rising left traverse and a short grass gully lead to a broad grass ledge. Cross the ledge leftwards to the foot of the main buttress; the rocks directly above are bulging and holdless, and the climber is forced leftwards into a groove which leads to a ledge (120 ft.). Ascend rightwards towards the edge of the buttress and up to a grassy recess (The Pulpit), climb the wall (or crack) at the back of The Pulpit and reach the final knife-edge arête which gives a pleasant scramble to the top of the buttress. The *Original Route* on Sugach Buttress (250 ft., D., W. Inglis Clark and J. G. Inglis) is on the grassy north-east flank of the buttress and leads by several short pitches to The Pulpit from where the Direct Route is followed to the top. The right-hand side of the Sugach Buttress is bounded by *Maclay's Gully* (300 ft., J. Maclay and party). The first part of the gully is a fairly easy scramble, but the final pitch is loose and rather dangerous, so this cannot be regarded as a summer climb. In winter, however, it gives an excellent climb provided good snow conditions prevail (Grade III, W. Skidmore, J. Crawford and J. Madden). From the foot of the final pitch of Maclay's Gully a left traverse under a bulge marks the start of *Slab and Groove* (130 ft., D., J. B. Nimlin, D. Easson and B. H. Humble). After the traverse, the climb goes up the right-hand corner of the slab to the final steep exit.

The best climb on Central Buttress is *McLaren's Chimney* (200 ft., V.D., A. C. McLaren, S. G. Shadbolt and C. P. Shadbolt), an obvious line of short, dark chimneys which gives a very interesting little climb. The start is near the foot of Maclay's Gully. The first pitch is the left-hand of two chimneys, and the chockstone at the roof of the cave provides a good running belay for the awkward move round the overhang. The next obstacle is a big chockstone jammed in the chimney (it may be avoided on the right), and a cave is entered. Climb onto the top of the huge chockstone and up the left wall to reach the continuation of the gully. The final pitch is also climbed on the left wall. The winter ascent of McLaren's Chimney (W. Skidmore, J. Crawford and J. Madden) is an excellent Grade IV route which poses considerable problems at all its pitches. The right-hand half of Central Buttress is very grassy and is bounded by *Curving Gully*, an Easy climb in summer, but probably much more interesting in winter when there may be two or three ice-pitches.

There are several climbs on the Upper Tier. Starting near the top of The Rake, *Eighty Foot Gully* is loose and vegetatious (Difficult). *Face Route* (120 ft., S., J. B. Nimlin) begins a few yards right of the previous route and after a slightly overhanging start ascends the wall diagonally towards the right-hand edge, which is climbed to the top. *V-Groove* (140 ft., V.D., P. Mitchell and J. Morrison) starts in a grassy bay 30 yards up The Rake from the lowest point of the Upper Tier. From the grassy bay climb to a sloping ledge and traverse left below a steep arête to enter the groove which is climbed, mainly on the left wall, to the top. *Hangover* (180 ft., S., P. Mitchell and J. Morrison) follows the wide groove immediately above the grassy bay, finishing on the right wall. *Solo Buttress* (250 ft., V.D., R. D. B. Stewart) starts just left of the lowest rocks of the Upper Tier; climb a crack and gully to a grass ledge, descend leftwards to the foot of a wide gully, climb it by the right branch and gradually work leftwards to the top of the crag. *Alfresco* (130 ft., S., D. McKelvie, C. Whyte, H. Martin and A. Burns) starts at the lowest point of the rocks of the Upper Tier and goes more or less directly up the wall above. Finally, *Arch Chimney* (200 ft., V.D., P. Mitchell and J. R. Ewing) is to the right of the foot of The Rake and is in two sections separated by a terrace. The first section is a good chimney, and the second section is a series of short pitches leading to a pillar which forms an arch leading to the final chimney.

A fine route on Creag Tharsuinn, and one that gives about 750 ft. of varied and interesting climbing, is the Direct Route on Sugach Buttress as far as the foot of the knife-edge arête, followed by a descending traverse across the slab of Slab and Groove into Maclay's Gully. Descend this for about 150 ft. and climb McLaren's Chimney, cross The Rake and finish by the Face Route. Although rather discontinuous, this is a good combination of three of the best routes on the crag.

A'Chrois, 2785 ft., is a fine little peak standing at the end of Beinn Narnain's north-east ridge. It is very steep on the north and south-east, and looks particularly impressive from Inveruglas. The north side of the peak dropping into Coiregrogain is rocky, but there are no cliffs large enough to attract the climber. On the south-east face there is a crag just below the summit, but the rocks are very vegetatious and the main interest lies in winter climbs in the gullies.

The panorama from A'Chrois is very fine, and the summit of the hill is one of the best viewpoints in the Arrochar Alps. The neighbouring peaks all look impressive, and there are fine views southwards to Loch Lomond and northwards across Loch Sloy towards Ben Lui.

A'Chrois is frequently climbed with Beinn Narnain, and the ridge connecting the two peaks is a delightful walk. The usual approach from Arrochar starts at Succoth Farm near the head of Loch Long. The path on the north-east side of the Allt Sugach is followed until one is above the trees, and then a fairly direct line to the summit is taken just west of north up a broad, grassy ridge. A Forestry Commission road starting in Glen Loin contours round the north-east side of A'Chrois and can be used as an approach from Arrochar to Coiregrogain and the north side of the hill, which is very steep and gives quite an interesting scramble. There are some remarkable fissures in the ground on the north-east and east sides of the hill, and care should be taken if one is descending in this direction in the dark.

The only recorded climbing on A'Chrois is on the crag on the south-east face. The main feature of the crag is the big central gully, Chrois Gully; on the left is South Buttress, and on the right are Centre Buttress, Pinnacle Buttress and North Gully. The approach to the crag may be made by the Allt Sugach to the tree-line, followed by a rising traverse due north to the corrie below the crag; alternatively, the Forestry Commission road to Coiregrogain may be followed until a break in the trees allows one to climb directly into the corrie.

The gullies can only be regarded as winter climbs. *Chrois Gully* is the best, and its difficulty depends on the amount of snow; if there is only a thin covering two or three short ice-pitches may appear, but with a lot of snow these will probably be masked, (Grade I to II). *Pinnacle Gully* is the shorter gully to the right of Chrois Gully, and it will almost certainly have a pitch (of steep grass or ice) at its foot, (Grade I to II). The north end of the crag is bounded by *North Gully*, a short, easy snow climb. The buttresses are all very vegetatious, and none of them give satisfactory rock-climbs. The only feature of interest is the Chrois Pinnacle situated high on Pinnacle Buttress (between Pinnacle Gully and North Gully); it has been climbed from Pinnacle Gully (100 ft., D., C. Walker and party), and it can also be reached from the top of the cliffs by a narrow neck.

Although not by any means the highest, **The Cobbler,** 2891 ft., is certainly the most interesting and important mountain of the Arrochar Alps. The extraordinary outline of its three rocky peaks is one of the strangest and most impressive sights in the Scottish mountains, and it is well seen by travellers passing in the train along the West Highland Line near Arrochar. By virtue of its position on the southern edge of the Arrochar Alps, The Cobbler is prominent in many views from the south and south-east, and from its summit the climber has grand views towards Ben Lomond, the Luss hills and the Firth of Clyde. Northwards, however, the view from The Cobbler is rather restricted by its higher neighbours.

The origin of the name Cobbler is obscure, but it is much more commonly used than the alternative name Ben Arthur. It is hard to find anything in the shape of the mountain which resembles a cobbler, but it is interesting to note that some of the peaks of the Eastern Alps, whose shapes are often spectacular, have the name Schuster (or Cobbler) applied to them. John Stoddart (*Local Scenery and Manners in Scotland, 1799–1800*) writes: 'This terrific rock forms the bare summit of a huge mountain, and its nodding top so far overhangs the base as to assume the appearance of a cobbler sitting at work, from whence the country people call it *an greasaiche cróm*, the crooked shoemaker.'

The name Cobbler properly refers only to the Centre Peak, which is also the highest, but the name is commonly applied to the whole mountain. The South Peak (on the left as seen from Arrochar) is familiarly known either as Jean or The Cobbler's Last; the North Peak is The Cobbler's Wife.

The summit of The Cobbler is formed by a huge block of rock (about twelve feet high) at the south-west end of the broad, grassy ridge which forms the backbone of the Centre Peak. Were it not for this block of rock, which is sheer on all sides, the summit would be as easy to reach as any in the Southern Highlands; however, there are many who get as far as the foot of the summit rock and go no further. Although the last few feet are no more than a scramble in rock-climbing terms, there is probably sufficient exposure to worry anyone with a bad head for heights, and a slip might result in a long fall. The route onto the topmost point goes through the window or gap at the north-west end of the summit rock, along a broad ledge on its south-west side and up at its south-east end.

The North Peak is probably the most impressive of the three as it is formed by two huge, overhanging beaks of rock. The small summit cairn is close to the edge of the higher of these beaks. The east face of the peak is entirely rocky, and there are many excellent climbs. The other three sides of the peak are much less steep, and the ascent from the col between the North and Centre Peaks is short and easy.

The South Peak is steep on all sides, and is the most difficult for the 'non-climber' to reach. The north-east and south-west faces are particularly formidable; the north-west face drops to the col between the South and Centre Peaks, and is only about 100 ft. high, but it also is quite steep. The south-east ridge is probably the easiest route to the top of this peak; it is long and easy-angled with a few short, steep sections.

The Cobbler is most popular on a warm, dry summer day when the rock-climbing is at its best. In winter, however, a covering of snow and ice adds to the scale and grandeur of the peaks, and there are some good climbs at that time of the year. At all seasons the traverse of the three peaks is a grand scramble (in winter it may be much more than a scramble), and when clouds swirl round the mountain and are wind-torn against the rocks, the peaks can assume weird and impressive forms as they appear fleetingly through gaps in the clouds.

The most popular approach to The Cobbler is up the Allt a' Bhalachain from Loch Long by either of the routes already described for Beinn Ime. The Cobbler path crosses the burn a few hundred yards beyond the Narnain Boulders and climbs into the corrie below the three peaks. The easiest route to the summit follows the path (which is steep in places) to the col between the North and Centre peaks, and then along the broad, grassy ridge to the summit rock. Another route goes to the col between the South and Centre peaks and up the narrow ridge to the top. This ridge has one or two rocky sections, but the path avoids all difficulties; however, if the crest of the ridge is followed, a not-too-difficult scramble leads to the top of the summit rock.

From Ardgartan the usual route is up the south-east ridge, climbing due north from the foot of Glen Croe to reach the ridge which is followed to the foot of the South Peak. If it is not intended to climb this peak, it is a simple matter to traverse round its foot on either side to reach the ridge leading to the Centre Peak.

The shortest, but least interesting route starts in Glen Croe three miles above Ardgartan, and follows the stream towards the Bealach a' Mhaim for three-quarters of a mile before bearing south-east. This approach leads easily to the summit or the col between the North and Centre peaks, but it lacks the grand views of the mountain which one enjoys on the approaches from the east.

The traverse of the three peaks is an excellent expedition which calls for a modest degree of rock-climbing ability, about Difficult standard. The best direction is from south to north. The South-east Ridge of the South Peak is a Moderate scramble and follows the crest of the ridge. The summit of the South Peak is a bare slab of rock with an impressive drop to the north. The descent to the next col is short, but in wet weather care is needed on the sloping holds near the bottom of this pitch. The ridge towards the Centre Peak is narrow and easy until a slab of rock bars the way; it can be climbed by a crack up its centre. The rocky crest of the ridge is followed for a short distance further to end on top of the summit block. Descend by the ledge on the south-west side of the block and crawl through the window. The remainder of the traverse is a walk, but the ascent of the North Peak can be given added interest by traversing rightwards from the col along a grass ledge under the first big overhang of the peak. The ascent can then be made by *Right-Angled Gully* (120 ft., V.D., W. W. Naismith and J. S. MacGregor), which is the open gully between the two overhanging beaks. Climb the gully for 60 ft., traverse right along an overhung ledge and finally climb a short, awkward corner to finish a few yards from the summit cairn.

No description of The Cobbler would be complete without reference to the many excellent rock-climbs on the mountain; however, it is not intended to describe these in detail as this is done in the Climber's Guide to *Arrochar* by J. R. Houston. In this chapter mention will simply be made of some of the principal routes, whose positions can be identified from the accompanying photographs.

The south face of the South Peak lies just left of the South-east Ridge, and consists of smooth, slabby walls crossed by grass ledges. *Ardgartan Wall* (200 ft., V.D., J. B. Nimlin and party) is the classic route on this face; it starts up a steep slab with well-polished holds and finishes on a quartz-studded wall. A few yards to its left, *Ardgartan Arête* (200 ft., S., J. Cunningham) follows the angle between the south and south-west faces. The south-west face is steep to the point of overhanging, and all the routes on it are Very Severe.

The north-east face of the South Peak is well seen as one approaches The Cobbler by the usual route up the corrie, and it has an impressive appearance. However, this face loses the sun early in the day and is rather vegetatious, so the routes on it (with one or two exceptions) are not as pleasant as elsewhere on the mountain.

Jughandle (350 ft., V.D., J. B. Nimlin and A. Sanders) is a rambling route which starts in a prominent groove near the foot of South-east Ridge and follows a series of upward pitches and rightward traverses (keeping always on the right of the ridge) to finish by two steep walls just below the summit. *Bow Crack* (100 ft., S., W. Smith, W. Dobbie and R. Hope) starts several yards right of Jughandle and gives a good, short climb. Moving rightwards, *S-Crack* (115 ft., V.S., J. Cunningham and W. Smith) and *Aeon* (150 ft., S., J. Cullen and C. Vigano) start to the right of an obvious gully, and end on the broad grass ledge of Grassy Traverse, a rake running across the face which gives a fair winter climb (200 ft., Grade II, R. Robb, P. McKenzie and W. Skidmore). Near the foot of this rake, *Sesame Groove* (100 ft., V.D., J. B. Nimlin, Miss J. Dryden and R. Peel) gives access to a steep, grassy shelf which rises to the north edge of the face. This is *North Wall Traverse* (180 ft., D., J. B. Nimlin, Miss J. Dryden and R. Peel); it is not a good summer route, being almost entirely on loose turf, but in good conditions it makes a fine winter route, possibly the best on The Cobbler (Grade III, W. Skidmore and P. McKenzie).

Above Sesame Groove there are two diverging lines of cracks and grooves. The left-hand one is *Deadman's Groove* (110 ft., V.S., J. Cunningham, W. Smith and S. Smith), and the right-hand one is *North Wall Groove* (200 ft., S., W. Smith and C. Wilson). Between them are *Grossen Zinnen* (130 ft., S., H. MacInnes and R. Hope) and *McLean's Folly* (100 ft., V.S., R. Carrington and J. Gardner). These four routes tend to be rather damp and slimy, and take a long time to dry out after rain.

The north edge of the north-east face forms a fine, steep ridge of clean rock leading very directly to the summit of the South Peak. The original route, *Nimlin's Direct Route* (250 ft., V.D., J. B. Nimlin and A. Sanders) gains the ridge by a rising traverse low on the north-west face and thereafter goes directly up the ridge to the summit. A more direct and harder variation, *Slack's Route* (300 ft., S., A. Slack and G. Fraser), starts at the foot of the ridge and goes directly upwards to join Nimlin's Direct Route.

The north-west face of the South Peak has several short routes of which the *Original Route*, near the west end of the face, is the one usually used for the ascent or descent when traversing the peak.

The Centre Peak is disappointing from the climbing point of view. The arête from the South Peak has already been mentioned in connection with the traverse of the three peaks, and the only other climb of note is the *Centre Gully*, a narrow gully in the middle of the east face which gives a good climb in winter (Grade I to II). The broad gully to its left which ends close to the summit gives an easy climb in winter.

The east face of the North Peak gives the best rock-climbing on The Cobbler, with a wonderful variety of short routes, many of them

46. Looking north from A'Chrois towards Loch Sloy and Ben Lui.

47. Beinn Ime from Butterbridge in Glen Kinglas.

48. Ben More and Stobinian from Strath Fillan.

49. Stobinian; approaching the summit by the south ridge.

50. Rob Roy's Putting Stone at the head of the Kirkton Glen.

51. Stobinian and Ben More from Leum an Eireannaich.

52. The Arrochar Alps from Beinn a' Chroin.

53. Stobinian and Ben More from the River Dochart.

in spectacular situations. There are few routes with the difficulty of those on the south-west face of the South Peak, but they are certainly better than the majority of the climbs on the north-east face of that peak. The face gets plenty of sunshine, and this combined with the excellent rock and spectacular situations give really enjoyable climbing which more than repays the long walk uphill from Loch Long.

Starting near the col, *Chimney Arête* (80 ft., S., J. Cunningham and I. Dingwall) is an exhilarating one-pitch climb, and *Right-angled Chimney* (100 ft., D.) is a more straightforward chimney with a delicate traverse at its top. *Cat Crawl* (120 ft., S., A. Lavery and another) and *Direct Direct* (100 ft., V.S., R. Muir, J. Wilson and J. Cunningham) both ascend the groove on the left of the big overhang. Round the corner below this overhang is a grassy bay, and at its back Right-angled Gully is a classic climb; at the point where the original route traverses right, the *Direct Finish* (60 ft., S., J. B. Nimlin) continues straight up the corner. To the left of the gully, *Punster's Crack* (160 ft., S., J. Cunningham and W. Smith) is a fine climb with a spectacular final pitch on a steep, wrinkled slab. *The Nook* (150 ft., V.S., J. Cunningham and M. Noon) is another spectacular route which links the top of the first pitch of Punster's Crack to the upper part of Direct Direct by a rising traverse under the overhanging beak.

To the right of Right-angled Gully, *Club Crack* (110 ft., V.S., P. Walsh and party) is probably the hardest climb on The Cobbler, and *Right-angled Groove* (150 ft., S., J. B. Nimlin) gives a delicate climb up the open groove immediately left of the overhanging beak of rock – the Ramshead – which forms the summit of the peak. *Whither Wether* (120 ft., S., H. MacInnes and W. Smith) is another spectacular route which goes up the north side of the Ramshead close to its outer edge. Other routes on the north wall of the Ramshead are (from left to right) *Grey Wall* (120 ft., S., W. Rowney and M. Noon), *Telepathy Crack* (80 ft., S., W. Smith and T. Paul) and *Ramshead Wall* (80 ft., D., J. B. Nimlin and A. Sanders).

Well below these routes, and finishing near them, is the prominent *Ramshead Gully* (200 ft., V.D., J. Muir and A. Muir). On its left is *Wether Wall* (100 ft., V.S., J. Cunningham and H. MacInnes) which, taken with Whither Wether, gives a very fine route. *Ramshead Ridge* (150 ft., D.) is an easier climb open to variation, and at its foot a large hole gives access to a deep cavern.

To the right of Ramshead Gully, *Incubator* (250 ft., S., J. Cunningham and party) and *Recess Route* (300 ft., V.D., J. B. Nimlin, J. Fox and R. Ewing) are the longest routes on the peak, and Recess Route is the most popular and probably the best route on the mountain. It is well scratched, and several short and interesting pitches follow one another in quick succession. The initial slab is followed by a short right traverse, a pull-up and an easy crack to the foot of a prominent deep chimney. This gives a good pitch with an awkward overhang at the top, and another chimney leads to the Halfway Terrace. From the right-hand end of the Terrace a short, steep wall (or the groove on its right) leads to a cave from which the exit on the left wall is quite hard. The last pitch is another cave, again climbed on the left wall.

To the right of Recess Route the rocks are steep, but rather vegetatious, and the routes – *Fold Direct*, *N'Gombi* and *Gangway* (all Severe) – do not have the same quality as the other routes on the North Peak. The big gully to the right of these climbs is *Great Gully*, not a summer route, but worth climbing in good winter conditions. *Maclay's Crack* (200 ft., D., J. Maclay and W. W. Naismith) starts on the left of the foot of the gully at an obvious smooth corner which is followed by a vegetatious chimney. After 60 ft. the chimney branches and the left fork is taken. On the other side of Great Gully the longest route is *North Rib* (200 ft., V.D., J. B. Nimlin and J. Fox) which starts 20 ft. right of the gully and goes up the rib crowning its north wall.

Ben Vane, 3004 ft., is an isolated and imposing looking mountain on the north side of Coiregrogain. The south face of the mountain overlooking the corrie is very steep for over two thousand feet, and there are considerable rock outcrops near the summit. The other sides of the mountain are not nearly so steep, and northwards a ridge leads out to Beinn Dubh, 2509 ft. The col between Ben Vane and its nearest big neighbour Beinn Ime is about 1600 ft., so although the two peaks can be climbed together, there is a fair amount of climbing between them. Probably the best route up Ben Vane is the east-south-east shoulder which rises from Coiregrogain at a fairly easy angle; the starting point for the ascent is a few hundred yards south-west of the bridge over the Inveruglas Water (where cars can be left). The cairn is at the south edge of the small summit plateau. The return can be varied by descending north-west and then north along the ridge to Beinn Dubh which can be easily climbed before descending eastwards to the Loch Sloy dam.

Although there is no recorded rock-climbing on Ben Vane, there must be many short climbs on the crags south of the summit. In hard winter conditions the direct ascent of the south face would probably give an interesting route; the face rises 2000 ft. in half a mile, which is as steep as many a well-known climb.

Ben Vorlich, 3092 ft., is the northernmost of the Arrochar Alps, and the largest in terms of size if not of height. It occupies the area between Loch Sloy and Loch Lomond. The main backbone of the mountain is a long crescent-shaped ridge running roughly from south to north, with a lateral ridge running eastwards from the summit over the Little Hills and then dropping steeply to Loch Lomond. These ridges enclose two beautiful corries – Coire Creagach and Coire na Baintighearna.

There are several possible routes to the summit of Ben Vorlich, of which possibly the most pleasant is by Coire Creagach. The road is left less than half a mile south of Ardlui Hotel, and a path beside the stream leads up the beautifully wooded corrie. Higher up one can either head directly towards the summit, or keep to the south and join the ridge which leads over the Little Hills. The north-east ridge rising above Ardlui is an easy ascent which includes the 3055 ft. North Top of Ben Vorlich. From the south the ridge rising above Inveruglas is rather tiresome as an ascent route because of its several false tops; however, the ridge does command a good view of the neighbouring Arrochar hills. Although the west slopes are generally steep and rough, there is an interesting ascent from the Loch Sloy dam. At this point there is an almost continuous line of crags and little buttresses rising one above the other, and it should be possible to get some rock-climbing on this route.

No description of the Arrochar Alps would be complete without a mention of the many howffs among these mountains. These natural shelters have for long been the refuge of climbers and other mountain dwellers. The caves on The Brack and Beinn an Lochain have already been mentioned. On The Cobbler the best known howff is under the lower of the two Narnain Boulders, but it is rather muddy and squalid. A short distance beyond the Boulders, on the opposite side of the Allt a' Bhalachain, there is a much better shelter under an overhanging crag close to The Cobbler path, and higher up in the corrie there are two or three big boulders with good caves under them. In Coire Sugach there is a howff at about 2000 ft. just below the Beinn Narnain–Creag Tharsuinn col, and another one beside the Allt Sugach not far above the upper Forestry Commission road. The best known howffs in the area are the A'Chrois caves which are located in the forest on the west side of Glen Loin; the track on the west side of the glen is followed past a cottage until it enters the forest, and at that point a path leads uphill through the trees to the caves. Finally, high up on Ben Vorlich above the Loch Sloy dam the Vorlich Fissures are the most remote and least visited of Arrochar's natural mountain refuges.

North and west of the Arrochar Alps there is a rather featureless area of low hills and rough moorland which is seldom visited by climbers or walkers. Binnein an Fhidhleir, 2658 ft., and its slightly higher neighbour Point 2680 ft. enclose the north side of Glen Kinglas with a continuously steep hillside. These tops can be easily climbed from Butterbridge in Glen Kinglas. North of them the landscape is rather barren and uninteresting as far as the Lairig Arnan. On the north side of this pass Troisgeach, 2407 ft., is a favourite short climb from Inverarnan, and its neighbour Meall an Fhudair, 2508 ft., commands a fine view of the Arrochar Alps, Beinn Bhuidhe and the Ben Lui group.

The Lairig Arnan was mentioned in the last chapter as a possible route from Inverarnan to Glen Fyne, and the only other cross-country walk of note in this area is that from Ardlui to Glen Kinglas. From a point half a mile north of Ardlui Hotel the stream up the Srath Dubh-uisge is followed, steeply at first. In less than two miles a hydro road is reached, and this road can be followed past the north end of Loch Sloy and down Glen Kinglas to Butterbridge, (8 miles).

Transport and Accommodation

Arrochar is well served by buses from Glasgow on the routes to Oban (W. Alexander and Sons (Midland) Ltd.) and Inveraray (Macbrayne's). The Oban service continues by Tarbet, Inveruglas and Ardlui, and the Inveraray service continues through Glen Croe and Glen Kinglas.

The West Highland railway has stations at Arrochar and Tarbet, and at Ardlui.

There are hotels at Arrochar, Tarbet, Ardlui and Inverarnan, and a Youth Hostel at Ardgartan.

BIBLIOGRAPHY

Notes on the Cobbler, W. W. Naismith, *S.M.C.J.*, Vol. 3, p. 161.
Ben Arthur, A. E. Maylard, *S.M.C.J.*, Vol. 3, p. 272.
The Cobbler Climbs, H. C. Boyd, *S.M.C.J.*, Vol. 5, p. 153.
The Cobbler, Central Buttress and South Peak, (Note), H. Raeburn, *S.M.C.J.*, Vol. 5, p. 141.
The Narnain Caves, (Note), H. Raeburn, *S.M.C.J.*, Vol. 5, p. 200.
The Arrochar Group, (Guide Book Article), *S.M.C.J.*, Vol. 6, p. 172.
Narnain and Vorlich, W. Inglis Clark, *S.M.C.J.*, Vol. 7, p. 66.
A Climb on the Rocks of Coire Sugach, J. Gall Inglis, *S.M.C.J.*, Vol. 7, p. 70.
Coire Sugach and Narnain, (Note), R. G. Napier, *S.M.C.J.*, Vol. 7, p. 179.
The Mystery of Crois, W. Inglis Clark, *S.M.C.J.*, Vol. 8, p. 309.
Rocks of Coire Sugach, (Note), S. G. Shadbolt, *S.M.C.J.*, Vol. 9, p. 143.
Rocks of Coire Sugach, (Note), J. A. Garrick, *S.M.C.J.*, Vol. 16, p. 90.
Eating Between Meals, J. A. Garrick, *S.M.C.J.*, Vol. 17, p. 190.
Cobbler Calling, B. H. Humble, *S.M.C.J.*, Vol. 21, p. 392.
Rock Climbs on The Cobbler, J. B. Nimlin, B. H. Humble and G. C. Williams, *S.M.C.J.*, Vol. 22, p. 221.
Climbers' Guide to Arrochar, J. R. Houston, (Scottish Mountaineering Club.)
Argyll Forest Park Guide, (H.M. Stationery Office).

11

The Crianlarich
and Balquhidder Hills

(1) **Beinn Chabhair,** 3053 ft., 3½ miles E.N.E. of Ardlui at the N. end of Loch Lomond.
(2) **An Caisteal,** 3265 ft., 1 mile N.E. of (1).
(3) **Beinn a' Chroin,** (West Top), 3078 ft., 1¼ miles E. by N. of (1).
(4) **Beinn a' Chroin** (East Top), 3104 ft., ½ mile E. of (3).
(5) **Beinn Tulaichean,** 3099 ft., 4 miles E.S.E. of Crianlarich.
(6) **Cruach Ardrain,** 3428 ft., 3 miles E.S.E. of Crianlarich.
(7) **Stob Garbh,** 3148 ft., ⅝ mile N.N.E. of (6).
(8) **Ben More,** 3843 ft., 3 miles E. by S. of Crianlarich.
(9) **Stobinian (Stob Binnein),** 3827 ft., 1 mile S. of (8).
(10) **Stob Coire an Lochain,** 3497 ft., ½ mile S.S.E. of (9).
(11) **Meall na Dige,** 3140 ft., 1 mile E. of (9).
(12) **Stob Creagach,** 2966 ft., ⅝ mile N.E. of (11).
(13) **Meall an t-Seallaidh,** 3 miles W. of Lochearnhead.
(14) **Creag MacRanaich,** 2600 ft. contour, 1¼ miles N. by E. of (13).
Maps: Ordnance Survey One-inch Series, Sheets 53 and 54 and Loch Lomond and the Trossachs Tourist Map.
Bartholomew's Half-inch Series, Sheet 48.

This very fine group of mountains is in the heart of the Southern Highlands and contains some of their best-known and most popular peaks. The area is well-defined geographically by Loch Voil, Loch Doine and the River Lochlarig on the south, Glen Ogle on the east, Glen Dochart on the north and Glen Falloch on the west. The area extends for about seventeen miles from east to west and six miles from north to south.

These hills are for the most part formed of massive grits and crumpled mica-schists belonging to the Highland Metamorphic Series. There are also many small intrusive dykes of basalt and other basic igneous rocks. The whole group has been weathered evenly to give grass covered hills with many small outcrops of rock, and consequently the area is not of much interest to the rock-climber. However, there is much excellent hill-walking and the position of these mountains, remote from the sea, ensures that the highest of them carry snow until late in springtime.

The mountains are sub-divided into several groups by glens which run from south to north between them. At the centre are the grand twin peaks Ben More and Stobinian which are the highest in the area described in this chapter, and are exceeded in height in the Southern Highlands only by Ben Lawers. South-east and east of Stobinian, and linked to it by a high ridge, are the subsidiary tops Stob Coire an Lochain, Meall na Dige and Stob Creagach. East of these, between the Monachyle and Kirkton Glens, there is a lower and rather featureless group of hills. North-east of the Kirkton Glen the highest hills are Meall an t-Seallaidh and Creag MacRanaich, but the best feature of these hills is the fine crag called Leum an Eireannaich at the head of the Kirkton Glen and the beautiful Lochan an Eireannaich at its foot. The southern slopes of the hills which overlook Lochs Doine and Voil are called the Braes of Balquhidder.

West of Ben More and Stobinian is the deep glen of the Benmore and Inverlochlarig burns, and on the west side of this glen are the three peaks Cruach Ardrain, Stob Garbh and Beinn Tulaichean which form a Y-shaped ridge. South west again, across the headwaters of the River Falloch, are An Caisteal, Beinn a' Chroin and Beinn Chabhair in a triangular group, the last-named peak overlooking Glen Falloch and the north end of Loch Lomond.

Ben More and Stobinian are the dominant mountains of this group, and they are among the finest of the Southern Highlands. They are prominent in the views from many places as far apart as Ben Nevis and Glasgow, and their very symmetrical twin peaks of almost equal height are easily recognised. Probably the finest view of them is to be had from Strath Fillan to the north-west, and the view down this beautiful glen to Ben More, Stobinian and Cruach Ardrain is one of the best-known mountain landscapes in the Scottish Highlands.

Access to the mountains in this group is quite easy as there are good roads around the entire perimeter except for an eight mile stretch between Inverarnan in Glen Falloch and Inverlochlarig two miles west of Loch Doine. In addition there are several footpaths crossing the range from north to south.

Loch Voil, on the south side of the area described in this chapter, is one of the loveliest lochs of the Southern Highlands and the view along its whole length from Balquhidder to the hills beyond the western end is very fine. Loch Doine, which is separated from Loch Voil by only a few hundred yards of sluggish river, is rather more bleak, and beyond it the River Lochlarig winds its way down a treeless and rather barren glen. The walk up this glen, over the pass on the south side of Beinn Chabhair and down the Ben Glas Burn to Inverarnan is trackless and very boggy for much of its length.

Glen Falloch is rather bare in its upper reaches just south of Crianlarich, and its desolate appearance is heightened by a few scattered pine trees, the last remnants of the Old Caledonian Forest. Lower down, the glen becomes narrower and wooded, and the River Falloch plunges down a series of falls and cascades which are a fine sight when in spate. Below the falls the glen becomes flat and beautifully wooded for three miles to the head of Loch Lomond.

Beinn Chabhair, 3053 ft., is the most westerly mountain of this group, and it provides the River Forth with its most remote source. The upper slopes of the mountain are quite steep, with rock outcrops on all sides except the north-west where a long ridge runs out to Ben Glas. Three quarters of a mile west of the summit, Lochan Beinn Chabhair lies in a very boggy corrie at 1650 ft.

The easiest starting point for the ascent of Beinn Chabhair is the bridge over the River Falloch just north of Inverarnan Hotel, and the mountain is a popular climb from there. After passing through Beinglas Farm there is a choice of routes. One way goes by a path which climbs south-eastwards beside the waterfall at the foot of the Ben Glas Burn. Above the waterfall the path continues along the burn for two miles to Lochan Beinn Chabhair, and from there a steep climb up grass interspersed with rock outcrops leads to the summit and a large cairn. The alternative route from Beinglas Farm is to climb north-east across the steep hillside, following a path which leads to a ruined cottage. Once flatter ground is reached at about 1000 ft. a course eastwards leads to Ben Glas. Near the top of this hill, which is really the terminal point of Beinn Chabhair's north-west ridge, is the beautifully situated Lochan a' Chaisteil. The route continues over (or round) Stob Creag an Fhithich and then along the very knobbly north-west ridge with many ups and downs. A good circuit can be made by ascending one of these routes and descending the other.

Beinn Chabhair can also be climbed from Inverlochlarig which is four and a half miles due east of the summit. A four mile walk up the River Lochlarig to the foot of the Coire a' Chuilinn is followed by a pleasant scramble up the south-east corner of the mountain. On the north-east side of Beinn Chabhair a 1000 ft. drop leads to the col separating the mountain from An Caisteal and Beinn a' Chroin; the way is steep and broken and the descent requires care, particularly in winter.

An Caisteal, 3265 ft., is formed by two long ridges rising from Glen Falloch, the summit being at their junction. On the other side of the summit the short south-east ridge drops about 600 ft. to the col separating An Caisteal from Beinn a' Chroin. Of the two main ridges (which are separated by the Allt Andoran) the longer one drops north-north-west from the summit and is called Twistin Hill. It ends at Sron Garbh, 2322 ft., below which grassy slopes fan out to the right-angled bend in the River Falloch. The other ridge drops steeply westwards from the summit for just less than half a mile and then turns north-west to Stob Glas, 2323 ft.; the upper part of this ridge just below the summit is quite steep and rocky.

The usual route to An Caisteal is up the Twistin Hill ridge, starting one and a half miles south-west of Crianlarich at the bend in the River Falloch where there is a footbridge. The lower slopes are inclined to be wet, but once the ridge proper is reached it gives a delightful walk. About two hundred yards north of the summit a prominent rocky knoll with a cairn is passed; this knoll is well seen from Glen Falloch and may well give the mountain its name. The Stob Glas ridge gives a similar route starting at Derrydarroch cottage.

The **West Top** of **Beinn a' Chroin,** 3078 ft., is separated from An Caisteal by a col at 2650 ft. This top is in fact an undulating ridge about four hundred yards long with two cairned points, and it could be confusing in misty weather. The **East Top,** 3104 ft., which is separated from the West Top by a drop of about two hundred feet, has a well-defined summit with a small cairn. The west and east ends of the summit ridge of Beinn a' Chroin are both steep for a few hundred feet. On the south side of the mountain a small loch, Lochan a' Chroin, nestles in a little corrie at 2450 ft., and on the other side a broad ridge drops northwards from the col between the two tops to Coire Earb and the headwaters of the River Falloch.

Beinn a' Chroin can be climbed easily from Glen Falloch by following the river into Coire Earb and climbing the north ridge of the mountain. Alternatively, from Inverlochlarig an easy route follows the River Lochlarig to its junction with the Ishag Burn and then climbs directly up the south-east slopes of the mountain to the East Top. The traverse combining these two routes is a good expedition.

The three mountains – Beinn Chabhair, An Caisteal and Beinn a' Chroin – can be climbed together in a good circuit. Derrydarroch cottage in Glen Falloch is probably the best starting and finishing point for this expedition.

Cruach Ardrain, 3428 ft., is a fine mountain and one of the most popular in the Southern Highlands, particularly in winter. Its steep north face and pointed summit are well seen from Crianlarich, and are very impressive when the Y Gully is snow-filled in winter. From the south also the mountain is very prominent in the view from, say, the Campsie Fells above Glasgow.

Three well defined ridges radiate from the summit of Cruach Ardrain. The north-west ridge terminates in the Grey Height, 2249 ft., above Crianlarich, and the north-east ridge runs out for half a mile before curving round northwards to the rocky summit of **Stob Garbh,** 3148 ft. These two ridges enclose Coire Ardrain whose head-wall is the north face of Cruach Ardrain itself. The long south-south-east ridge drops to 2750 ft. and then rises to the top of **Beinn Tulaichean,** 3099 ft., beyond which uniform grass slopes with rock outcrops drop to the River Lochlarig. There is also a short spur south-west of Cruach Ardrain which ends at Stob Glas, 2675 ft., and the south face of this spur overlooks the head of the Ishag Glen. It is rocky, but not steep enough to offer continuous rock-climbing; however, the most obvious gully, *Hollow Gully* (400 ft., Grade II, E. Fowler and G. Skelton), has been climbed in winter, and is a good route.

On the north side of Cruach Ardrain there are extensive Forestry Commission plantings along the lower slopes from the River Falloch to the Benmore Burn. There are two access routes to the mountain through the trees, one from the bridge over the railway half a mile south of Crianlarich southwards towards a prominent boulder on the skyline below Grey Height, and the other from Inverardran up the Coire Ardrain. The former route is the best approach for hill-walkers, for whom the Grey Height ridge is a very pleasant route to Cruach Ardrain. The route up the corrie is more suitable as an approach to Stob Garbh and the Y Gully.

The climbing route on Cruach Ardrain is the Y Gully which is directly below the summit on the headwall of Coire Ardrain. The gully is usually a perfectly straightforward snow-climb by either branch, with little or no cornice.

Beinn Tulaichean is very easily climbed from Inverlochlarig, and can be combined with Cruach Ardrain to give a pleasant traverse from there to Crianlarich. The slopes of Beinn Tulaichean just below the summit on the south-east side are strewn with huge boulders which form some deep caves and fissures.

Ben More, 3843 ft., and **Stobinian,** 3827 ft., are the highest mountains south of Strath Tay, and are among the best known of all Scotland's mountains. From most viewpoints they appear as almost identical twin summits; however, Stobinian has rather more elegance and Ben More appears bulkier because of the long drop of its northern slopes for over three thousand feet from its summit to Loch Iubhair. Because of their height and distinctive appearance Ben More and Stobinian are easily recognised from many viewpoints far and near, and the view from their summits on a clear day embraces half of Scotland from the Cairngorms to Galloway and from Edinburgh to the Western Isles.

The usual route of ascent for Ben More starts at Benmore Farm two miles east of Crianlarich and goes directly up the north-west ridge of the mountain – a long and unrelenting climb. (To call this route a ridge is slightly misleading as it is really the rounded angle between the north and west faces.) On the south-west side of this ridge there is a shallow hanging corrie a few hundred feet below the summit on its north-west side. The upper part of this corrie is very steep and has been the scene of several accidents (at least one of them fatal) in winter. Great care should therefore be taken when descending the north-west side of the mountain in conditions of hard snow or ice and also when the snow is soft and liable to avalanche. (This corrie is not clearly shown on the One-inch Map; however, it is at the head of the little stream which flows down the north-west side of Ben More to join the Benmore Burn.)

An alternative route to Ben More which is probably rather more pleasant, though longer, is the north-east ridge. The starting point is about five miles east of Crianlarich, and the angle of ascent is quite gentle compared with the north-west ridge. The lower slopes are wooded and the upper part of the ridge is quite narrow with small cliffs on the south-east side. The third ridge of Ben More, the south ridge, drops to the Bealach-eadar-dha-Beinn (the col between Ben More and Stobinian) and is broad and easy.

From most viewpoints Stobinian appears as a conical mountain, only the cone has been cut off at its tip to leave a small level summit.

The mountain has two principal ridges – the north ridge dropping to the Bealach-eadar-dha-Beinn, and the south ridge which leads out to **Stob Coire an Lochain,** 3497 ft., and continues to Stob Invercarnaig above the west end of Loch Doine. There is also a short, steep ridge dropping eastwards from the summit, and the north-east face of the mountain holds snow until late in spring; however, it is hardly steep enough to provide interesting winter climbing.

Stobinian can be climbed from Crianlarich by ascending the Benmore Burn for a mile and a half and then climbing steeply eastwards to reach the Bealach-eadar-dha-Beinn. From there the north ridge leads easily to the cairn which is at the southern edge of the flat little summit plateau.

From the south Stobinian can be climbed by two or three routes. The shortest starts at Ardcarnaig cottage half a mile west of Loch Doine, climbs directly up the steep grassy slopes of Stob Invercarnaig and continues along the delightful ridge to Stob Coire an Lochain and Stobinian. Alternatively, from the farm at Monachylemore one can climb steeply to Meall Monachyle, 2123 ft., and continue north-westwards along a broad ridge to **Meall na Dige,** 3140 ft. From there a short descent and reascent leads to Stob Coire an Lochain. Another route from Monachylemore follows the beautiful Monachyle Burn for a mile and a half and then climbs up beside the waterfalls of the Allt Coire Cheathaich. From the corrie at the head of this stream Meall na Dige can be climbed directly or one can include **Stob Creagach,** 2966 ft., in the traverse.

If the snow conditions are right, the ski-ascent of Stobinian from the south is very pleasant. The best route is up Glen Carnaig for about a mile and a half, and then westwards to reach the Stob Invercarnaig ridge which gives an easy route to within a few hundred feet of the summit of Stobinian. The traverse may be continued to Ben More and down its north-east ridge to give a very interesting tour.

The Monachyle Glen is the eastern limit of the high mountains in the area described in this chapter. There is a good walk through the glen from Monachylemore to Luib in Glen Dochart; the path is easy to follow in the Monachyle Glen, but becomes indistinct as one crosses the pass south of Stob Luib and descends the Luib Burn (6 miles).

East of the Monachyle Glen the hills are lower and less interesting, although their southern slopes above Loch Voil are beautifully wooded and there are some fair-sized crags that might be worth investigating. The Kirkton Glen, north of Balquhidder, is forested and a road goes up the glen for almost two miles. (The start of this road is some distance west of Balquhidder, but a path starting behind the churchyard in the village also leads up the glen.) Beyond the end of the road a good path continues through the trees and onto the open hillside at the head of the glen, passing the foot of the impressive little crag called Leum an Eireannaich. The view back down the glen towards Strathyre and Ben Ledi is very fine. At the watershed the path passes the beautiful Lochan an Eireanniach and then continues down the Ledcharrie Burn to Glen Dochart; however, the north side of the hills lacks the beauty of the Kirkton Glen.

Leum an Eireannaich and the huge boulder below it which is called Rob Roy's Putting Stone offer possibilities for several short climbs. Taking the Putting Stone first, the obvious crack and flake on the south side is the easiest route and was climbed by W. Inglis Clark and J. G. Inglis in 1899, standard Difficult. The well-defined slanting crack on the west side is *Bumper Crack* (40 ft., Severe), and the lower (right-hand) crack on the same side ends just below the top of the boulder and looks harder.

Leum an Eireannaich is an impressive little crag. Its profile is well seen from the main road just north of Strathyre, and the foot of the cliff has a pronounced overhang. On closer inspection the crag is found to be rather vegetatious, and this applies particularly to the section north of the overhanging nose. To the south of the nose there is a grassy bay; its most prominent feature is a big overhang two-thirds of the way up the right-hand wall, while the left-hand wall is more vegetatious. The following routes have been recorded by T. Low of the Ochils Mountaineering Club:

1. *Garden Wall* (70 ft., V.D.). This route is on the vegetatious wall some distance north of the nose and the start is below two prominent little overhangs. Climb up past a grass ledge to a narrow ledge below the overhangs, then traverse right to reach a line of weakness which leads towards some detached blocks on the skyline.
2. *Old Man's Groove* (120 ft., S.). This route starts at a mossy slab just left of the nose of the crag. Climb up to the top right-hand corner of the slab and avoid the overhang above by a right traverse onto a slab. Above this a groove is climbed until an exposed move rightwards leads to a good ledge and easier ground.

3. *Stella Crack* (60 ft., V.S.). To the right of the nose there is an open corner. This is the line of the route which ends on a grass ledge below the left wall of the big bay.

4. *Stella Major* (70 ft., S.). This route starts just above the finish of Stella Crack. An overhanging start leads to a crack and a small cave; from the cave traverse left for a few feet until it is possible to climb upwards.

5. *Kirkton Wall* (60 ft., V.S.). This is the clean south facing wall at the foot of the crag. Climb a groove to a grass ledge on the right of the wall, then make a rising traverse across the wall to its left edge which is followed to the top, (near an old fence post).

6. There is an easy scramble up grass to the back of the bay followed by a left traverse into a little grassy gully which is climbed to the top of the crag.

7. *November Crack* (60 ft., H.S.). From the traverse of the preceding route climb directly up a narrow crack, (some loose rock at the start).

8. *Corrugated Wall* (70 ft., S.). This route starts below the big overhang on the right-hand wall of the bay. Climb up to the right-hand end of the overhang, which is avoided by a severe traverse rightwards, and finish directly up a steep wall.

LEUM AN EIREANNAICH

From the top of Leum an Eireannaich a short walk leads to the small cairn marking the summit of Meall an Fhiodhain, 2595 ft. This hill is the north-west end of a broad grassy ridge whose south-eastern end is **Meall an t-Seallaidh,** 2795 ft. This hill stands directly above Balquhidder village, and the grass slopes which drop south-east from the summit towards Kingshouse Hotel are remarkable for their uniformity.

Finally, at the eastern end of the mountains described in this chapter there is **Creag MacRanaich,** 2600 ft. contour. This hill has a south-east facing corrie ringed by broken crags, but there are no records of any worthwhile routes on them either in summer or winter, although the top of the crags is sometimes heavily corniced in winter. This corrie and the summit of the hill can be reached by the track up the east side of the Kendrum Glen, starting at Edinchip. By keeping to the left near the head of the glen the pass at 2000 ft. on the south-west side of Creag MacRanaich can be crossed and a descent made to Glen Dochart by the path on the east side of the stream in Gleann Dubh. (6 miles from Edinchip to Ardchyle in Glen Dochart.)

Transport and Accommodation.

Railway: There are about five trains per day (Sundays excepted) between Glasgow and Crianlarich. Some of these trains stop at Ardlui at the head of Loch Lomond.

Buses: The bus services from Glasgow to Oban and Fort William (operated jointly by W. Alexander and Sons (Midland) Ltd. and Highland Omnibuses Ltd.) go up Glen Falloch to Crianlarich. The service from Callander to Crieff passes through Lochearnhead, and the service from Stirling to Crianlarich goes by Lochearnhead, Glen Ogle and Glen Dochart. (Both these services are operated by W. Alexander and Sons (Midland) Ltd.)

There are hotels at Inverarnan (Glen Falloch), Crianlarich, Suie Lodge (Glen Dochart), Lochearnhead and Kingshouse (Balquhidder). There are Youth Hostels at Crianlarich and Balquhidder.

BIBLIOGRAPHY

Cruach Ardrain by N.W. Face, (Notes), *S.M.C.J.,* Vol. 3, p. 306.
Creag MacRanaich, A. W. Russell, *S.M.C.J.,* Vol. 4, p. 247.
Leum an Eireannaich, J. Gall Inglis, *S.M.C.J.,* Vol. 5, p. 246.
The Crianlarich Group, (Guide Book Article), *S.M.C.J.,* Vol. 6, p. 195.
Avalanche on Ben More, W. G. Macalister, *S.M.C.J.,* Vol 12., p. 124.

Creag MacRanaich, W. Inglis Clark, *S.M.C.J.*, Vol. 14, p. 203.
The Highlands in June, J. G. Stott, *S.M.C.J.*, Vol. 14, p. 259.
Day Trips by Rail, J. Dow, *S.M.C.J.*, Vol. 19, p. 33.
In Defence of Ben More, E. C. Thomson, *S.M.C.J.*, Vol. 19, p. 238.
Beinn a' Chroin, (Notes), *S.M.C.J.*, Vol. 20, p. 453.

54. Looking west along Loch Voil. The twin-topped hill in the distance is Stob a' Choin.

55. Ben Lui.

56. Approaching the summit of Beinn Dubhchraig.

57. Looking south from Beinn Tulaichean, Ben Lomond in the distance.

58. Beinn Chuirn from the east.

59. The Summit of Ben Lui.

12

Ben Lawers and the Tarmachans

(1) **Ben Lawers,** 3984 ft., on the north side of Loch Tay 2¾ miles N.W. of Lawers Hotel.
(2) **Creag an Fhithich,** 3430 ft., ½ mile N. of (1).
(3) **An Stuc,** 3643 ft., 1 mile N. of (1).
(4) **Meall Garbh,** 3661 ft., 1½ miles N.N.E. of (1).
(5) **Meall Greigh,** 3280 ft., 2¾ miles N.E. of (1).
(6) **Beinn Ghlas,** 3657 ft., 1 mile S.W. of (1).
(7) **Meall Corranaich,** 3530 ft., 1¼ miles W.S.W. of (1).
(8) **Meall a' Choire Leith,** 3033 ft., 2 miles N.W. of (1).
(9) **Meall nan Tarmachan,** 3421 ft., 3¾ miles N. by E. of Killin.
(10) **Meall Garbh,** 3369 ft., ½ mile S.W. of (9).
(11) **Beinn nan Eachan** (W. top), 3265 ft., 1 mile W.S.W. of (9).
(12) **Beinn nan Eachan** (E. top), 3110 ft., ½ mile E. of (11).
(13) **Creag na Caillich,** 2990 ft., ¾ mile S.W. of (11).
Maps: Ordnance Survey One-inch Series, Sheet 48.
Bartholomew's Half-inch Series, Sheet 48.

These two groups of mountains lie between Loch Tay and Glen Lyon, and are bounded on the west by the well-defined pass called the Lairig Breisleich. Ben Lawers is at the centre of a continuous ridge of seven distinct peaks over three thousand feet; the connecting ridge is about seven miles long and never drops below 2500 ft. The whole range is the biggest single mountain massif in the Southern Highlands above 2500 ft.; the Cairn Mairg range on the opposite side of Glen Lyon may rival it for area, but certainly not for height or grandeur.

The Tarmachan Hills are separated from Ben Lawers by the road from Loch Tay to Glen Lyon over the Lochan na Lairige pass. There are four distinct peaks in this range, and the highest, Meall nan Tarmachan, gives its name to the whole group.

The traveller going northwards from Lochearnhead has a grand view of these mountains as he crosses the pass at the head of Glen Ogle and descends towards Glen Dochart. Near at hand, above the town of Killin, the four peaks of the Tarmachans show their distinctive knobbly outline, and beyond them Ben Lawers and its satellites have a very different appearance with long, grassy ridges rising from Loch Tay to their high summits.

Ben Lawers and the Tarmachans are among the most popular mountains of the Southern Highlands, and access to both groups is easy from the Lochan na Lairige road which reaches 1750 ft. at the lochan. The southern side of Ben Lawers is owned by the National Trust for Scotland who have an Information Centre and car-park on this road about a mile south of the lochan at MR 609377; the 'tourist route' to the mountain starts at this point. Both mountain groups are famous for their alpine flowers which attract botanists as well as climbers and walkers in early summer. Some of the Ben Lawers peaks, in particular Beinn Ghlas, are very popular for skiing and ski-mountaineering in winter, and the Scottish Ski Club has a small private hut in Coire Odhar. When one adds to these attractions the fact that Ben Lawers, despite its height, is one of the easiest mountains in the Southern Highlands to climb (there is a good path all the way) it is not surprising that it is also one of the most popular.

The Tarmachans are quite different in character from Ben Lawers. Whereas the ridges and summits of the latter are rather smooth and regular in outline, the Tarmachans are knobbly peaks with some craggy faces, and the linking ridges are themselves in places mazes of little knolls and hollows. These hills have a character all of their own.

Ben Lawers, 3984 ft., is the central and highest point of the seven-mile ridge which connects all the peaks of the range. As a glance at a map will show, this ridge is not straight but rather S-shaped; in places it is quite narrow and well-defined, elsewhere it is broad. The complete traverse of the range is a grand and fairly energetic day's hill-walking, and the peaks will be described from the point of view of a climber traversing them from west to east.

Meall a' Choire Leith, 3033 ft., is the terminal peak at the north-west end of the range. It is an undistinguished, rounded hill with a flat top from which a broad ridge descends south-south-east to a col at 2550 ft. On the west side of this col the Coire Gorm is shallow and grassy, but on the other side Coire Liath is steep, and might give some short climbs in winter. The main ridge continues south from the col to **Meall Corranaich,** 3530 ft., which has a flat top and a small cairn. At this top the main ridge turns south-east and drops steeply along the line of a broken fence to the col (ca. 3050 ft.) at the head of Coire Odhar. This corrie is the most popular part of Ben Lawers for skiers, and the Scottish Ski Club's hut is about half a mile south-south-west of the col.

The main ridge continues south-east up a rather steep slope to **Beinn Ghlas,** 3657 ft., whose summit is marked by a very small cairn on the edge of the steep northern face of the mountain. The main ridge turns north-east and drops gradually to the col (ca. 3300 ft.) below Ben Lawers. This part of the ridge is marked by a path which is broad and usually muddy; at the time of writing it is considerably eroded by the passage of many feet and the path is a very unsightly scar on the ridge. The final ascent to Ben Lawers is quite steep and there is a large cairn and an indicator on the top. The present cairn is all that remains of a 20 ft. cairn built by thirty men and two masons one summer's day in 1878. Presumably the organiser of this feat, one Malcolm Ferguson of Glasgow, hoped to raise Ben Lawers to the select company of Scotland's 4000 ft. mountains, but his cairn has failed to survive the ravages of time.

From the summit of Ben Lawers a subsidiary ridge branches eastwards and gradually merges with the grassy flank of the mountain above Lawers village and Loch Tay. The main ridge turns north and drops to a very minor top **Creag an Fhithich,** 3430 ft., (known locally as Spicean nan Each). This top involves hardly any climb less than 100 ft., and it would be easy to miss it in misty weather; however, when seen from the east it is easily recognized as the top of a prominent little rock buttress. Beyond it the ridge drops more steeply to the next col, the Bealach Dubh (3042 ft.).

The next top along the ridge, **An Stuc,** 3643 ft., has some claim to be considered the finest of the Ben Lawers peaks. It is steep on all sides and has quite a sharp little grassy summit; the south-east face drops precipitously to the beautiful Lochan nan Cat. The ridge over An Stuc gradually turns towards the north-east and a very steep descent followed by a more gradual ascent leads to **Meall Garbh,** 3661 ft. There is a small cairn at the north-west edge of Meall Garbh's broad summit ridge, and from it a long ridge drops north-north-west towards Roromore in Glen Lyon; however, the main backbone of the range curves round towards the east in a very broad ridge which drops to 2802 ft. at the Lairig Innein, the last col on the main ridge. From

there the ridge rises very gradually to the last peak, **Meall Greigh,**
3280 ft., whose summit has two cairns about 150 yards apart, the
south-eastern one marking the highest point.

The flanks of the Ben Lawers massif are in general smooth and
grassy, with three or four well-defined ridges dropping northwards to
Glen Lyon. The south-east slopes above Loch Tay are remarkably
uniform and uninteresting, and one does not get a good impression of
the mountain from the main road along the north side of the loch; the
minor road along the south side gives better viewpoints. The finest
feature of the range is the corrie which holds Lochan nan Cat, the
source of the Lawers Burn. This beautiful corrie is enclosed by
Meall Garbh, An Stuc and Ben Lawers itself, and Lochan nan Cat is
probably the most beautiful of the high mountain lochans in the
Southern Highlands. The grassy crags surrounding the lochan are
notable for the profusion of alpine flowers, and the corrie can well be
regarded as the true heart of the Ben Lawers range. There is a good
path up the Lawers Burn starting at Machuim Farm, and although
it eventually becomes rather indistinct the lochan is easily reached by
keeping alongside the burn.

The few cottages and farms near the foot of the Lawers Burn are
all that now remain of the once-thriving village of Lawers which at
one time had a population of about a thousand and was a centre of the
flax spinning industry in Scotland. There were once, it is said, about
a dozen mills along the lower part of the Lawers Burn, but only three
or four remain, none of them working.

The most popular route to Ben Lawers starts at the National Trust
Information Centre and car park on the Lochan na Lairige road.
A good track leads up the west side of the Burn of Edramucky, but
within a mile one crosses the burn and climbs towards the grassy
south ridge of Beinn Ghlas. The path is marked (at the time of writing)
by red-painted rocks and is easy to follow in summer over the summit
of Beinn Ghlas and along the connecting ridge to Ben Lawers.

The Lawers Burn path to Lochan nan Cat is probably a pleasanter
route and avoids the crowds of the 'tourist route'. From the south-
west corner of Lochan nan Cat a little stream is followed to reach the
upper part of the east ridge of Ben Lawers, and this ridge is followed
to the top. There is also a path (the original Pony Track) from Lawers
Hotel directly towards the summit of Ben Lawers, but there is little
variety or interest in this route which ascends the featureless grassy
hillside above the hotel.

The Lawers Burn is also the best approach to the three north-eastern peaks – An Stuc, Meall Garbh and Meall Greigh. An Stuc may appear rather steep and formidable, and the easiest route is from the west end of Lochan nan Cat to the Bealach Dubh and then up the south ridge.

The track up the Edramucky Burn from the National Trust Information Centre leads quite high into Coire Odhar. Continuing up the burn, the Scottish Ski Club hut is passed and the col at the head of the corrie is reached. Beinn Ghlas and Meall Corranaich can both be easily climbed from this point, but the ridge to the latter peak is steep for a short distance and in icy conditions it is preferable to keep some distance south of the line of fence posts which marks the ridge.

A shorter route to Meall Corranaich can be made by starting near the highest point of the Lochan na Lairige road. This point is marked by a conspicuous cairn, and is also a good starting point for Meall a' Choire Leith; from the cairn a rather rough walk over peat bogs leads north-east over a low bealach and (losing as little height as possible) into Coire Gorm from where it is a short climb to the flat top of the hill.

There are easy routes onto most of the Ben Lawers peaks from Glen Lyon, although the distances are rather longer than the southern approaches just described. Camusvrachan is the best starting point in Glen Lyon, and the Allt a' Chobhair gives access to all the peaks except Meall Greigh.

The complete traverse of the Ben Lawers range is the best day's high level hill-walking in the Southern Highlands, the ridge itself being seven miles long and involving about four thousand feet of ascent between the end peaks. If the climber is committed to returning on foot to his starting point at the end of the traverse, Milton Roro in Glen Lyon is probably the best starting and finishing point. Otherwise the traverse is most easily made from the cairn on the Lochan na Lairige road to Machuim at the foot of the Lawers Burn.

There are no recorded rock-climbs on Ben Lawers, which is surprising when one considers the extent of the mountain. The crag overlooking the head of Lochan nan Cat is probably the biggest one on the mountain, but it is vegetatious and no routes have been recorded on it. In the same corrie *Cat Gully* (500 ft., Grade I) is the best winter climb on the mountain. It rises above Lochan nan Cat directly to the summit of An Stuc. The gully is really more like a big groove as it has no right-hand containing wall; however, the climb is steep and well-defined, and near the top there are two or three branches in the left wall which give steeper variations than the straightforward finish.

On Creag an Fhithich the *Raven's Gully* (400 ft., J. McCoss) starts in the high corrie below Bealach Dubh and splits the north face of the crag. There is a steep pitch of about 20 ft. half-way up.

If Ben Lawers has little to offer the rock or ice-climber, the same cannot be said for its skiing potential. For some reason (which the author will not attempt to explain) the best snow conditions seem to occur in the early part of the winter, and there is seldom much snow for late spring skiing. Downhill skiers congregate in Coire Odhar where there are many easy slopes; if there is enough snow, the run from the col at the head of the corrie down to the car park gives two miles of very pleasant and easy skiing.

It is for ski-mountaineering rather than downhill skiing that Ben Lawers is well known. Every peak except An Stuc can be reached quite easily on skis by a competent skier, and most of the main ridge can be traversed with occasional minor diversions. The most popular ascent is Beinn Ghlas from the Scottish Ski Club hut in Coire Odhar, and the continuation to Ben Lawers is straightforward if there is plenty of snow. The easiest route to Ben Lawers is probably the ascent from Lawers Hotel direct to the ridge a short distance east of the summit.

The north-west face of Meall Corranaich gives good steep skiing, and the north ridge of this peak leads easily to Coire Gorm (known in the skiing fraternity as Charlie's Gully), and this shallow corrie gives a fine, easy ski-run. Finally, the traverse of Meall Garbh and Meall Greigh is quite easy, with plenty of scope for variation.

The best expedition is the traverse of the whole ridge; this is a magnificent expedition, one of the best in Scottish ski-mountaineering. It is unlikely that any but fast and very competent skiers could hope to complete the whole traverse in a short winter's day, and Beinn Ghlas to Meall Greigh would satisfy most people. An Stuc is the biggest obstacle in the traverse, and this peak can be bypassed quite easily by a traverse across its north-west face into the head of the Fin Glen followed by an easy ascent of Meall Garbh's north-north-west ridge. Alternatively, a descent from the Lawers–Creag an Fhithich col south-eastwards gives an exciting run down to Lochan nan Cat from where a steep climb leads to Meall Garbh.

The Tarmachan Hills are a much more compact group, it being only two miles between the end peaks. The traverse of the four peaks is a fairly short, but nevertheless very enjoyable hill-walking expedition with sufficient variety to make it always interesting.

The approach to these hills can be made directly from Killin or from the Lochan na Lairige road near the lochan. A private road (locked gate) leaves this road half a mile south of the lochan and contours across the southern slopes of the Tarmachans to end at a disused quarry at about 2150 ft. in the Coire Fionn Lairige.

Meall nan Tarmachan, 3421 ft., is the highest of the four peaks and lies at the north-east end of the range. It is very steep to the south and east, but much less so to the north and west where grassy slopes drop into Coire Riadhailt. The shortest route of ascent starts at the Lochan na Lairige dam and climbs almost due west by a steep little stream to the corrie below the summit of Meall nan Tarmachan. The final slopes can be taken directly, a pleasant route if there is good snow, or avoided by a diversion onto the easier north-east ridge. The steep hillside and grassy crags on the west side of Lochan na Lairige are notable for their profusion of alpine flowers.

One third of a mile south-east of Meall nan Tarmachan there is a small conical peak marked by the 3000 ft. contour on the One-inch Map, but this height is probably an over-estimate, otherwise the peak would qualify for inclusion in Munro's Tables as a top. The ridge connecting Meall nan Tarmachan to Meall Garbh, 3369 ft., is broad and grassy, descending southwards and then bending south-west to the col where there are three little tarns set among knolls – a confusing place in misty weather. From the col a short steep climb leads to Meall Garbh with an occasional iron fence post to mark the way.

Meall Garbh is not named on the One-inch Map, but is marked by the 3250 ft. contour. The summit is a sharp knob of rock dropping steeply on all sides; there is not enough room for a cairn. The south ridge of Meall Garbh, which is a well-defined route of ascent or descent, joins the main crest about fifty yards east of the summit.

Continuing in a westerly direction from Meall Garbh, the main ridge is narrow and nearly level for about fifty yards before dropping to the next col, the Bealach Riadhailt, 2950 ft., which is a narrow defile. Beyond the col the ridge again becomes broad and knolly and confusing in misty weather. The **East Top** of **Beinn nan Eachan,** 3110 ft., is the largest of these knolls and is marked by a small cairn;

to its west there is a steep drop of nearly 100 ft. before the **West Top** of **Beinn nan Eachan,** 3265 ft., is reached. This summit is flat and grassy, but drops very steeply to the south into Coire Fionn Lairige.

From Beinn nan Eachan the main ridge drops westwards and then turns south-west to become fairly level for a third of a mile at the next col; then it turns south and rises to **Creag na Caillich,** 2990 ft., the lowest of the four Tarmachan peaks. The summit of this peak is an undulating ridge running from north to south with three tops, the northern one being the highest. The south end of the ridge and the east and south-east face of the peak drop very steeply for a few hundred feet, the profile of this crag being well seen from Killin. Difficulties in ascending or descending the ridge can be avoided by keeping well to the west of its crest at the steep part.

The south-east side of the Tarmachans have a discontinuous line of crags running almost the whole length of the two-mile summit ridge. These crags are steepest and highest on the east face of Creag na Caillich, continue in a more broken way across the face of Beinn nan Eachan and finally present a more continuous line of crags and narrow gullies below the ridge between Meall Garbh and Meall nan Tarmachan. This last section is called Cam Chreag on the One-inch Map. By contrast, the north side of the hills dropping into Fionn Ghleann and the Coire Riadhailt are grassy and much less steep.

There are several possible routes to the Tarmachan peaks. The one from the south end of Lochan na Lairige has already been described. The private road mentioned earlier which starts half a mile south of the lochan gives easy access to the south side of the hills. Alternatively, one can climb directly from Killin into the Coire Fionn Lairige, leaving the roadside near Bridge of Lochay. On this side of the Tarmachans the south ridge of Meall Garbh, the Bealach Riadhailt, the col between Beinn nan Eachan and Creag na Caillich and the south ridge of the latter peak (avoiding difficulties on the west) are all easy routes. On the north side the approaches are longer and less interesting; however, the ridge of Creag an Lochain, 2742 ft., is easily reached from the top of the Lochan na Lairige road and gives a pleasant high-level route to Meall nan Tarmachan with impressive views of the lochan.

There are considerable rock outcrops and crags on the south and east faces of the Tarmachans, but most of them are very vegetatious and no summer rock-climbs of any merit have been recorded. The best climbing is to be had in winter when frost grips the grassy crags and snow and ice fill the many gullies and chimneys, and the following notes refer mainly to winter climbs.

The east face of Creag na Caillich is the most impressive feature of the Tarmachans from the climbers' point of view. At the north end of this face there is a wide gully which gives an easy climb. Left of this gully there is a broad buttress, crossed by discontinuous ledges and very vegetatious; an indeterminate summer route has been made near the left side of this buttress by shallow gullies and ledges, but the rock is loose and the exposure considerable, (400 ft., D.). South of the buttress is *Great Gully*, (400 ft., Grade II to III); the lower half was climbed by H. Raeburn and Lawson in 1898, and the complete climb was done by G. W. Young, A. M. Mackay and S. A. Gillon in 1902. The lowest part of the gully can be avoided by a left traverse, and there follows a narrow rocky section which leads to a ledge running across the face by which an escape may be made to the left. The gully continues in a straight line and is steep. Good snow conditions and hard frost are desirable for this climb, otherwise it may be a nasty climb up steep grass and vegetatious rock.

Lower down in the corrie below the cliffs of Creag na Caillich there is a semicircle of clean schist which gives some short rock-climbing problems of about 50 ft.

The south face of Beinn nan Eachan is steep and there are one or two gullies which give pleasant snow climbs. The best defined of these gullies ends steeply just to the west of the summit cairn. There are many gullies and chimneys in the crags of Cam Chreag on the south-east side of the Meall Garbh–Meall nan Tarmachan ridge. These have probably all been climbed in winter and give good sport, but no great difficulty. The steepest climbs are at the south-west end of the crag where two narrow gullies cut through the broken rocks below Meall Garbh (Grade I to II). The gully descending from the Meall Garbh–Meall nan Tarmachan col is very easy, and north-east of this col there are several gullies of moderate steepness, (Grade I). High up on the left wall of one of these gullies there are some steep, narrow chimneys which give good winter ascents.

Finally, there is the steep, south-facing crag above the south end of Lochan na Lairige. In summer this crag looks (and is) very grassy, but closer inspection reveals a more or less continuous chimney near the west side. This is *Arrow Chimney*, (350 ft., Grade II to III, H. Raeburn and Lawson), which gives rather a hard winter climb. The lowest section can be avoided on the left and the chimney is regained at a chockstone. Thereafter the climb follows the very steep chimney directly to the top. Good snow and ice conditions are necessary if one is to get the best from this climb, otherwise it is likely to be a struggle up steep, snow covered grass. To the right of Arrow Chimney a wide depression in the crag (barely a gully) gives an easier climb, and at the right-hand (east) end of the crag there is an obvious slanting gully topped by an overhang, but there is no record of an ascent.

Although the Tarmachans are not as well-known as Ben Lawers for their skiing possibilities, there is some very good terrain in the corrie below Cam Chreag which is easily reached from the Lochan na Lairige road. A very pleasant short day can be had by 'skinning' up to the foot of Cam Chreag, doing a climb and finally enjoying the delightfully easy run back to the road. Coire Riadhailt also appears to be good skiing country, and it is easily accessible from near the summit of the Lochan na Lairige road.

Transport and Accommodation
Bus services: Aberfeldy to Killin (school days only) and Aberfeldy to Lawers (Monday to Saturday); both operated by Aberfeldy Motor Coaches Ltd. Aberfeldy to Lubreoch (Loch Lyon dam), (Monday to Saturday); operated by Malcolm R. Stewart, Aberfeldy.

There are several hotels at Killin, also at Morenish, Lawers and Fearnan on the A827 road and at Fortingall. There is a Youth Hostel at Killin.

BIBLIOGRAPHY

BEN LAWERS

Ben Ghlas and Ben Lawers, J. M. Macharg, *S.M.C.J.*, Vol. 1, p. 158.
Note on Ben Lawers, W. Brown, *S.M.C.J.*, Vol. 2, p. 276.
Ben Lawers, (Guide Book Article), *S.M.C.J.*, Vol. 7, p. 23.
A Tale of Two Days' Tramp, F. S. Goggs, *S.M.C.J.*, Vol. 9, p. 229.
The Highlands in June, J. G. Stott, *S.M.C.J.*, Vol. 14, p. 259.
Cairn on Ben Lawers, (Note), H. MacRobert, *S.M.C.J.*, Vol. 23, p. 94.
The Cairn on Ben Lawers, (Note), H. R. J. Connacher, *S.M.C.J.*,
    Vol. 23, p. 191.

THE TARMACHANS

The Killin Hills, J. G. Stott, *S.M.C.J.*, Vol. 1, p. 270.
Two Climbs on the Tarmachans, H. Raeburn, *S.M.C.J.*, Vol. 5, p. 70.

The Tarmachans, (Note), A. W. Russell, *S.M.C.J.*, Vol. 5, p. 88.

A Winter Climb on the Tarmachan Cliffs, W. I. Clark, *S.M.C.J.*, Vol. 5, p. 242.

TheKillin Hills, (Guide Book Article), *S.M.C.J.*, Vol. 7, p. 25.

Tarmachan and the Creag na Caillich Gully, A. M. Mackay, *S.M.C.J.*, Vol. 7, p. 61.

The Heights of the Tarmachan Peaks, (Note), J. G. Inglis, *S.M.C.J.*, Vol. 7, p. 115.

A Climb on the Tarmachans, (Note), J. Macmillan, *S.M.C.J.*, Vol. 7, p. 298.

A Winter Climb on Creag na Caillich, (Note), H. Walker, *S.M.C.J.*, Vol. 7, p. 365.

13

The Tyndrum Hills

The principal mountains in this group are:
(1) **Ben Lui (Beinn Laoigh),** 3708 ft., 4¾ miles W.S.W. of Tyndrum.
(2) **Ben Oss,** 3374 ft., 4 miles S.W. of Tyndrum.
(3) **Beinn Dubhchraig,** 3204 ft., 1¼ miles E. of (2).
(4) **Beinn a' Chleibh,** 3008 ft., 1 mile W.S.W., of (1).
(5) **Beinn Chuirn,** 2878 ft., 2 miles N.N.E. of (1).
(6) **Beinn Odhar,** 2948 ft., 2¼ miles N. of Tyndrum.
(7) **Beinn Udlaidh,** 2759 ft., 3½ miles N.W. by W. of Tyndrum.

Maps: Ordnance Survey One-inch Series, Sheets 47 and 53 and the Loch Lomond and the Trossachs Tourist Map.
Bartholomew's Half-Inch Series, Sheet 48.

The mountains described in this chapter, which lie on or near the main watershed between the east and west coasts, are all within a six mile radius of Tyndrum village. The main mountains of the group, namely Ben Lui and its surrounding peaks lie to the south-west of Tyndrum and south of the A85 road through Glen Lochy, while Beinn Odhar lies north of Tyndrum on the east side of the A82 road to Fort William, and Beinn Udlaidh lies north-west of Tyndrum between Glen Lochy and Glen Orchy.

The group is dominated by Ben Lui which has some claim to be considered the most beautiful mountain in the Southern Highlands, particularly in its winter garb of snow and ice when the grand north-east corrie presents one of the finest sights in the Scottish mountains. The snowfilled gullies and their enclosing ridges sweep upwards in perfect harmony to the level summit ridge with its twin tops, and it is no wonder that this mountain and the winter climbs in the north-east corrie have for over seventy years been among the best known and most popular in Scotland.

The three other 3000 ft. mountains are linked to Ben Lui by high ridges, Beinn a'Chleibh on the south-west, and Ben Oss and Beinn

Dubhchraig on the east. Beinn Chuirn is to the north of Ben Lui, and these five mountains form a compact and impressive group which is conspicuous in many views. Their northern slopes overlooking Glen Lochy and the River Cononish are in general rather steep, while the southern flanks dropping to the Allt nan Caorrunn (Dubh Eas) are more gradual, with wide expanses of featureless moorland below 2000 ft.

Beinn Odhar, north of Tyndrum, is a shapely little conical peak lying very close to the summit of the A82 road. Beinn Udlaidh is an undistinguished hill with a broad, flat summit; its main interest from the climber's point of view is a fine semicircular corrie, the Coire Daimh, overlooking Glen Orchy.

There are several other features of interest in the area covered by this chapter. Dailrigh (MR 343290) is the site of a battle in 1306 between Robert the Bruce and the MacDougals of Lorne in which the Bruce was forced to retire. A mile south-west of Dailrigh, at the junction of the River Cononish and the Allt Gleann Achrioch, there is a small but very beautiful pine wood, the Coille Coire Chuilc, which is one of the few remnants of the Old Caledonian Forest in the Southern Highlands. A mile west of Tyndrum, on the hillside south of the main road, there are the remains of old lead mines which are worth a visit with a torch and rope on an off-day, and there are also remains of lead workings on the south-cast shoulder of Beinn Chuirn above Cononish Farm. Finally, there are indications at the time of writing that the Nature Conservancy intend to establish a small nature reserve in the Fionn Choirein on the north-west side of Ben Lui and this may create an area of interest for the naturalist.

Access to the mountains is quite easy from several directions. Tyndrum is the best centre from which to explore the group as all the mountains are within easy walking distance. Other starting points for the Ben Lui group include the Dubh Eas and Allt Fionn Ghlinne in Glen Falloch, Dailrigh in Strath Fillan from where there is a very rough road to Cononish Farm, and the foot of the Eas Daimh in Glen Lochy (seven miles from Tyndrum along the A85 road to Dalmally). It is also possible to reach these mountains from Glen Fyne, but this involves a very long walk, the last part of which crosses the desolate country between the head of the glen and the southern slopes of Ben Lui. Beinn Udlaidh can be reached from either Glen Lochy or Glen Orchy.

The best view of the Ben Lui group is had from the hillside to the east of Tyndrum above Strath Fillan or, better still, from the summit of Beinn Odhar. From the roadside half a mile north-west of Dailrigh, Ben Lui looks very fine early on a spring morning, but Ben Oss is hidden behind the north ridge of Dubhchraig. There is another fine view of Ben Lui, with Beinn a'Chleibh beside it, from the northeast end of Loch Awe. Ben Oss and Beinn Dubhchraig look their best from the south, and stand out well in the view from Loch Lomond just south of Ardlui.

There is a fine cross-country route along the southern edge of these hills following the line of an old drove road from Dalmally to Glen Falloch. From Dalmally the Tyndrum road is followed for two miles, and then one takes the private road to Succoth Lodge. Beyond the lodge the Eas a'Ghail and Allt a' Chaorain are followed to the pass between Beinn a'Chleibh and Meall nan Tighearn, and on the south-east side of the pass the Allt a' Mhinn is followed past a bothy. (Avoid straying to the south in thick weather as this might lead one down Glen Fyne.) In two miles from the pass the Allt nan Caorrunn is reached and a hydro road high on the south side of the burn leads down to Glen Falloch. The distance from Dalmally is 12½ miles.

The only other walking route of note in this area is much shorter, but takes one through grand scenery in the heart of the mountains. Starting at Dailrigh one follows the rough road to Cononish Farm, (alternatively, a path from Tyndrum Lower Station leads round the hillside to join this road). From Cononish a good path continues south-westwards, and a short digression up a zigzag track on the hillside on one's right leads to the old lead mines on Beinn Chuirn. The path ends near the junction of the Allt an Rund and the Allt Coire Laoigh, and the former stream is followed westwards to the low pass (ca. 1400 ft.) on the north side of Ben Lui. On the west side of the pass one soon enters newly planted forest and follows a fair path on the north side of the Eas Daimh to its junction with the River Lochy where there is a footbridge, 7 miles from Dailrigh.

Ben Lui (Beinn Laoigh), 3708 ft., is a magnificent mountain, and many would consider it to be the finest in the Southern Highlands. It may lack the height of Ben Lawers and the symmetrical simplicity of Ben More and Stobinian, but it more than makes amends by its perfect form and by the beautiful north-east corrie – the Coire Gaothaich – which holds snow until long after the other mountains of the Southern Highlands are bare. Ben Lui has four corries – facing west, north, north-east and south-east – and five ridges radiate outwards between these corries. The south-west side of the mountain drops away in uniform stony slopes towards the desolate moorland at the head of the Allt nan Caorrunn.

The best route to Ben Lui, and one which gives a grand view of the mountain as one approaches it, is along the River Cononish from Dailrigh or Tyndrum. The path beyond Cononish ends at the Allt an Rund near a sheep fank. Immediately above this a little stream tumbles steeply down from Coire Gaothaich, and one climbs up a faint path beside it. Once in the corrie, the hill-walker should bear either to left or right to reach one of the bounding ridges of the corrie which (in summer at least) can be climbed easily to the summit.

A shorter route, but one which lacks the view of the mountain as one approaches it, is from Glen Lochy. Starting at the foot of the Eas Daimh, where there is a footbridge, one follows this stream for just over a mile to the foot of Ben Lui's north ridge. The giant rock steps at the foot of this ridge, known as the Ciochan Beinn Laoigh, can be easily avoided on the west, and a steepish climb up the broad, stony ridge leads directly to the slightly lower north top only a hundred yards from the summit. Alternatively one may cross the Eas Daimh at the beautiful little fall Eas Morag near the foot of the stream and head south-eastwards into Fionn Choirein. The last two or three hundred feet to the Ben Lui–Beinn a'Chleibh col are quite steep, but once on the col the south-west ridge of Ben Lui (which is hardly a ridge, but more a broad shoulder between the south and west faces) leads easily to the summit.

The Eas Daimh also gives a quick approach from Glen Lochy to the Coire Gaothaich. The stream is followed to the upper limit of the forest and then a rising traverse below the Ciochan Beinn Laoigh leads by an obvious and natural line round the north side of the mountain and into the corrie. This route passes below a little water-fall in the stream tumbling from Ben Lui's northern corrie, and the direct ascent of this corrie is another pleasant route, particularly in good winter conditions.

None of the routes described thus far are in any way difficult in summer, nor would they be difficult for a competent party in winter. Nevertheless, they all involve a certain amount of quite steep climbing on ground that might become awkward in icy conditions. The only route of ascent that does not involve any steep climbing is the long and rather tedious approach from Glen Falloch by the Allt nan Caorrunn. From the end of the hydro road (four miles up the stream) one can head west of north directly towards Ben Lui, passing close to the Ben Lui–Ben Oss col and climbing the easy-angled south-south-east ridge.

The best climbing on Ben Lui is to be had in winter in the Coire Gaothaich. The corrie itself is bounded by two ridges, one dropping from the summit and the other from the north top, and between these ridges the corrie forms a huge bowl in which the most prominent features are the Central Gully which runs up to the level summit ridge, and the crescent-shaped South Rib on its left (south-east). On the left of the South Rib, the South Gully ends on the east ridge some distance below the summit. On the right of the Central Gully there is a broad snowfield and a broken buttress adjoining the north-east ridge which rises from a level shoulder called Stob Garbh to the north top. Most of the climbs in this corrie were pioneered by members of the Scottish Mountaineering Club between 1891 and 1896 in the days when Tyndrum (by virtue of its two railway stations) was one of Scotland's main climbing centres. Although easy by modern standards, these climbs (and in particular the Central Gully) have retained their popularity ever since then. They are summarised as follows:

1. *East Ridge*. This, the bounding ridge on the south side of the corrie, is an easy scramble.
2. *South Gully*, (Grade I). This broad gully has two or three possible finishes. The obvious line is straight up a narrow gully to the East Ridge. An alternative finish on the left reaches this ridge lower down by easy rocks. The right-hand finish leads onto the upper part of South Rib.
3. *South Rib*, (Grade I to II). In summer the lowest rocks can be climbed directly, but this may be quite difficult in winter, in which case the Rib can be reached from the South Gully a short distance above its foot. The upper part of the Rib is a scramble.
4. *South-Central Gully*, (Grade I). This ill-defined gully on the immediate right of South Rib is parallel to Central Gully, with which it shares the same finish.
5. *Central Gully*, (Grade I). This is the classic winter climb on Ben Lui; the line is directly up the centre of the corrie. The gully is narrow and well-defined for a few hundred feet and then opens out so that there is plenty of scope for variation as the cornice (which is often large) is approached.

60. Ben Lui from Loch Awe; Kilchurn Castle in the foreground.

61. Beinn Oss and Ben Lui from Beinn Odhar.

62. Ben Lui from Beinn Oss.

63. In the Centre Gully of Ben Lui.

64. Ben Lui from the north ridge of Beinn Dubhchraig.

6. *Upper Snowfield*, (Grade I). This route is not well defined, but it lies to the right of Central Gully up a broad snowfield. The finish may be made at the north top by a narrow little gully, or alternatively on the north-east ridge a short distance below the top.

7. *North Rib*, (Grade I). This route is up the indeterminate buttress which adjoins the north-east ridge. In winter it is likely to be a climb of no great merit on steep snow, rocks and frozen turf.

Below, and to the right of North Rib, there is a broad, easy gully leading to the north-east ridge just above Stob Garbh.

A note of warning should be sounded about climbing in Coire Gaothaich in thaw conditions such as frequently occur in spring. Collapsing cornices and snow avalanches are not uncommon, and the snow and ice debris that can often be seen in spring at the foot of the corrie testify to the size of these avalanches.

Ben Oss, 3374 ft., is rather overshadowed by Ben Lui, but from certain viewpoints to the north and south (for example, from the north end of Loch Lomond) it presents a fine appearance as a steep conical peak. It is usually climbed in conjunction with Beinn Dubhchraig, and the ascent from the Oss–Dubhchraig col is quite straightforward over a small top at the point where the ridge turns from west to south-south-west. (This top is not clearly shown on the One-inch Map, but it is marked by a cairn.) The summit of Ben Oss is a fairly level ridge with a large cairn at its south end.

From the south there are two possible approaches to Ben Oss. The hydro road up the Allt nan Caorrunn can be followed to its end and then one heads northwards up rather featureless and uninteresting slopes. Alternatively, a rather more pleasant route lies up the Allt Fionn Ghlinne, starting about two miles up Glen Falloch from Inverarnan. The burn can be followed all the way to Loch Oss from where Ben Oss is easily reached. The going along the burn is rather wet in places.

The north and north-west sides of Ben Oss are steep and rough, and not often visited. In winter there might be some interesting climbing on this side of the mountain, but no definite routes have been recorded. The quickest route to the summit from Cononish is by way of the Oss–Dubhchraig col; the slopes on the north side of this col are steep for a short distance.

Beinn Dubhchraig, 3204 ft., is the easternmost mountain of the group surrounding Ben Lui. It looks its best from the south, from where the crags just under the summit give the hill an impressive appearance, but on closer acquaintance these crags are found to be very broken and unsuitable for climbing. The north side of the hill is formed by a big, grassy, easy-angled corrie, the Coire Dubhchraig, which is enclosed by two broad ridges, the north and north-east ridges. At the foot of this corrie the ancient pines of the Coille Coire Chuilc are remnants of the Old Caledonian forest.

Beinn Dubhchraig can be climbed from Glen Falloch by the Allt Fionn Ghlinne and Loch Oss. From the loch one can either climb directly and steeply towards the summit, or make a more circuitous route by the Oss–Dubhchraig col and the easy north-west ridge along which there is a faint track. On the north side of this ridge, in the corrie facing north-west to Beinn Chuirn, there is a short, narrow gully which gives an easy climb in winter. It is best approached from Cononish.

The most popular route to Beinn Dubhchraig, however, is up the Coire Dubhchraig or one of its bounding ridges. From Dailrigh the Cononish road is followed for three-quarters of a mile to a railway bridge, and then a path leads down to the River Cononish which is usually easy to cross at this point. Alternatively, starting at the bridge over the River Fillan a quarter of a mile below Dailrigh, a track along the railway leads to a footbridge over the Allt Coire Dubhchraig. There is a delightful path through the trees on the north side of this stream which continues a short distance westwards above Creag Bhocan towards the north ridge of Dubhchraig. This is possibly the most pleasant route by virtue of the grand view of Ben Lui as one gains height on the ridge. The Coire Dubhchraig is a very pleasant ski-route, and the ascent of the mountain by this corrie is one of the most popular ski tours in the Southern Highlands. There are practically no difficulties, and the corrie gives delightfully easy skiing on the descent.

Beinn a' Chleibh, 3008 ft., is rather dwarfed by Ben Lui, with which it is connected by a col at about 2550 ft. It is easily climbed from this col which can be reached from Glen Lochy by the Fionn Choirein. Alternatively, the hill can be climbed from Succoth Lodge (3 miles east of Dalmally) by the long west ridge. This ridge is smooth and grassy, and as one approaches the top two small cairns on the summit plateau are passed before the true top, marked by a larger cairn, is reached.

The north-east face of Beinn a' Chleibh overlooking Fionn Choirein is very steep, with crags and several narrow gullies. (These crags are not adequately shown on the One-inch Map.) Although this face gives some good climbing in winter, it must definitely be avoided as a route of descent. The north-west side of the hill is also broken by low crags, and the best descent route towards Glen Lochy is on the west side of the north-north-west shoulder which drops towards the foot of the Eas Daimh.

Beinn Chuirn, 2878 ft., is separated from Ben Lui by the Allt an Rund. It has a steep little east-facing corrie, and as one approaches from the east up Strath Fillan, Beinn Chuirn looks rather like a small version of Ben Lui. The easiest ascent is probably from Cononish Farm up the zigzag track on the south-east shoulder of the hill. This track leads to the old mines, and from there one continues north-west past the top of the Eas Anie and so to the summit. The eastern corrie can also be reached by ascending the stream that comes down at the back of the farm. There are some gullies in this corrie, the most prominent ones being at the south end of the cliff which forms the headwall of the corrie. One of these gullies is wide and has been described as being similar to the Centre Gully of Ben Lui, though much shorter, (B. Bain and E. Whitelaw). Another narrower and steeper gully has also been climbed, (M. Boyle and R. Mann). Both these climbs were done in winter conditions, and it is unlikely that there is any rock-climbing in this corrie. The Eas Anie might make a very sporting winter climb when the big waterfall is well frozen. An alternative and shorter approach can be made to Beinn Chuirn and its eastern corrie from Glen Lochy, provided the river can be crossed at a suitable point.

The western spur of Beinn Chuirn is Beinn Dubh, 2300 ft. contour. It has a steep and rocky north face overlooking Glenlochy Crossing, and there are three shallow gullies on this side which have been reported by J. Mackenzie to give climbs of Grade II to III standard, with some ice-pitches. Considering the low altitude of this face, it must be rather rare to find these gullies in good condition.

Beinn Odhar, 2948 ft., is a smooth, conical hill on the east side of the A82 road from Tyndrum to Bridge of Orchy. A long, grassy ridge drops southwards from the summit towards Tyndrum, while the west and north sides of the hill are uniformly steep. Although the hill is not of much climbing interest, it does command a magnificent view in all directions and is worth climbing on a clear day for this alone. The quickest route is up the grassy south-south-west spur, leaving the A82 road at a bridge over the railway one mile north of

Tyndrum, and following a faint grassy track almost all the way to the summit. The ascent by this route takes little more than an hour. The view from the summit encompasses almost all the high mountains of Perthshire and Argyll. Ben Lui and its neighbours stand up grandly to the south-west, and to the west Ben Cruachan dominates the horizon. North-westwards the Black Mount peaks make a fine array, while closer at hand to the north and north-east Beinn Dorain, Beinn a'Chreachain, Creag Mhor and Beinn Heasgarnich show their bulk. Eastwards there is a glimpse of Ben Lawers and the Tarmachans, and to the south-east is the familiar outline of the Crianlarich mountains. Finally, Ben Lomond and the Arrochar Alps appear in the distant south. Altogether it is a wonderful panorama which more than repays the small effort required to climb the hill.

Beinn Udlaidh, 2759 ft., is the highest hill between Glen Lochy and Glen Orchy. It is not a particularly striking hill, with an extensive, flat summit surrounded by steep and, in many places, craggy flanks. The summit plateau is grassy and featureless, and the top is marked by a large cairn of flat stones. An interesting feature of the hill is a prominent quartzite dyke which crosses the north ridge, and can be clearly seen from the north around Loch Tulla.

The shortest ascent is from Glen Lochy, starting about two and a half miles west of Tyndrum. However, this side of the hill has recently been planted by the Forestry Commission, and this approach should probably be avoided; it is, in any case, rather uninteresting.

A better approach can be made from Glen Orchy. Starting at the foot of the Allt Daimh, a track up the north-east side of the stream can be followed for three-quarters of a mile and then one should head south-east to avoid the steep ground in Coire Daimh. The north ridge of Beinn Udlaidh is reached near the quartzite dyke, which at this point forms a broken line of crags about 20 ft. high. From the summit one can continue south-westwards across the grassy plateau until, after three-quarters of a mile, a descent can be made down the broad ridge on the west side of Coire Daimh.

The main interest in Beinn Udlaidh for the climber is the Coire Daimh, a semicircular corrie ringed by low cliffs. The main features are a 100 ft. high line of quartzite crags low down and a higher line of dark schist rocks just below the rim of the corrie. At the west end of these crags there are two larger gullies, and north-west of these the cliffs become very broken and vegetatious. The rocks in the corrie tend to be rather damp as water drains over them from the grassy summit plateau, so it is advisable in summer to make a visit after a long dry spell. The first ascents of the summer rock-climbs were all made by J. B. Nimlin, Hutchison and Slack. It is probable that the best climbing in this corrie can be had in winter when the water which drains continuously down the gullies gives a good build-up of ice in frosty weather; however, in view of the low altitude of the corrie, such conditions rarely last for long.

The low quartzite crag is vertical and the rock looks very loose. At the west end of the crag (and not readily visible from below) there are two chimneys. The left-hand one, *100 ft. Chimney* (V.D.) is a good climb and the rock is fairly sound. The right-hand one, *West Chimney*, is short and easy. Just to the right of these chimneys is the foot of *Central Gully*; the start consists of two or three pitches of boulders (the last pitch may be climbed by a slab on the left) and then the gully becomes an easy grass slope slanting left. Central Gully has also been climbed in winter; the lower pitches may be icy, or with sufficient snow they are completely masked (Grade I to II). West Gully starts near the foot of Central Gully and slants rightwards; there is a pitch some distance up the gully which may be obliterated if there is sufficient snow (Grade I to II).

The upper line of crags, which is two to three hundred feet high, extends for a few hundred yards eastwards from the top of Central Gully. The rock is generally vegetatious, and the most obvious routes are in the gullies. Starting at the west end of the crags and working eastwards, the first feature is an open, leftward-slanting gully, *Sunshine Gully*, which has been climbed in winter, but is not a summer route, (300 ft., Grade II, E. Fowler, F. Jack, R. McGowan and G. Skelton). A short distance further east is the narrow *Rams-head Gully* (300 ft., D.) which gives a good climb in summer on generally sound rock. It has also been climbed in winter (G. Skelton and party) and is reported to give an excellent Grade II climb.

The line of crags gradually curves round to the north, and the main feature is a big, dark wall of rock with few ledges or grass patches. This is the Black Wall. Its south edge is defined by a narrow little gully, South Gully of Black Wall (200 ft., V.D.). The winter ascent has also been made, the climb being a series of short ice-pitches, (Grade III, R. McGowan and G. Skelton). The right-hand end of Black Wall close to the South Gully is broken up and gives an easy scramble from ledge to ledge. The main wall is very steep and gives a good climb trending right, with the most difficult pitch near the top (250 ft., V.D.). The left side of Black Wall is bounded by an open groove, *Quartzvein Scoop,* which is climbed on the left of the line of quartz rocks in the corner of the groove (170 ft., D.).

To the north of Black Wall the rock becomes much more broken by grass ledges. There are two deep fissures at this point, and to the north of them *Fissure Slab* (60ft., D.) is a very pleasant short climb. Near these fissures, *Zigzag Gully* is a winter route up the left-hand edge of the crags, (300 ft., Grade II, A. Agnew and J. Jewel).

On the east side of Beinn Udlaidh there is a long line of crags overlooking Coire Ghamhnain, but there does not seem to be much worth climbing. The prominent dark gully at the north end of these crags has been climbed by D. D. Stewart. Three-quarters of a mile north of the summit, where the quartzite dyke crosses the north ridge, there is a line of crags up to 80 ft. high which gives some good little climbs.

Transport and Accommodation

The bus services from Glasgow to Oban and Fort William give access to all the mountains described in this chapter. Both services are operated jointly by W. Alexander and Sons (Midland) Ltd. and Highland Omnibuses Ltd. There is also a bus service from Edinburgh to Tyndrum.

The Glasgow to Oban and Glasgow to Fort William railways pass through the area, with stations at Ardlui, Crianlarich, Tyndrum, Bridge of Orchy and Dalmally.

There are hotels at Inverarnan (Glen Falloch), Crianlarich, Tyndrum, Bridge of Orchy and Dalmally, and Youth Hostels at Crianlarich and Cruachan (Loch Awe).

BIBLIOGRAPHY

Ben Lui, T. F. S. Campbell, *S.M.C.J.,* Vol. 1, p. 207.
Old and New Routes on Ben Lui, J. Maclay, *S.M.C.J.,* Vol. 4, p. 106.
Ben Lui, (Note), H. C. Boyd, *S.M.C.J.,* Vol. 4, p. 177.
A Blizzard on Ben Lui, W. W. Naismith, *S.M.C.J.,* Vol. 4, p. 276.
Ben Lui, (Guide Book Article), *S.M.C.J.,* Vol. 6, p. 192.
Ben Lui Revisited, W. Douglas, *S.M.C.J.,* Vol. 8, p. 95.
Some Hill Walks from Tyndrum, J. H. Bell, *S.M.C.J.,* Vol. 9, p. 1.
The Spell of Ben Lui, C. R. P. Vandeleur, *S.M.C.J.,* Vol. 21, p. 93.
Beinn Chuirn, (Note), *S.M.C.J.,* Vol. 27, p. 285.
Beinn Dubh, Glen Lochy, (Note), *S.M.C.J.,* Vol. 29, p. 321.

14

The Glen Lochay Hills

(1) **Beinn Heasgarnich,** 3530 ft., 3½ miles W.N.W. of Kenknock Farm in Glen Lochay.
(2) **Stob an Fhir-Bhoga,** 3381 ft., ½ mile S. of (1).
(3) **Creag Mhor,** 3387 ft., 2 miles S.W. of (1).
(4) **Stob nan Clach,** 3146 ft., ⅝ mile S. by W. of (3).
(5) **Beinn Chaluim** (N. top), 3354 ft., 2½ miles S. of (3).
(6) **Beinn Chaluim** (S. top), 3236 ft., ½ mile S. of (5).
(7) **Meall Ghaordie,** 3407 f.t, 5½ miles N.W. of Killin.
(8) **Meall Glas,** 3139 ft., 2¾ miles E. of (5).
(9) **Beinn Cheathaich,** 3074 ft., ⅞ mile E.N.E. of (8).
(10) **Sgiath Chuil,** 3050 ft., 2 miles E. by S. of (8).
(11) **Meall a' Churain,** 3007 ft., ½ mile N. of (10).
(12) **Beinn nan Oighreag,** 2978 ft., 5½ miles N.N.W. of Killin.
Maps: Ordnance Survey One-inch Series, Sheets 47, 48, 53 and the Loch Lomond and the Trossachs Tourist Map.
Bartholomew's Half-inch Series, Sheet 48.

The mountains described in this chapter are on the north and south sides of Glen Lochay, and round its head. The area is bounded on the north by the River Lyon and on the south by the River Fillan (which becomes the River Dochart below Crianlarich). On the east the area is separated from the Tarmachan Hills by the Lairig Breisleich, and the western boundary is the Abhuinn Ghlas (the true headwater of the River Lyon) and the Allt Gleann a' Chlachain which flows into the River Fillan. Thus all the mountains in this area are within the catchment area of the River Lochay, and all can easily be climbed from Glen Lochay. Killin is the best centre for these hills, or, better still, a tent about seven miles up Glen Lochay from which point they are all within fairly easy walking distance.

Glen Lochay is rather an attractive and quiet glen, and as there is no public through road it is usually free of much traffic. For the first seven miles above Killin it is beautifully wooded, the river flows through some quiet rocky pools and there are farms every mile or so. At Kenknock Farm the public road ends and the glen becomes desolate and almost treeless. A private road continues up the glen for a further three miles to the shepherd's cottage at Batavaime, and another private road from Kenknock crosses the Learg nan Lunn pass to Lubreoch in Glen Lyon, (the gate at the north end of this road is usually locked).

The mountains in this area are not particularly striking, nevertheless they provide the hill-walker with some fine, wild country well off the beaten track, and the ski-mountaineer has the choice of three or four excellent tours. There is nothing for the rock-climber, but the enthusiastic searcher after winter climbs might find something to repay his efforts in the corries of Beinn Heasgarnich and Creag Mhor, or on the north side of Beinn Chaluim.

The three mountains just mentioned, all of which stand at the head of Glen Lochay, comprise the Forest of Mamlorn which was once one of the best known of the royal deer forests. The Gaelic poet Duncan Ban MacIntyre lived for a few years at the head of the glen as keeper in Coire Cheathaich on Creag Mhor. These three are also the finest of the mountains described in this chapter: Beinn Chaluim's steep north face and the twin spurs of Creag Mhor are the features of the view up Glen Lochay from Kenknock, but the summit of Beinn Heasgarnich is hidden behind the uninteresting lower slopes and the mountain must be seen from the north to be fully appreciated.

The other hills around Glen Lochay are rather less imposing. Meall Ghaordie is the highest of the group between glens Lochay and Lyon to the east of the Learg nan Lunn; the slopes above Glen Lochay are grassy and featureless, and the most impressive parts of this hill are the two steep spurs overlooking Glen Lyon. Meall Glas, Beinn Cheathaich and Sgiath Chuil are the highest points in an extensive area of rather uninteresting hills and moorland between Glen Lochay and Glen Dochart.

For the walker there are several routes from glen to glen through the hills. The Lairig Breisleich is a well-defined pass between Glen Lochay and Glen Lyon, and it is also possible to strike southwards and south-westwards from the head of Glen Lochay towards Crianlarich and Tyndrum by trackless passes.

Beinn Heasgarnich, 3530 ft., occupies a considerable area between glens Lyon and Lochay to the west of the Learg nan Lunn; on its south-west the Bealach na Baintighearna separates it from Creag Mhor. The backbone of the mountain is a broad ridge which rises north-eastwards from the Bealach na Baintighearna to the south top, **Stob an Fhir-Bhoga** (which is not shown on the One-inch Map, but is marked by the 3300 ft. contour line) and then continues half a mile north to the highest point. Beyond the summit the main ridge divides and its two arms enclose the Coire Heasgarnich, the finest feature of the mountain. The western slopes fall very steeply to the Allt Fionn a' Glinne, but elsewhere (apart from the headwall of Coire Heasgarnich) the sides of the mountain are not particularly steep, and from most viewpoints Beinn Heasgarnich appears as a massive, flat-topped mountain lacking in distinctive features. However, being very remote from the sea, it carries plenty of snow which lingers in the high corrie east of the summit, Coire Ban Mor, until late in spring. The lochan in this corrie is one of the highest in Scotland, and there are several other tiny lochans high on the mountain.

The shortest approaches to Beinn Heasgarnich are from Glen Lochay. From Badour (two miles beyond Kenknock) a perfectly straightforward climb north-north-westwards leads to the main ridge a short distance south of the summit. If it is possible to drive to the top of the Learg nan Lunn road this gives a higher starting point, and the line of the Allt Tarsuinn can be followed across a wide, peaty plateau to the Coire Ban More and so to the top. This route can be particularly recommended as a ski route; the high starting point reduces ski-carrying, the Allt Tarsuinn holds snow well and the terrain is good for skiing.

The approach to Beinn Heasgarnich from Glen Lyon has become rather more difficult since the building of the dam at Lubreoch has created a greatly enlarged Loch Lyon which now extends almost six miles up the glen. From Lubreoch the Learg nan Lunn road can be used to reach the Allt Tarsuinn route just described. Alternatively, a three mile walk along the trackless south shore of Loch Lyon leads to the Allt Heasgarnich which can be followed into Coire Heasgarnich. In winter it is possible that the gullies at the head of this corrie might give enjoyable, but probably easy climbs. A third possible route takes a direct line from Lubreoch over Meall a' Chall, past Lochan nan Cat and finally up the north-east ridge to the top.

Creag Mhor, 3387 ft., is lower but more shapely than its bulky neighbour just described. The summit stands at the junction of three ridges, two of which form a horseshoe enclosing Coire Cheathaich between the steep spurs that are well seen from Glen Lochay. **Stob nan Clach**, 3146 ft., (not named on the One-inch Map, but shown by the 3100 ft. contour) is the highest point on the south-western rim of this horseshoe. The third ridge of Creag Mhor drops north-west then north from the summit, rises briefly to Meall Tionail, 2937 ft., and then continues down to the shore of Loch Lyon.

Creag Mhor can be reached from Glen Lyon, Tyndrum and Crianlarich, but these starting points all involve long approaches and in some cases a good deal of up and downhill work as well. The simplest approach is undoubtedly from Batavaime in Glen Lochay, and if it is not intended to combine the ascent of Creag Mhor with any of its neighbours, the best expedition is the circuit of the horseshoe round Coire Cheathaich. From Batavaime an easy ascent leads to Sron nan Eun, 2747 ft., and from there a pleasant walk leads on to the summit. Westwards, the ridge is broad and drops gradually before turning south-east and rising to Stob nan Clach. The north-east face of this peak is steep, and one or two gullies might give winter climbs. The south-east end of the Stob nan Clach ridge is steep, but there are no apparent possibilities for any climbing; however, care is needed when descending the end of this ridge.

If Creag Mhor is being combined in a traverse with Beinn Heasgarnich, the steep north-east face of the mountain dropping from the summit to the Bealach na Baintighearna must be negotiated. In summer this will cause no difficulty, but in winter the descent of this face should be tackled carefully. It might be preferable in conditions of hard snow or ice to descend north-north-west from the summit of Creag Mhor for a quarter of a mile before turning east to descend to the bealach.

Cam Chreag, 2887 ft., lies south-west of Creag Mhor, with which it is linked by a col at about 2400 ft. It is an undistinguished hill with a flat mile-long summit ridge which is rarely climbed for itself, but may be included in a traverse from Creag Mhor to Beinn Chaluim.

Beinn Chaluim, 3354 ft., (spelt Ben Challum on the One-inch Map) is the pointed peak which is prominently seen in the view up Glen Lochay from Kenknock. From the Strath Fillan side the mountain looks less impressive as the broad and rather uninteresting lower slopes rising above the West Highland railway detract from the twin summits. The south top is the culminating point of the broad, featureless hillside rising above the railway, and from it a narrow ridge with steep drops on both sides leads to the main summit. Two other ridges radiate from the summit, one to the north-west and the other to the east. Between these ridges the steep north face of Beinn Chaluim rises a thousand feet above the Allt Challum, one of the headwaters of the River Lochay.

From the south-west Beinn Chaluim can be ascended most easily from Auchtertyre Farm, a mile and a half south-east of Tyndrum. One can either climb directly towards the south top by easy grass slopes, or follow the Allt Gleann a' Chlachain for a mile and a half and then climb eastwards to the south top. In winter it might be worthwhile to ascend into Coire nan Each in search of a more interesting route to the summit. The direct route from Auchtertyre to the south top is an easy ski ascent in the right conditions, with some nice slopes for the descent on the south-west side of the top.

From Glen Lochay the ascent of Beinn Chaluim starts at Batavaime. By climbing a few hundred feet above the cottage, the line of an aqueduct is reached and this may be followed to its end at the Allt Challum. From there one heads south-west to reach the east ridge of the mountain which is followed to the top. The north face of Beinn Chaluim is not particularly well suited for climbing as it lacks definite features such as buttresses and gullies, and the face is for the most part steep grass and broken rock. However, there is a fairly well defined and long gully which reaches the north-west ridge a short distance below the summit, and this is probably the most promising winter line on the mountain.

Meall Ghaordie, 3407 ft., stands by itself on the north side of Glen Lochay, five and a half miles north-west of Killin. From most points of view it appears as a rather conical hill, but on the north side it throws out two ridges towards Glen Lyon which terminate in the steep buttresses Creag Laoghain and Creag an Tulabhain.

The farm at Duncroisk in Glen Lochay is as good a starting point as any on the south side of the hill, and a path leads up the west side of the Allt Dhuin Croisg. This may be followed for half a mile or so until it is convenient to head north-westwards up the uniform grassy slopes of the mountain. This can also be recommended as a good ski route in winter.

The ascent from Glen Lyon is more interesting, and the deserted farm at Stronuich is a good starting point. Some scrambling might be found on the faces of Creag Laoghain or Creag an Tulabhain to add interest to the climb; alternatively, the burn between them, the Allt Laoghain, can be followed to its source about half a mile northeast of the summit of Meall Ghaordie. There are gullies on both

Creag Laoghain and Creag an Tulabhain, and although they are not steep they might give interesting climbs in winter.

West of Meall Ghaordie there is a rather uninteresting group of hills stretching towards the Learg nan Lunn. They can all be climbed easily from the south, but they have no features of interest.

North-east of Meall Ghaordie is **Beinn nan Oighreag,** 2978 ft., a featureless hill with a long, hummocky summit ridge; there are three distinct tops, of which the middle one is the highest and is marked by a fairly large cairn. The hill can be climbed easily from either Duncroisk in Glen Lochay or from Glen Lyon, starting from the Lochan na Lairige road near the foot of the Allt Breisleich.

The Lairig Breisleich on the east side of Beinn nan Oighreag provides a low level route from Glen Lochay to Glen Lyon. Starting at Duncroisk, the Allt Dhuin Croisg is followed, (there are paths on both sides of the burn, but the one on the east side goes further before fading out). As the pass is approached, the going becomes trackless and boggy over peat hags; however, the descent on the north side of the pass is drier and the Allt Breisleich is followed down to the Lochan na Lairige road. The distance from Killin to Bridge of Balgie by this route is 11 miles, 2 miles shorter than the Lochan na Lairige road.

An alternative and much shorter crossing from Glen Lochay to Glen Lyon can be made by a trackless but otherwise easy pass between Meall Ghaordie and Beinn nan Oighreag. Follow the path on the west side of the Allt Dhuin Croisg for a mile and then head northwards along the Allt na h-Iolaire, over the pass at about 2100 ft. and down the Allt Lairig Luaidhe to Glen Lyon half a mile above Kenknock Farm, where there is a bridge over the river.

The hills on the south side of Glen Lochay have few distinctive features, although Sgiath Chuil and its lower top Sgiath Chrom have steep south-facing buttresses which give the hill a characteristic appearance when seen from the head of Glen Falloch. The four 3000 ft. summits of this group can easily be climbed together in one day, the two possible starting points being Auchessan in Glen Dochart and Lubchurran in Glen Lochay (the latter being nearer to the foot of the hills).

Meall Glas, 3139 ft., and **Beinn Cheathaich,** 3074 ft,. form a broad, crescent-shaped ridge enclosing Coire Cheathaich, a grassy corrie overlooking Glen Lochay. From Lubchurran a track leads a short distance towards the north ridge of Beinn Cheathaich, and this ridge is a quick and easy route to the summit which is marked by a triangulation pillar and a small cairn. The ridge continues south-west to a small cairn marking Point 2980 ft., and then a slight drop leads to the col which is flat and featureless, and might be confusing in misty weather. A short ascent leads to Meall Glas, marked by a fair-sized cairn. If one is returning to Lubchurran, a direct descent can be made north-eastwards into Coire Cheathaich and diagonally downwards across the hillside.

From the south the approach to Meall Glas from Auchessan involves a longer approach over rough country along the Allt Riobain. Two miles up this burn one can strike north-westwards and reach the ridge between Meall Glas and Beinn Cheathaich.

The approaches to **Sgiath Chuil,** 3050 ft., and **Meall a'Churain,** 3007 ft., are similar in character to the routes just described. From Lubchurran one can climb easy grass slopes on the east side of the Lubchurran Burn to reach the north ridge of Meall a'Churain which gradually narrows and steepens towards the summit. An almost level ridge leads a further half mile southwards to Sgiath Chuil.

From Auchessan in Glen Dochart the approach along the Allt Riobain is rough and there is no continuous track. After two miles one leaves the burn and heads north-east to the steep bluff below the summit of Sgiath Chuil.

If the four 3000 ft. summits are to be climbed in one expedition, there is a descent and reascent of just over a thousand feet across the pass between the Lubchurran Burn and the Allt Riobain. This pass also gives a trackless, but otherwise easy walk from Lubchurran to Auchessan, or vice versa. The distance is 5 miles, and this is the easiest crossing through the mountains between glens Lochay and Dochart.

These hills are not high enough to be particularly well-known for ski-mountaineering; nevertheless, in the right conditions there is some good terrain for skiing in Coire Cheathaich, Coire Lobhaidh and along the upper part of the Allt Riobain. These are hills which, although rather featureless for hill-walking in summer, have plenty of interesting and generally easy country for the ski-mountaineer in winter; however, there should be snow down to about 1000 ft. to make it worthwhile taking skis onto them.

Eastwards from Meall a'Churain a broad, undulating ridge forms the watershed between Glen Lochay and Glen Dochart, but it has few features of interest and none of the tops exceed 3000 ft. The best approach to this ridge is from Glen Lochay, and the highest tops (all those over 2000 ft.) can most easily be traversed by starting at Lubchurran and descending to Corrycharmaig, or vice versa. The eastern point on this ridge, Sron a' Chlachain, overlooks Killin and can be easily climbed by a track leading uphill from the town. It commands a grand view towards Loch Tay, Ben Lawers and the Tarmachan Hills.

Transport and Accommodation
Bus Services: Aberfeldy to Lubreoch (Loch Lyon dam), operated by M. R. Stewart, Aberfeldy.

Callander to Crianlarich via Glen Dochart, operated by W. Alexander and Sons (Midland) Ltd.

Glasgow to Crianlarich and Tyndrum, operated by W. Alexander and Sons (Midland) Ltd., and Highland Omnibuses Ltd.

Train: Glasgow to Crianlarich and Tyndrum.

There are hotels at Killin, Suie Lodge (Glen Dochart), Crianlarich and Tyndrum. There are Youth Hostels at Killin and Crianlarich.

BIBLIOGRAPHY

The Tyndrum Hills, (Note) J. G. Stott, *S.M.C.J.*, Vol. 1., p. 325.
The Glen Dochart Hills, (Note), J. G. Stott, *S.M.C.J.*, Vol. 2., p. 31.
The Killin Hills, (Note), H. B. Watt, *S.M.C.J.*, Vol. 2, p. 137.
Guide Book Articles, *S.M.C.J.*, Vol. 7, p. 28.
Beinn Heasgarnich, Creag Mhor and Beinn Chaluim, (Note), F. S. Goggs. *S.M.C.J.*, Vol. 7, p. 366.
Some Hill Walks from Tyndrum, J. H. Bell, *S.M.C.J.*, Vol. 9, p. 1.
The Highlands in June, J. G. Stott, *S.M.C.J.*, Vol. 14, p. 259.
Beinn nan Oighreag, (Note), J. A. Parker, *S.M.C.J.*, Vol. 19, p. 208.
Beinn nan Oighreag, (Note), J. G. Inglis, *S.M.C.J.*, Vol. 19, p. 361.

15

The Bridge of Orchy Hills

The principal summits described in this chapter are:
(1) **Beinn Dorain,** 3524 ft., 2 miles S.E. by E. of Bridge of Orchy.
(2) **Beinn an Dothaidh,** 3283 ft., 2¼ miles E.N.E. of Bridge of Orchy.
(3) **Beinn Achaladair,** North Top, 3404 ft., 1¾ miles N.E. by N. of (2).
(4) **Beinn Achaladair,** South Top, 3288 ft., ¾ mile S. by W. of (3).
(5) **Beinn a' Chreachain,** 3540 ft., 1¾ miles E.N.E. of (3).
(6) **Meall Bhuidhe,** 3193 ft., 1 mile W. of (5).
(7) **Beinn Mhanach,** 3125 ft., 1¾ miles S. of (5).
(8) **Beinn a' Chuirn,** 3020 ft., ¾ mile W. of (7).
(9) **Beinn a' Chaisteil,** 2897 ft., 1½ miles E.N.E. of Auch.
Maps: Ordnance Survey One-inch Series, Sheet 47.
Bartholomew's Half-inch Series, Sheet 48.

The arca described in this chapter includes the mountains between the head of Glen Lyon and the headwaters of the River Orchy. The western boundary is formed by the West Highland railway which contours round the foot of the mountains between Auch (three and a half miles north of Tyndrum) and Gorton Siding (MR 394480); the eastern boundary goes south from Gorton to Gleann Meran, along Loch Lyon to its head, up the Abhuinn Ghlas to its source and finally down Gleann Choillean to Auch. Whereas the western side of the mountains in this area are easily accessible and a familiar sight to travellers between Tyndrum and Glencoe, the eastern hillsides above Loch Lyon and Gleann Meran are remote and lonely.

The finest mountains of this group are the four highest which form a more or less continuous, twisting ridge from Beinn Dorain to Beinn a' Chreachain. The western and north-western sides of these peaks drop steeply and without interruption to Loch Tulla and the headwaters of the River Orchy, and this continuous and impressive rampart forms the north-western perimeter of the mountains of Breadalbane and the Southern Highlands. From their summits the climber looks out across the south-west corner of the Moor of Rannoch to the Black Mount and the mountains of Lochaber.

These peaks are themselves well seen by the traveller between Tyndrum and Glencoe. In particular the view of the great cone of Beinn Dorain from the summit of the A82 road just north of Tyndrum is one of the grandest sights in the Southern Highlands, and the upsweep of the mountainside completely dwarfs the railway line which contours round its base. Further north, the three other mountains are well seen from the road where it climbs above the north end of Loch Tulla.

The other mountains of the group are almost hidden behind their big western neighbours. However, from a point on the road near Auch Farm, Beinn a' Chaisteal looks impressive with its steep, rocky buttresses rising above the viaducts of the West Highland railway, and the twin rounded tops of Beinn Mhanach and Beinn a' Chuirn fill the head of the Auch Gleann.

Access to the mountains of this group is easy from three points on the A82 road. Auch is a good starting point for the southern and eastern peaks, and there is a good track up the Auch Gleann. Bridge of Orchy is the best starting point for the western peaks, and Achallader Farm (three miles N.N.E. of Bridge of Orchy) is the third point of access, suitable for the northern end of the group. All the mountains may also be approached from the head of Glen Lyon, but this route involves a long and tiresome walk along the shore of Loch Lyon from Lubreoch, and only the most energetic of hill-walkers are likely to favour this approach. However, this route has its rewards to offer the searcher of solitude, for there are few lonelier places in the Southern Highlands than Gleann Meran and the head of Loch Lyon.

There is a right-of-way from Glen Lyon to Auch which was once the funeral route for the MacGregors of Glen Lyon to their clan burial ground at Glenorchy Church near Dalmally. The motor road in Glen Lyon now ends at the Loch Lyon dam, and from there it is probably best to walk along the north side of the loch which involves a diversion up Gleann Meran to get round an arm of the loch which now extends for a mile up this glen. This part of the way is trackless as the old right-of-way has been flooded. From the west end of Loch Lyon the route strikes westwards up the Allt Tarabhan along the line of an aqueduct which carries the waters of Coire a' Ghabhalach to Loch Lyon. Once over the pass half a mile west of the loch, the route follows a path along the Allt a' Chuirn to the roofless

65. Beinn Chaluim from Glen Lochay.

66. Ben Lawers from Meall Greigh.

67. Glen Lyon and Meall Ghaordie.

68. On Beinn Ghlas, looking north.

69. Beinn nan Eachan from Meall Garbh, Tarmachans.

70. The summit of Meall Garbh, Tarmachans.

cottage at Ais-an t-Sithein and so to Auch along a good track. The distance from the Loch Lyon dam to Auch is twelve miles, and the only shelter is a bothy half way along Loch Lyon.

Beinn Dorain, 3524 ft., is not quite the highest mountain of the group, but the impressive upsweep of its sides above Bridge of Orchy and Auch and its sharp conical summit make it the best known landmark in this area. The shape of the mountain is starkly simple; from the summit it drops steeply for almost three thousand feet to the west, south and east, while to the north a broad, boggy hillside drops gradually towards the Coire a' Ghabhalach.

The usual approach to the summit is from Bridge of Orchy. After crossing the railway line at the station, one can follow a fair path up the south side of the Allt Coire an Dothaidh. The head of the corrie is rather rough, and the route keeps on the south side of the stream to reach the col at the head of Coire an Dothaidh. Turning south, the route continues up the very broad north ridge of Beinn Dorain. There is a faint track in places, and eventually a large, well-built cairn is reached. Beyond this point a short drop and re-ascent leads to the summit where the cairn is rather smaller. In clear weather it is worth descending a short distance south of the top to get the very impressive view downwards of the railway line curving round the foot of Beinn Odhar and over the Gleann Choillean viaduct; this view puts the work of man into its proper perspective.

From Auch the direct ascent of Beinn Dorain is shorter, but it is an unrelentingly steep climb. It is probably more rewarding to walk up the Auch Gleann for a mile and then climb up the Coire Chruitein which is wild and rugged at its head. The southern and western slopes of the mountain may not be ideal as routes of ascent because of their continuous steepness and lack of variety; however, in the right snow conditions there are excellent glissades to be had down the long, shallow gullies which furrow the hillside. The direct descent from the summit due south to Auch should only be undertaken with caution as there are two rather steep gullies and some rock bands on this route.

The only recorded rock-climbing on Beinn Dorain is on the buttress at the head of Coire an Dothaidh. This cliff faces north-west and is clearly seen from Bridge of Orchy. Its left side is defined by a steep, narrow gully which is usually wet. From the foot of this gully a broad grass ledge leads rightwards below the buttress, and about twenty or thirty yards along this ledge (just beyond the point where it rounds the nose of the buttress) the steep rocks above the ledge relent somewhat. This is the starting point of a route which takes the line of least resistance upwards on good rock, with some grassy pitches and traverses first to the left and then to the right (300 ft., V.D., D. D. Stewart). Another climb of similar standard has been done a few yards right of this route. The most impressive looking line on the buttress is further right again, and consists of three sections, each one a hundred feet or more high, separated by grass ledges. The highest of these three sections appears from below to be a very steep wall of clean, grey rock.

Just above the Dorain–Dothaidh col on the Beinn Dorain side there is a line of rocks which is almost a hundred feet high in places. The rock is rather steep and holdless, but there may be a possibility of some short climbs. There are also some cliffs on the east side of Beinn Dorain overlooking the Auch Gleann, but this side of the mountain is seldom visited and there are no records of any climbs.

The top of **Beinn an Dothaidh**, 3283 ft. (pronounced Ben Doe) is a rather flat plateau with three bumps. The West Top, 3267 ft., is marked on the One-inch Map, and a quarter of a mile east of it is the highest point, 3283 ft., which is indicated on the Half-inch Map. A quarter of a mile south-east of the summit is a third and lower top, and beyond it a broad ridge drops south-east and then east to the Dothaidh–Achaladair col. The west and north-west sides of the mountain drop in long concave slopes towards Loch Tulla, but the finest feature is the north-east face which is steep and forms quite an impressive corrie, especially when snow-clad in winter.

The ascent of Beinn an Dothaidh can be easily made from Bridge of Orchy by the Coire an Dothaidh. The route up the corrie is the same as that just described for Beinn Dorain, and the two mountains can be conveniently climbed together. From the col at the head of the corrie an easy climb northwards leads to the summit plateau of Beinn an Dothaidh. An alternative route starts at Achallader Farm. A track leads southwards from the farm and crosses the railway by a footbridge; thereafter it becomes indistinct, but the route is perfectly straightforward and continues due south over steepening moorland to reach the north-west end of Beinn an Dothaidh's summit plateau at a point where it overlooks a fine little corrie. Finally, an easy walk up the gently sloping plateau leads to the West Top.

The route from the summit of Beinn an Dothaidh to the Dothaidh–Achaladair col passes over the lower south-east top and continues in that direction for a short distance before turning east to the broad, grassy col.

The north-east corrie is well suited for winter climbing as it holds snow well, and there are several gully climbs, mostly of easy standard. The main feature of the corrie is *Central Gully*, the wide gully in the middle of the corrie which is sometimes heavily corniced at its exit on the col between the summit and the West Top. East of this gully there is another wide and ill-defined gully, *East Gully*, which debouches on the plateau close to the summit. Central and East gullies are both of Grade I standard, the only possible difficulties being at their cornices. East Gully is bounded on its east by a well-defined ridge which drops from the summit to the floor of the corrie and gives a pleasant route of ascent. South-east of this ridge the face of the mountain is less steep, and an easy-angled slope running up to the col between the summit and the south-east top gives an easy line of ascent or descent.

The north-west end of the corrie is much more impressive although it is not seen from below until the climber is well up Coire Achaladair. The narrow *West Gully* is the most prominent feature; it is separated from Central Gully by a broad and rather broken buttress, and gives the best of the easy gully climbs in the corrie (Grade I, W. Ramsay and party). On the left wall of West Gully, starting at about one third of its height, there is a steep, twisting gully. This is the line of the winter route *Taxus* (600 ft., Grade III, A. W. Ewing and A. J. Trees), which starts with three or four steep pitches of ice or snow. At a bifurcation the left branch is taken to reach a snow ridge which is followed until a left traverse leads to a narrow gully which is climbed to its finish near the West Top.

On its north-west side West Gully is bounded by a very steep north-facing cliff which might aptly be named the North-West Buttress. Two short but very steep gullies split this buttress; the left-hand one is wide and has an overhanging section near its foot, the right-hand one is much narrower, more in the nature of a chimney. These gullies cannot, judging by their appearance, be recommended as summer routes, but may well give very hard winter climbs when in condition. The main buttress between them is very steep and vegetatious, but at least one route has been made on it, starting a few yards down from the narrow right-hand gully where a large boulder leans against the wall. After a difficult overhanging start, the route becomes rather indeterminate and follows the line of least resistance;

the rock is lichenous and there is a good deal of grass (300 ft., V.D., J. Crosby and T. Allan). This route is probably close to *Ghyll Buttress* (370 ft., V.D., R. Peel) reported in the last edition of this guide book.

There is a fair sized crag on the Beinn an Dothaidh side of Coire an Dothaidh, but it is vegetatious and often wet, and no climbs have been recorded on it. Two gullies to the north-west of this crag might give good winter climbs and are more or less on the direct route between Bridge of Orchy and the summit.

The crest of **Beinn Achaladair,** 3404 ft., is a mile-long curving ridge from which the north-west side drops in continuous, and in places rocky slopes towards Achallader Farm. The south-east side of the summit ridge encloses Coire nan-Clach, whose gentle slopes drop towards the bealach separating Beinn Achaladair from Beinn Mhanach and Beinn a' Chuirn. The mountain has two tops, of which the summit is at the north end of the ridge and the lower top, 3288 ft., is at the south end. The summit cairn stands at the edge of the north-east face, and another cairn about a hundred yards south-west of it is only imperceptibly lower. The north-east face forms the headwall of a fine corrie which is split by several gullies, and the western edge of this corrie is bounded by a narrow, rocky ridge which drops northwards from the summit directly towards Crannach Wood.

From Achallader Farm there are two or three routes to the mountain. The direct ascent of the north-west face is a long, steep grind, devoid of interest. This side of Beinn Achaladair has been the scene of at least two serious accidents in winter, and should be treated with caution at that time of year. Probably the finest approach (though not by any means the shortest or most direct) is to walk up the Water of Tulla for almost two miles to Crannach Wood, a beautiful remnant of the Old Caledonian Forest which is well worth a visit. From Crannach there is a choice of routes, either directly up the north ridge to the summit, or up the Allt na Crannaich to the col between Beinn Achaladair and Meall Bhuidhe and finally up the short east ridge of Achaladair.

The traverse of the mountain can be continued over the south top to the Achaladair–Dothaidh col and then down Coire Achaladair. (The direct descent from the south top into the corrie requires care, particularly in winter, as the slope is steep and there are several rock bands.)

The most interesting feature of Beinn Achaladair from the

climbers' point of view is the beautiful north-east corrie which lies at the head of the Allt na Crannaich. No routes have been recorded in summer, and it is doubtful if there is any rock-climbing of interest. In winter, however, there are several gullies that give snow climbs of a generally easy standard. Immediately below the summit there is a narrow little gully which looks impressive from below but turns out to be quite straightforward. A hundred yards south-east of the summit there are two parallel, broad gullies at an easy angle; the only possible difficulties might be their cornices. To the left of these gullies there is a stretch of steep, vegetatious rocks, and a not very well-defined gully near the left end of these rocks has been climbed by H. C. Boyd, W. Brown and A. E. Robertson. The climb is steep, with a few short pitches of rock or ice. The snow slope leading to the Beinn Achaladair –Meall Bhuidhe col is quite easy, and the climbing interest of the corrie is completed by a narrow gully well to the left of this col. Although there is no record of an ascent, it is probable that this gully has been climbed; its main difficulty may well be at the cornice.

From the col just mentioned, whose height is about 2700 ft., a broad, grassy ridge rises to **Meall Bhuidhe**, 3193 ft., which is itself an almost level ridge of smooth, springy moss, half a mile long. Two small cairns at the south-west end mark the highest point, and there is another cairn at the north-east end just before the ridge drops to the next col.

Beinn a' Chreachain, 3540 ft., is the highest mountain of this group. From the south and south-west it appears as rather a rounded mountain, but from the north-west it shows a more pointed summit above the crags of Coire an Lochain. Possibly the best view of the mountain is had from the east, and it can be particularly fine when the remote little north-east corrie is filled with snow.

The usual route to Beinn a' Chreachain starts at Achallader Farm and follows the Water of Tulla to Crannach Wood; one continues through the wood among ancient pines and emerges onto the hillside above with its scattered birches. Soon the Allt Coire an Lochain is joined and followed to the beautiful Lochan a' Chreachain. From the lochan one can climb one of the two scree (or snow) gullies which lead from the water's edge to the 3050 ft. col between Meall Bhuidhe and Beinn a' Chreachain, and from there a broad, easy slope leads to the summit. Alternatively, by bearing well to the east from the lochan, one reaches the north-east ridge of Beinn a' Chreachain near Point 3145 ft.; this ridge is particularly beautiful in winter as it is quite narrow and may form a lovely wind-blown edge of snow, but the ascent is perfectly easy.

The rocks on the north-west face of Beinn a' Chreachain overlooking the lochan are quite steep, but very broken, and there are no well-defined climbs; however, winter ascents of this face have been recorded, and there may be good climbing in the right conditions.

It is apparently no longer possible (as it once was) to arrange for the Fort William train to stop at Gorton, and the ascent of Beinn a' Chreachain from there by its north-east ridge is now out of fashion. The only other possible route of ascent is from the Loch Lyon dam, following the north side of the enlarged loch to Gleann Meran and then climbing the south-east side of the mountain, possibly by the Coire Dubh in which a little lochan lies at a height of 3000 ft.

Standing as it does at the edge of the Southern Highlands, overlooking the Moor of Rannoch, Beinn a' Chreachain commands a very fine view northwards and north-westwards to the mountains of Glencoe and Lochaber. The Cairngorms, too, are visible to the north-east.

Beinn Mhanach, 3125 ft., and **Beinn a' Chuirn,** 3020 ft., lie between the main mountain chain just described and the head of Loch Lyon. They are among the more remote hills of the Southern Highlands, hidden from most viewpoints by their higher neighbours. The best impression of these hills is gained from a point on the A82 road about three miles north of Tyndrum. From there the two rounded hills are well seen at the head of the Auch Gleann framed between the steep sides of Beinn Dorain and Beinn a' Chaisteil; the left-hand summit is Beinn a' Chuirn and the right-hand one is Beinn Mhanach. The latter hill is also seen prominently from the Loch Lyon dam as one looks westwards up the loch.

The two summits are connected by a broad, stony ridge which drops at its lowest point to about 2800 ft. On their north-west side a col at about 2050 ft. connects these hills to Beinn Achaladair, and on all other sides grassy slopes, in some places quite steep, fall towards Gleann Cailliche, Loch Lyon and the head of the Auch Gleann. These hills have no outstanding features, and this, combined with their remoteness, accounts for their being seldom climbed.

The easiest approach to these two hills is up the Auch Gleann, starting from Auch Farm. The track alongside the Allt Chonoghlais is good as far as the ruined cottage at Ais-an t-Sithein, where once the celebrated Gaelic poet Duncan Ban MacIntyre lived as shepherd and keeper on the slopes of Beinn Dorain. Beyond the cottage one can climb directly up the steep, grassy south-west shoulder of Beinn a' Chuirn, crossing the line of an aqueduct feeding Loch Lyon at about 1250 ft.; the summit is flat and marked by a very small cairn. An easy walk of a mile leads to Beinn Mhanach and a rather larger cairn.

From Achallader Farm a longer approach to these hills can be made by Coire Achaladair, there being an indistinct path for most of the way up the east side of the stream to the Dothaidh–Achaladair col. From there a traverse north-eastwards across the steep flank of Beinn Achaladair leads to the 2050ft. col already mentioned, from which Beinn a' Chuirn and Beinn Mhanach are easily reached. If this approach is used, it is a simple matter to combine the ascent of these two hills with Beinn Achaladair.

The Glen Lyon approach to these hills is even longer. Starting at the Loch Lyon dam, the north shore of the loch is followed to the head of the inlet that reaches almost a mile up Gleann Meran; from there Beinn Mhanach can be climbed by its north-east shoulder.

From Beinn a' Chuirn there is a fine glimpse through the Dorain–Dothaidh col to the twin pointed peaks of Ben Cruachan, and looking down the Auch Gleann one sees Ben Oss and Ben Lui to good advantage. From Beinn Mhanach there is a good view down Glen Lyon to the distant spurs of Meall Ghaordie, while nearer at hand Beinn Heasgarnich and Creag Mhor show their full size on the opposite side of Loch Lyon.

Beinn a' Chaisteil, 2897 ft., and Beinn nam Fuaran, 2632 ft., are seldom climbed, although the former hill certainly looks impressive from the A82 road near Auch. The sides of this hill overlooking Gleann Choillean and the Auch Gleann are very steep and rocky; however, on closer acquaintance the rock is found to be very vegetatious and there is little or no good climbing.

The big gully above the Auch Gleann viaduct was climbed in summer conditions in 1899 by E. M. Corner and J. O. Cuthbertson, but it gave a rather unsatisfactory climb with only one point of difficulty where it was necessary to escape rightwards from the gully for a hundred feet. This gully might well give a much better climb in good winter conditions. Further up the Auch Gleann there is a fairly continuous line of cliffs for half a mile or so, but they are so indeterminate that no distinct routes have been recorded. The crag called Creagan Liatha overlooking Gleann Choillean is also very broken.

The direct ascent of Beinn a' Chaisteil from Auch by its western buttress is mainly very steep grass with a few short rock pitches. Easier routes can be made either up the little corrie immediately south-east of this buttress, or by walking up the Auch Gleann until the crags on one's right fall back enough to allow a steep scramble up to the broad ridge between Beinn a' Chaisteil and Beinn nam Fuaran. The 2897 ft. point has a small cairn, but the true summit is about a hundred yards away to the south-east and has no cairn.

Transport and Accommodation
The Glasgow to Fort William bus service passes along the A82 road round the western perimeter of these hills, and the West Highland railway takes a parallel route with stations at Tyndrum and Bridge of Orchy.

An infrequent bus service from Aberfeldy up Glen Lyon to Lubreoch at the Loch Lyon dam is operated by M. R. Stewart, Aberfeldy.

There are hotels at Bridge of Orchy (the best centre for these hills), Tyndrum and Inveroran (Loch Tulla). It may also be possible to get lodging at Achallader Farm. The nearest Youth Hostel is at Crianlarich.

BIBLIOGRAPHY

Beinn an Dothaidh and Beinn Doireann, G. Thomson, *S.M.C.J.*, Vol. 3, p. 76.
A Long Day on the Hills in March, J. Coats *S.M.C.J.*, Vol. 3, p. 127.
The Corries around Achalladair, H. C. Boyd, *S.M.C.J.*, Vol. 4, p. 92.
Beinn a' Chaisteil, (Note), J. Maclay, *S.M.C.J.*, Vol. 5, p. 263.
Ben a' Chaisteil etc., (Notes), E. M. Corner, *S.M.C.J.*, Vol. 5, p. 315.
Guide Book Article, *S.M.C.J.*, Vol. 7, p. 29.
Some Hill Walks from Tyndrum, J. H. Bell, *S.M.C.J.*, Vol. 9, p. 1.
The Achallader Accident, G. Sang, *S.M.C.J.*, Vol. 17, p. 179.

71. Beinn Dorain.

72. Looking up the Auch Gleann to Beinn a' Chuirn and Beinn Mhanach.

73. Looking down the Auch Gleann from Beinn a' Chuirn.

74. The Crianlarich Hills from Beinn an Dothaidh.

75. Beinn Achaladair from Crannach Wood.

76. An Stuc and Ben Lawers from Glen Lyon.

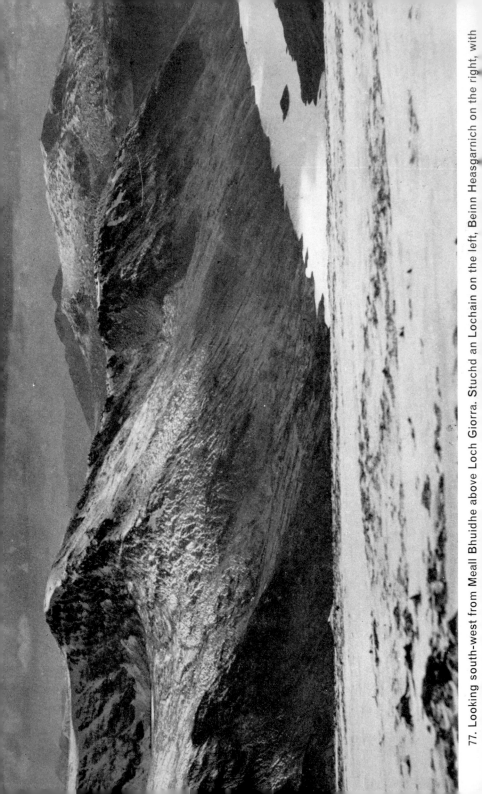

77. Looking south-west from Meall Bhuidhe above Loch Giorra. Stuchd an Lochain on the left, Beinn Heasgarnich on the right, with

79. Dumbarton Rock. The north face climbs are at the left with Monsoon Gully prominent. The overhanging west face is in sunlight with the boulders at its foot.

16

Glen Lyon to Loch Rannoch

The 3000 ft. summits in this area are:
 (1) **Schichallion,** 3547 ft., 4 miles S.E. by E. of Kinloch Rannoch.
 (2) **Carn Mairg,** 3419 ft., 4 miles N.W. by W. of Fortingall.
 (3) **Meall Liath,** 3261 ft., ½ mile E. by S. of (2).
 (4) **Meall a' Bharr,** 3315 ft., approx ¾ mile W.N.W. of (2).
 (5) **Creag Mhor,** 3200 ft., 3¼ miles W.N.W. of Fortingall.
 (6) **Meall Garbh,** 3200 ft., 2¼ miles W. of (2).
 (7) **Meall Luaidhe,** 3035 ft., ¾ mile S.E. by E. of (6).
 (8) **An Sgor,** 3002 ft., ⅝ mile S.W. of (6).
 (9) **Carn Gorm,** 3370 ft., 3¼ miles W.S.W. of (2).
 (10) **Stuchd an Lochain,** 3144 ft., 1¾ miles N.N.W. of Cashlie in Glen Lyon.
 (11) **Sron Chona Choirein,** 3031 ft., ¾ mile E. by S. of (10).
 (12) **Meall Bhuidhe,** 3054 ft., 2¼ miles N.W. by N. of the east end of Loch Giorra.
 (13) **Meall Bhuidhe** (S.E. top), 3004 ft., ⅝ mile S. by E. of (12).
Maps: Ordnance Survey One-inch Series, Sheets 47 and 48.
Bartholomew's Half-inch Series, Sheet 48.

The extensive area covered by this chapter forms the north-eastern corner of the Southern Highlands. It is bounded on the south by Glen Lyon, on the east by the road from Coshieville to Tummel Bridge (B846), on the north by the River Tummel and Loch Rannoch, and on the west by the eastern edge of the Moor of Rannoch and the low pass between Gorton Siding (on the West Highland railway) and Gleann Meran.

The principal mountains of this area are Schichallion in the northeast corner, the Carn Mairg group a few miles south-west of Schichallion, and Stuchd an Lochain some twelve miles west-south-west of Carn Mairg. With the exception of Schichallion, whose conical peak is one of the best known features of the Highlands, the other mountains just mentioned, and many other lower ones in this area are rather flat-topped and lacking in distinctive features. Only on Stuchd an Lochain is there a corrie of any size or steepness. These mountains and their surrounding moors are extensively used for deer stalking

185

and grouse shooting, and should be avoided by climbers in the stalking and shooting season.

The hills at the western end of this area above the head of Loch Giorra are just about the most remote and least visited of all the hills in the Southern Highlands, and the head of Loch Giorra is a most desolate place.

In general the southern sides of the mountains overlooking Glen Lyon are quite steep; however, on the north the hillsides above Loch Rannoch are more in the nature of heather covered moorland with some extensive areas of forest. If the mountains, Schichallion excepted, lack outstanding character or features, the same certainly cannot be said of Loch Rannoch on their north or Glen Lyon on their south. Loch Rannoch is one of Scotland's best known inland lochs, and it enjoys a fairly open situation with a beautifully wooded shoreline. The birch trees in autumn are particularly lovely, and the pine forest on the south shore of the loch, known as the Black Wood of Rannoch, is one of the remnants of the Old Caledonian Forest.

Glen Lyon is without question the grandest glen in the Southern Highlands, and ranks with Glen Affric (with which it has many features in common) as one of the finest of all Scotland's glens. It is about thirty miles long from its headwaters to the confluence of the Rivers Lyon and Tay, and in this distance there is almost every type of Highland scenery from the high mountains around Loch Lyon to the woodland and farms of the lower reaches.

The village of Fortingall near the foot of the glen has many features of interest, including several thatched houses and the oldest tree in Europe, a yew tree which is thought to be over three thousand years old growing in the churchyard. The standing stone Carn na Marbh on the south side of the village marks the spot where victims of the Black Plague were buried in the fourteenth century. Fortingall is also said to have been the birthplace of Pontius Pilate.

Half a mile west of the village the road enters the narrow Pass of Lyon where the outlying spurs of Ben Lawers and Carn Mairg close in and the River Lyon rushes through a narrow, twisting defile. The gorge is magnificently wooded, the beech trees being particularly fine, and five great larch trees stand at the point in the gorge where, in the sixteenth century, Gregor MacGregor leapt across the river to escape from pursuing Campbells and their bloodhounds. The place is still known as MacGregor's Leap, but the only person who has tried to repeat the feat died in the attempt.

Above the Pass of Lyon the glen opens out, and for about nine miles the river flows more gently between farms, fields and woodland. Between Invervar and Bridge of Balgie there is a minor road on the south side of the river; it is not suitable for cars, but makes a very delightful walk. At Bridge of Balgie, where the road from Loch Tay crosses the river, the character of the glen begins to change again. Meggernie Castle (once the stronghold of the Campbells of Glenlyon) stands in the centre of the glen flanked by avenues of lime and beech trees, and the public road climbs high on the hillside as it approaches the wild upper reaches of Glen Lyon. There is a beautiful pine wood where the Allt Conait tumbles down from Loch Giorra, and beyond this point the glen becomes more bare, with few trees.

A mile below Cashlie there is a new hydro-electric power station and reservoir, and just beyond Cashlie are the remains of the forts of Glen Lyon. There were four of these forts, but all that now remain are some not very obvious piles of stones which were once the circular walls. The most obvious remains (on the north side of the road) are of the fort called Caisteal an Duibhe, the Castle of the Black Hero. Tradition associates these forts with Fionn, the legendary Scottish king of the Iron Age, whose stronghold was in Glen Lyon. There is an old Gaelic saying:

'Twelve castles had Fionn
In the crooked glen of the stones.'

The crooked glen of the stones can only be Glen Lyon.

At Pubil the road passes a group of grey cottages (hardly a village) and it ends below the huge concrete face of the Loch Lyon dam. The new and greatly enlarged Loch Lyon is six miles long, with a side arm up Gleann Meran, and it completely fills the head of Glen Lyon. The old right-of-way to Auch and the River Orchy (along which the MacGregors carried their dead to the clan's burial ground at Glenorchy Church) is completely flooded, and the walker heading westwards must find a way along the steep hillside above the loch by sheep-tracks. The western end of the loch is a lonely and desolate spot, surrounded by hills and seemingly remote from civilization.

A side road leaves the main Glen Lyon road just east of the Allt Conait and climbs to the dam at the eastern end of Loch Giorra. This is now also a hydro-electric reservoir whose waters include the former Lochs Giorra and Daimh. The old farm and house at Lochs have been submerged and the new Loch Giorra (which is not correctly shown on the One-inch Map) is just over three miles long.

Access to the hills described in this chapter is gained by the Glen Lyon road just described, the road along the south side of Loch Rannoch, and the road from Coshieville which passes round the north-east shoulder of Schichallion to Kinloch Rannoch. There are a number of private roads on the south side of Loch Rannoch which lead into the hills, but permission should be sought before driving along them.

Schichallion, 3547 ft., (alternatively Schiehallion) is the outstanding mountain of this area, and it is one of the best known of all Scottish peaks. It is quite isolated, with deep glens on all sides, and it has a simplicity of shape which is quite striking, consisting as it does of a single hump-backed ridge running from east to west with steeply falling slopes to north and south. The finest view of Schichallion is seen from the north side of Loch Rannoch from where the mountain has a perfect conical appearance. It also shows up well from the Queen's View near the east end of Loch Tummel, although the symmetry of the mountain is lost from this viewpoint. Another striking view of the mountain is had from the Buachaille Etive Mor over thirty miles away to the west; from there the isolated peak of Schichallion is easily recognised beyond the vast expanse of the Moor of Rannoch.

The evenly weathered quartzite of which Schichallion is composed has given the mountain its regularity of outline, and it was this regularity that led Maskeleyne, then Astronomer-Royal, to carry out his pendulum experiment on the mountain to determine the earth's mass. The upper part of the mountain is largely composed of quartzite boulders and small outcrops. Lower down the slopes are heathery and where these two regions meet there are some areas of mixed heather and boulders, a most unpleasant combination.

Schichallion is easily climbed from three or four possible starting points on the road which goes from Coshieville to White Bridge (B846), and then by Braes of Foss to Kinloch Rannoch. Glengoulandie Farm is the starting point of a good path up Gleann Mor. This path can be followed for a mile and a quarter and then one bears north over heather to reach the foot of Schichallion's east ridge (marked Aonach Ban on the One-inch and Half-inch Maps). Once on the ridge, which is broad and heathery, one follows a path which becomes well-defined and leads without any difficulty to the summit. For the last half mile the way over quartz scree and boulders is marked by cairns at regular intervals.

The path marked on the Half-inch Map starting at White Bridge and leading westwards is not recommended as the hillside west of the road has recently been planted by the Forestry Commission. A good and easy route starts a short distance east of Braes of Foss Farm and follows a well-defined path southwards and then south-westwards to join the route just described above the Aonach Ban. The ascent by this route should not take much more than two hours. An even shorter ascent starts from the road a mile and a half west of Braes of Foss and climbs beside a dry stone wall to reach the east ridge half a mile east of the summit. This route is a good deal steeper and rougher than the ones just described.

From the north-west the standard route up Schichallion starts at Tempar, two miles east-south-east of Kinloch Rannoch. There is a rough road up the Tempar Burn, and above this a well-marked path leads to the summit. The north-west slopes of Schichallion have recently been planted by the Forestry Commission and a forest road starting near Lassintullich climbs up to almost 1500 ft. on this side; however, it is probably no better than the Tempar Burn route as an approach to the mountain.

As already hinted, the northern and southern slopes of the mountain are best avoided as they are steep, and in places are composed of a mixture of heather and boulders which is just about the most unpleasant type of terrain to be found in the Scottish hills.

The view from the summit of Schichallion is extensive in most directions: westwards across Loch Rannoch to the mountains of Glencoe and Lochaber, north to the wooded strath of Rannoch and Tummel and south-east to the lowland hills. Only to the south-west, where the bulk of Carn Mairg looms close, is the view restricted.

There is a pleasant walk round the south side of Schichallion from Kinloch Rannoch to Coshieville (11 miles). The Tempar Burn road is followed to its end where there is a small bothy. From there an easy descent along a narrow path leads round the flank of Schichallion to Gleann Mor and down to Glengoulandie. Alternatively, one can make for Fortingall (the same distance). From the bothy near the Tempar Burn–Gleann Mor watershed descend south-east to the confluence of the two streams at the head of Gleann Mor (MR 708533). The cave called Uamh Tom a' Mhor-fhir near this point is rather difficult to find as its entrance is an inconspicuous hole in the ground about a hundred and fifty yards north-west of the junction of the two streams. The route to Fortingall now goes up to the lonely

Glenmore Bothy half a mile south-east of the cave, and from there a good track continues in a south-easterly and then southerly direction to cross the ridge and descend to Gleann Muilinn. In due course the track (which continues eastwards) is left and one descends to the Allt Odhar and so to Fortingall. On the west side of the Allt Odhar there is a good path leading to a bothy high up in Gleann Muilinn.

The **Carn Mairg** range, of which Carn Mairg, 3419 ft., itself is the highest point, is a continuous broad ridge, in places almost a plateau, which extends for about six miles from east to west on the north side of Glen Lyon. The ridge is not straight, but rather forms a semi-circle so that most of the burns flowing southwards converge above Invervar which is the focal point of the range.

Although they might be compared with the Cairngorms because of their extensive flat summits, the Carn Mairg group lack the height or grandeur of the Cairngorms and their magnificent corries. Only the southern slopes of Creag Mhor, rising steeply above Chesthill and the wooded Pass of Lyon, give much impression of grandeur. Elsewhere, and particularly on the north, these hills appear rather unimposing and the summit ridges are featureless. Nevertheless the complete traverse of these hills is a good hill-walking expedition, and in suitable conditions in winter or spring the traverse on skis is one of the best expeditions of its kind in the Southern Highlands. Because of the broad ridges and generally gentle gradients, this ski-traverse does not call for a high standard of skiing, and for this reason it can be recommended for skiers of moderate ability and good stamina.

The most convenient way to describe these hills is from the point of view of a walker (or skier) making the traverse of all the tops. The most convenient starting and finishing point is Invervar in Glen Lyon, and the traverse will be taken from east to west. A zig zag path climbs the steep hillside north-east of Invervar and leads to a good bothy at about 1800 ft. beside the Allt Coir' Chearcaill. This stream and its southern tributary are followed towards the Carn Mairg–Creag Mhor col, and **Creag Mhor** is reached over easy ground. (The route just described is probably the best one for the skier. The walker may prefer to climb directly up the west ridge of Creag Mhor after climbing just over a thousand feet above Invervar.) Creag Mhor is marked on the One-inch Map by the 3100 ft. contour, but it is rather higher than this and has two tops a quarter of a mile apart, both just over 3200 ft.

To continue the traverse one descends a third of a mile north-west to the broad col leading to Carn Mairg. A short diversion to the north-east is necessary to include the small, rounded top of **Meall Liath,** 3261 ft., and from there it is less than half a mile to Carn Mairg. There is a big cairn on the flat, stony summit, and a few yards south-west of the cairn there is a sudden drop towards Coir' Chearcaill.

Continuing the traverse westwards, a broken fence runs along the broad ridge of **Meall a' Bharr,** 3315 ft. The highest point is at the east end of this very flat and featureless ridge, and at the western end the ridge drops north-west to a broad col at about 2800 ft. From this col the ridge turns south-west to **Meall Garbh,** 3200 ft., and a short diversion south-eastwards has to be made to include **Meall Luaidhe,** 3035 ft. (This top is not named on the One-inch Map, but it is at MR 656510.) The flat summit of Meall Garbh has three more or less distinct tops in addition to Meall Luaidhe; of these the highest is about 70 yards south of the fence and is marked by a fair sized cairn.

The main ridge continues west from Meall Garbh, and then drops south-west at the point where the fence turns north-west. The next col is well-defined and beyond it the ridge rises to **An Sgor,** 3002 ft., which has the sharpest summit of all the Carn Mairg group. The peak looks very steep and prominent from the Invervar Burn, but it is easy-angled on the north-west side. From An Sgor the ridge drops slightly and continues to the last summit, **Carn Gorm,** 3370 ft., which is probably the shapeliest of the Carn Mairg group. The north-west ridge runs out to a shoulder just over 3000 ft., but the intervening drop is not sufficient to justify its being classified as a top in Munro's Tables. The descent from Carn Gorm follows the broad south-east ridge until it flattens out and one can descend by the east-flowing stream to the Invervar Burn. Alternatively, the spur Meall Garbh just south of this stream may be followed. Either way one has to descend finally through recently planted trees, but there is at least one break which provides a route down to Invervar.

Needless to say, the tops of the Carn Mairg group can be climbed singly from Invervar by any of the streams or broad ridges that descend from the main ridge, and there are several stalkers' paths that make access easier.

An alternative and longer approach to the eastern summits, Creag Mhor and Carn Mairg, can be made from Fortingall. As already mentioned, a good path on the west side of the Allt Odhar leads to a bothy in Gleann Muilinn, and beyond it the stream can be followed to the col between Carn Mairg and Creag Mhor.

From the north there is an easy approach to Carn Gorm by the Carie Burn, starting at Carie three miles west of Kinloch Rannoch. A driveable road leads almost three miles up Coire Carie, ending at about 1700 ft. If permission is given to drive up this road, one can in winter or spring make a pleasant ski-ascent of Carn Gorm. The upper slopes of Coire Carie give excellent skiing.

West of Carn Gorm there is a large expanse of rather featureless hill country. Nothing exceeds three thousand feet and this may account for the lack of interest shown by hill-walkers. There is a right-of-way through these hills from Innerwick in Glen Lyon to Loch Rannoch which follows the old burial route of the MacGregors from Rannoch to Glen Orchy. Starting at Innerwick, a good track leads up the east side of the Allt Chalbhath and crosses the Lairig Chalbhath. On the north side of the pass the path divides, one way going through the forest to Dall and the other along the Allt na Bogair to Carie (7 miles).

The remaining three thousand foot mountains in the area described in this chapter are several miles up Glen Lyon from Innerwick, and are situated on the north and south sides of Loch Giorra. The road end at the Loch Giorra dam is probably the best starting point for these mountains.

Stuchd an Lochain, 3144 ft., occupies a commanding position between Loch Giorra and Glen Lyon, and its bulk fills the view as one looks up the glen from Bridge of Balgie. The summit is at the west end of a broad, crescent-shaped ridge which encloses the north facing Coire nan Cat. This corrie is the finest feature of the mountain, with the little Lochan nan Cat nestling seven hundred feet below the summit; but although the headwall of the corrie is steep, it is grassy and rather indeterminate and there are no recorded climbs of any interest.

The first recorded ascent of Stuchd an Lochain appears to have been made around 1590 by Colin Campbell, he who built the original tower of Meggernie Castle. It is recorded that 'On the brow of the hill, Stuic-an-Lochain – a huge rock beetling over a deep circular mountain tarn – they encountered a flock of goats'. It is one of the first accounts of the ascent of any Scottish mountain.

The ascent of Stuchd an Lochain may easily be made from the Loch Giorra dam. A steepish climb southwards leads to the east ridge of Creag an Fheadain, and this ridge is followed along a broken fence to the cairn which is about a hundred yards east of the highest point, 2909 ft. There the ridge turns south-west and is followed across a slight dip to **Sron Chona Choirein**, 3031 ft., (marked on the One-inch Map as a 3000 ft. contour line at MR 494445). The ridge then turns west over another very slight bump (marked as 2971 ft. on the Half-inch Map and by the 3000 ft. contour line on the One-inch Map), and finally rises to the summit of Stuchd an Lochain which is at the very edge of the precipice overlooking Lochan nan Cat and a few yards beyond the highest point of the fence.

On its south side Stuchd an Lochain throws out two spurs, An Grianan and Meall Dubh, which overlook Glen Lyon near Cashlie. There is a path up the east side of the Allt Cashlie between these spurs, and from its end a course north-north-west over easy ground leads to the summit. There is also an easy ascent from Pubil following tracks beside the Allt Camaslaidh to the rather boggy but otherwise easy ground near its source from where a north-easterly course leads to the summit.

The feature of the panorama from Stuchd an Lochain is the view eastwards down the whole length of Glen Lyon with the ridges of Ben Lawers and Carn Mairg almost closing its far end. Looking westwards one has a fine view of the seldom visited east face of Beinn a' Chreachain.

Meall Bhuidhe, 3054 ft., is a rather undistinguished hill two miles north of Loch Giorra. (It is named Garbh Mheall on the Half-inch Map, but on the One-inch Map this name is applied to the 2991 ft. north top of Meall Bhuidhe.) The hill is essentially a north-south ridge about a mile and a half long; the west side of the hill drops in a gentle, featureless slope towards the Moor of Rannoch and the east side drops more steeply into the Glas Choire. The summit is near the north end of the ridge, and the **South-east Top**, 3004 ft., is very flat. From the Loch Giorra dam the ascent to this top is very straightforward; it would probably be a pleasant ski-route in winter. The ridge to Meall Bhuidhe is broad and flat, and beyond the highest point there is a drop of a couple of hundred feet followed by a smaller rise to Garbh Mheall. The north side of this hill is, as the name implies, rather rough with some rock outcrops.

Meall Bhuidhe can also be approached from Loch Rannoch and there are two or three private roads leading into the hills south of Camghouran and Bridge of Gaur. Permission might be obtained to drive from Camghouran to the foot of the Allt Easan Stalcair (MR 510527), and a rough road leads up this burn for a further mile. Thereafter a course south-west leads into the corrie below Meall Bhuidhe and the ridge just north of the summit is easily reached. Alternatively, the road south of Bridge of Gaur can be followed for three and a half miles to the Allt Sloc na Creadha and the ascent made up the north-west side of Meall Bhuidhe.

The Allt Easan Stalcair gives a walking route from Camghouran to Loch Giorra (8 miles). The track on the east side of the burn is followed to steeper ground below the Glas Choire and then a course south-east is taken to reach the flat and featureless pass, the Lairig Meachdainn. On the south side of the pass the easy hillside is descended to the east end of Loch Giorra.

The west end of Loch Giorra is one of the few truly remote corners of the Southern Highlands although it is only three miles across the hills from Pubil. The highest hill in this area is another Meall Bhuidhe, 2976 ft., which is best climbed from Pubil by the broad ridge which terminates in Meall Phubuill. South-east of Meall Bhuidhe is Meall Daill, 2858 ft., whose steep western side drops into Gleann Meran, the western boundary of the area described in this chapter. These two hills are very seldom climbed, especially since the creation of the enlarged Loch Lyon has flooded the road that once reached as far as the foot of Gleann Meran; however, anyone climbing to the top of Meall Daill on a clear day will be rewarded with a grand view of the wild hills around the head of Loch Lyon and the seldom visited corries of Beinn Heasgarnich and Beinn a' Chreachain.

Transport and Accommodation
Bus services: Aberfeldy to Lubreoch (at the Loch Lyon dam) via Coshieville and Fortingall. Operator, M. R. Stewart, Aberfeldy.

Pitlochry to Kinloch Rannoch. Operator, W. Alexander and Sons (Midland). Kinloch Rannoch to Rannoch Station via north side of Loch Rannoch. Operator, J. Duncan, Kinloch Rannoch.

There are hotels at Fortingall, Coshieville and Kinloch Rannoch, and a Youth Hostel at Garth (near Fortingall).

BIBLIOGRAPHY

The Glen Lyon Hills, J. G. Stott, *S.M.C.J.*, Vol. 1, p. 131.
Deep Glen Lyon, J. G. Stott, *S.M.C.J.*, Vol. 2, p. 113.

Schichallion and Carn Mairg (Guide Book Article), S.*M.C.J.*, Vol. 6, p. 245.

From Ballinluig to Lawers over Schichallion, W. Garden, S.*M.C.J.*, Vol. 7, p. 15.

Stuchd an Lochain and the Upper Part of Glen Lyon, F. S. Goggs, S.*M.C.J.*, Vol. 8, p. 235.

The Cashlie Forts, F. S. Goggs, S.*M.C.J.*, Vol. 8, p. 245.

Mheall Garbh, Glen Lyon, E. M. Corner, S.*M.C.J.*, Vol. 11, p. 120.

The Carn Mairg Range, J. Gall Inglis, S.*M.C.J.*, Vol. 16, p. 161.

Highland Perthshire, D. Frazer, (Standard Press, Montrose).

The Whangie

The Whangie is a curious rock formation on the west side of Auchineden Hill in the Kilpatricks. It is reached by a well signposted and much frequented path which starts at the Queen's View on the Glasgow to Drymen road (A809) and contours round the north side of the hill for just over a mile. The rock formation consists of a large flake of rock and a smaller flake called the Gendarme which have been separated from the main hillside, probably by the action of 'glacier plucking' in the Ice Age. The Flake and the Gendarme are narrow slices of rock, almost vertical on both sides and a yard or less wide along their crests. The outside of the Flake is about 50 ft. high. There is a narrow defile between the Flake and the vegetatious rock wall of the main hillside. The rock of the Flake and Gendarme is more or less free of grass, but is very lichenous and slippery when wet; the inside faces take a long time to dry after rain as they get very little sunshine.

Making allowances for the shortness of the climbs (none of which exceeds about 60 ft.) and their tendency to be lichenous and slippery, the Whangie nevertheless offers excellent sport and a very wide range of climbs of all types and standards of difficulty. The outlook on a fine summer evening towards Arran, Cowal, the Luss hills, Loch Lomond and the mountains to the north-west is very fine.

The following list of climbs and grades has been taken from the original Whangie Guide published privately in 1950 by J. M. Cullen of the Creag Dhu Mountaineering Club, assisted by C. Vigano and I. McBain. The original guide has been unavailable for some time, and it is hoped that the present publication of material which appeared in that guide will be a valuable addition to this guide book. The author acknowledges the original work of J. M. Cullen and his helpers.

The original grading system for the Whangie used a numerical system which does not correspond exactly with the current numerical system of the U.I.A.A. To avoid possible confusion between the two systems, the traditional adjectival system has been used, but it should be borne in mind that the Whangie climbs are very short (20 to 60 ft.), and comparison of such climbs with long, exposed climbs is difficult and may be misleading. In addition to giving the grade of each climb, an attempt has been made to assess the quality of the rock which varies from excellent to very loose and unreliable (P, poor; F, fair; G. Good; Ex, excellent).

Inside the Gendarme
The angle of this face is just right for balance climbing on small holds.

	Grade	Rock		Grade	Rock
1. Spider Slab	S.	G.	8. Bird's Nest Route	V.D.	Ex
2. Blaeberry Crack	V.D.	Ex	9. Red Crack Route	V.D.	Ex
3. Mossy Slab (right)	S.	Ex	10. Red Slab Route	V.D.	Ex
4. Mossy Slab (left)	D.	Ex	11. Windswept Wall	S.	G.
5. Staircase Crack	M.	Ex	12. Upturned Flake	S.	Ex
6. The Bulge (right)	M.S.	G	13. Direct Finish	V.S.	F
7. The Bulge (left)	S.	Ex	14. Upturned L	V.D.	F

Outside the Gendarme

15. Angel Corner	V.S.	F	19. Easy Crack	M.	G
16. Heartbreak Corner	V.S.	G	20. Barrowland Bulge	S.	G
17. Hangover Overhang	V.S.	Ex	21. Backsnapper Crack	S.	G
18. Trench Wall	S.	F			

Outside the Flake (No. 1 Face)

22. Cave Route	V.D.	F	31. Horror Route	V.S.	F
23. Cave Chimney	V.D.	F	32. Bluebottle	V.S.+	F
24. Easy Chimney	D.	G	33. Curving Crack	V.S.+	
25. Easy Wall	V.D.	G	34. Sloping Ledge Route	S.	F
26. Easy Groove	M.	Ex.	35. Overhanging Cleft	V.S.	F
27. Vampire Crack	V.S.	G	36. Toenail Traverse	V.S.	F
28. Ivy Crack	V.S.	Ex	37. Rowan Rib	V.S.	F
29. Backstep Chimney	S.	Ex	38. Sunshine Crack	V.S.	F
30. Backbreak Wall	V.S.	G			

Inside the Flake (No. 2 Face)

39. Arrowhead Arête	D.	Ex	51. McBain's Wall	S.	G
40. Jughandle Arête	M.	Ex	52. Varsity Groove	V.D.	Ex
41. Novice Crack	D.	G	53. Mantelshelf Wall	S.	G
42. Novice Overhang	D.	G	54. Gremlin Groove	V.D.	Ex
43. Needle Route	M.	F	55. Whippenwoof Wall	H.S.	G
44. Hutch's Route	H.S.	G	56. Ruth's Route	V.S.	G
45. Long John's Wall	V.S.	Ex	57. Nocibur Wall	S.	G
46. Allison's Route	V.S.	Ex	(Start on Face No. 3 and stride		
47. Young's Route	H.S.	G	across to Face No. 2)		
48. Fallen Tree Groove	H.S.	F	58. Ladybird Layback	V.D.	Ex
49. Fallen Tree Arête	V.D.	G	59. Bebop	M.S.	G
50. Rowan Tree Groove	V.D.	Ex			

No. 3 Face
Nearly all the climbs on this face are vegetatious.

	Grade	Rock		Grade	Rock
60. Heather Wall Scoop	H.S.	F	69. Ginomie Arête	V.D.	G
61. Heather Overhang	V.S.	F	70. Ginomie Variation	S.	G
62. Nonchalant Route	V.S.	F	71. Garden Wall	V.D.	F
63. Manky Crack	M.S.	P	72. Earthquake Arête	S.	F
64. Suicide Wall	V.S.	F	73. Slantin Crack	H.S.	F
65. Grand Traverse	V.S.	Ex	74. Charity Arête	S.	P
66. Jungle Groove	V.D.	P	75. Rotten Rock Route	S.	P
67. Weed Groove	H.S.	P	76. Cancer Wall	S.	P
68. Tartan Traverse	S.	G			

THE WHANGIE

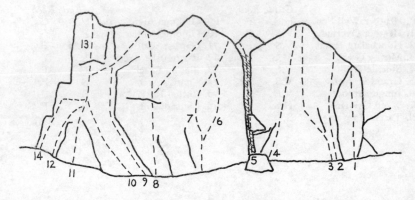

Inside The Gendarme

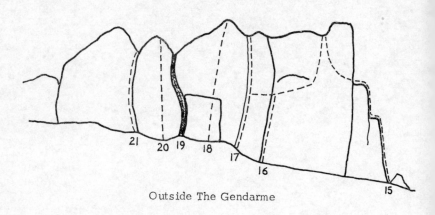

Outside The Gendarme

THE WHANGIE

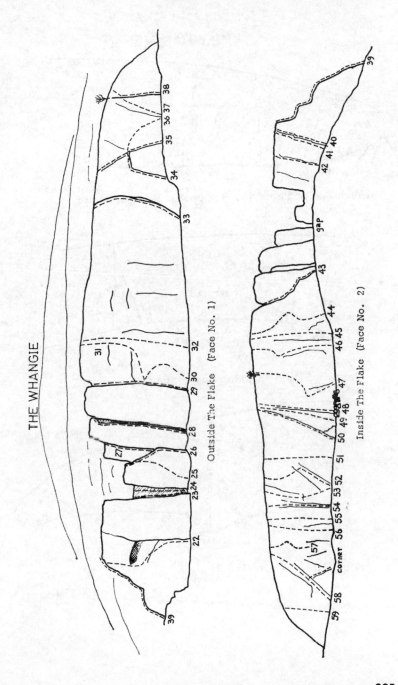

Outside The Flake (Face No. 1)

Inside The Flake (Face No. 2)

201

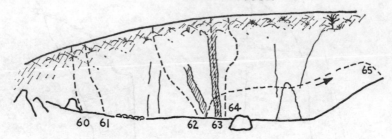

North End of Face No. 3 opposite The Gendarme

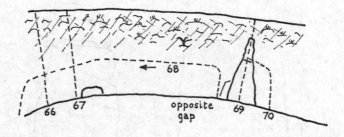

Centre of Face No. 3 opposite the Gap

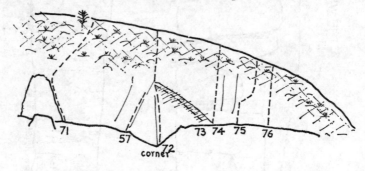

South End of Face No. 3

Dumbarton Rock

Dumbarton Rock stands in a prominent position on the bank of the River Clyde just at the point where the River Leven flows in from Loch Lomond. It is this strategic position of the Rock that made Dumbarton at one time the stronghold of the Britons in Strathclyde.

For many years the Rock was neglected by climbers, and only recently have its cliffs and boulders been explored. The climbs which have been recorded so far are on the north and west sides of the Rock. There are some short climbs on the south-west side, but these may be inaccessible when the tide is in, and the east side of the Rock, although very steep, does not seem to have been explored.

A footpath leads round the north side of the Rock, and the north face climbs start from this path. The west side of the Rock is characterised by a smooth, overhanging wall with several large boulders at its foot. Further round towards the south-west corner one can walk along the beach at the foot of the rocks, or at high tide traverse about 30 ft. above beach level by easy rocks and a path.

Most of the climbs (as distinct from the boulder problems) are very hard and quite serious. Many of them end on steep grass which provides poor belays, and if it is not possible to traverse onto easy ground the climber may either have to scramble upwards and climb the castle wall or abseil back to the foot of the cliffs. Generally, the rocks dry quickly after rain, but in places (particularly on the north face) water drips down the rocks from the grass above for some time after wet weather.

Apart from its boulders and a very few routes of Very Difficult standard and less, Dumbarton Rock does not have much for climbers of modest ability, and in this respect the Whangie, with its greater variety of climbs, is superior. On the other hand, the Whangie has no climbs comparable with the longest and hardest routes on Dumbarton Rock.

The following descriptions are taken from notes compiled by

B. Shields which first appeared in *S.M.C.J.*, Vol. 28, No. 156, (1965), with additional information supplied by I. Fulton. The climbs are described in sequence as one walks along the path round the north side of the Rock from the main road (Victoria Street). Climbers should be familiar with any local bye-laws which affect climbing on Dumbarton Rock.

1. *Executive Wall* (30 ft., S., M. Connolly). About 80 yards along the path one comes to a small wall beside a crack. The original route on the wall bears slightly left. The direct ascent is V.S.

2. *The Neilweg* (110 ft., V.S., B. Shields and M. Connolly). About 50 yards beyond (1) there is a thin vertical crack in a greenish wall with a corner on its right. Climb the crack (piton runner) to a grass ledge and belay, and continue by the crack to the top.

3. *Boulevard* (100 ft., V.S., N. McNiven). Two yards right of (2) a sloping shelf runs diagonally upwards from left to right; climb it and continue by turf ledges to the top. There are hard moves at the start, half way up and at the top.

4. *Hailstone Climb* (100 ft., V.D., M. Connolly). About 13 yards beyond (3) and just left of a big gully there is a groove. Climb it to a small ledge, step left and continue straight up. At the top there is a pull up onto vertical grass. (Not recommended as the turf at the top is unstable, and the protection poor.)

5. *Monsoon Gully* (120 ft., M.S., B. Shields and M. Connolly). This is the big gully which is usually wet. At the top there is a delicate step left round a block, and the finish is on nearly vertical grass with a piton belay necessary. (At the top of the gully the overhanging crack on the right would give a direct finish, so far unclimbed.)

6. *Nameless Crack* (80 ft., D., N. McNiven). Ten yards right of the gully there is a slanting crack which gives a pleasant route joining Monsoon Gully just below its crux.

7. *Alleyway* (80 ft., V.S., N. McNiven). Starting at the same point as (6), near the end of the north face, there is a sloping shelf. Climb the shelf, which is awkward, to a grass ledge; then step left and continue by blocks to the top.

8. *Sunset Groove* (100 ft., V.S., I. Fulton and I. Nicolson). At the west end of the north face there is a short dark groove. This is climbed, followed by a line of cracks to the top.

9. *Angel's Pavement* (300 ft., V.S., N. McNiven). This is the traverse of the north face from Alleyway to Executive Wall. The climber is

seldom more than 15 ft. from the ground, and the crux is the very awkward move at the foot of Boulevard.

Round the corner from the north face a steep grass slope leads up to the castle wall. The next four routes are on the wall on the left of this slope; there is a large patch of ivy on the lowest part of this wall.

10. *Ganglion Grooves* (60 ft., V.S., K. Haggerty and B. Shields). Two yards right of the patch of ivy there is a bulging groove. Climb the bulge for 15 ft., reach for a dubious flake, swing right onto a slab, surmount another bulge and continue by the groove to a grass ledge. From it traverse delicately left and finish by a crack.

Near its top, the grass slope narrows to a gully and the wall on its left is characterised by a small patch of ivy and a small black overhang. There are three unnamed routes on this wall.

11. (50 ft., S., I. Nicolson). The groove on the left of the ivy patch.

12. (50 ft., V.S., I. Nicolson and R. McFarlane). Climb between the ivy patch and the black overhang.

13. (40 ft., V.S., S. Belk and J. Dalrymple). Climb the crack passing to the right of the overhang.

The path continues round to the west side of the Rock where several huge boulders lie below an overhanging wall. There are many short problems on the boulders which do not require description. The next routes, which are the most impressive on the Rock, are on the overhanging wall. The first prominent crack is Stonefall Crack.

14. *Route Three* (65 ft., V.S., B. Shields and K. Haggerty). Start a few feet left of Stonefall Crack and climb direct to piton runner below overhang, traverse right and climb left wall of 15 ft. chimney. Climb over castle wall and belay.

15. *Stonefall Crack* (70 ft., V.S., N. McNiven). Start at the foot of the crack, then traverse diagonally left to the piton runner of the previous route which is then followed.

16. *Stonefall Crack Direct* (65 ft., V.S., N. McNiven and B. Shields). Climb the crack direct, very much harder than the original route.

The three following routes are on the overhanging wall and are largely artificial. A narrow ledge, in places little more than a flake, gives access to the starts of these routes. Although pitons and wedges are in place, some have been there for so long that they should be regarded as unreliable.

17. *The Big Zipper* (100 ft., V.S. and A.3., B. Shields and A. Baillie) This climb goes up the clean-cut corner right of Stonefall Crack. Mantelshelf onto the ledge and climb the corner by artificial technique.

18. *Chemin de Fer* (110 ft., V.S. and A.2., N. McNiven). The route follows the left-hand of two cracks in the overhanging face; the crack curves leftwards at its top. Starting near the foot of Stonefall Crack, traverse rightwards along the narrow ledge to the foot of the crack. The climb is very exposed and the angle is 110 degrees. At the top, mantelshelf onto a ledge and belay. To escape, a long free abseil is necessary; a piton has been left on the floor of the ledge for this purpose.

19. *Requiem* (150 ft., V.S. and A.3., B. Shields and M. Connolly). This crack is in the centre of the face and appears to fade out just below its top. Start as for the previous route and traverse right to gain the foot of the crack. Climb this with pitons, wedges and expansion bolts in a single run-out.

Moving further right past the boulders, one comes to the foot of two prominent, dark grooves. The right-hand one is divided in its upper half.

20. *Longbow* (110 ft., V.S., B. Shields and J. R. Houston). This is the left-hand of the two grooves. Climb for 20 ft. to reach a small ledge. Continue by the crack, using pitons and wedges, and revert to free climbing in the upper part. An awkward and strenuous route.

21. *Windjammer Crack* (110 ft., V.S., B. Shields and J. R. Houston). This route follows the right-hand branch of the right-hand groove. Climb the crack (wedge runners used on first ascent) and turn the overhanging flake at the top by a layback on the right.

Continue round the west side of the Rock by descending onto the beach. The next landmark is a gully (West Face Gully) with a big bramble thicket in its lower part. The next routes start in the gully above the thicket, and may be most easily reached by traversing into the gully from the right just above the thicket.

22. *Frendo* (120 ft., V.S., B. Shields). Immediately above the brambles on the left wall of the gully there is a clean slab. Climb this for 35 ft. There follows several feet of grass and rock, a delicate move on a slab, and a finish on good holds.

23. *Frendo Variation* (100 ft., S., B.Shields,). The delicate upper section of the slab of (22) is avoided by a traverse left, followed by a pull up on steep grass. A rightward traverse over loose blocks leads to the original route where it moves onto the upper slab.

24. *Grey Slab* (80 ft., V.S., B. Shields and M. Connolly). To the right of (22), near the top of the gully, there is a steep slab. Climb it by the line of least resistance, and finish by (22).

25. *West Face Gully* (100 ft., V.D., or S. by direct finish). Continue upwards from the bramble thicket by the deep chimney in the right side of the gully. The Direct Finish can be made by traversing left from the top of the gully to the corner between natural rock and the castle wall. Climb the corner.

26. *Plunge* (90 ft., D., L. Mitchell). Fifteen yards right of West Face Gully a rib of rock rises from the beach to the castle wall. Climb the rib, and at the top traverse right, climb over the castle wall and belay.

27. *Old Socks* (30 ft., S., B. Shields). A few yards right of (26) there is a crack leading up to an overhang. Climb the overhang direct.

28. *Poison Ivy* (30 ft., V.S., B. Shields). Several yards right of (27) there is a steep red slab, topped with ivy. Climb the centre of the slab, which is very delicate but affords good friction.

Twenty yards to the right of and above (28) there is a small crag just below the castle wall. Two routes have been reported on this crag.

29. *Banana* (50 ft., V.S., I. Nicolson and R. McFarlane). This route ascends the dark groove in the centre of the crag.

30. The rib on the left of the groove is Very Difficult.

31. *The West Face Girdle* (B. Shields and M. Connolly). This traverse goes from the railings on the south side of the Rock to the foot of West Face Gully, usually not more than 15 or 20 ft. above the beach. For most of its length the traverse is Difficult, but midway there is a 35 ft. V.S. section and there is a severe section near Poison Ivy. The traverse is entertaining when the tide is in.

Gaelic Names of Mountains and other Features

The following list of Gaelic names and their meanings includes most of the important mountains and other features mentioned in this guide book. The spellings are those used on the Ordnance Survey One-Inch maps. In many cases the names and their spellings are corrupted from the original Gaelic, and some names are of purely local significance.

A'Chrois   *The Cross*
An Caisteal   *The Castle*
An Creachan   *The Rock*
Am Binnein (Stobinian)   *The Pinnacle*
An Sgor   *The Rocky Peak*
An Stuc   *The Steep Rock*
Allt, Amhainn   *stream, river*
Bealach   *col, pass*
Bealach-eadar-dha-Beinn   *The Pass between the Mountains*
Bealach nan Corp   *The Pass of the Corpses*
Bealach a' Mhaim   *The Pass on the Ridge*
Ben, Beinn, Bheinn   *mountain*
Beinn Achaladair   *The Mountain of the Mower*
Beinn Bheag   *The Little Mountain*
Beinn Bhreac   *The Mottled Mountain*
Beinn Bhuidhe   *The Yellow Mountain*
Beinn Chabhair   *The Mountain of the Antler*
Beinn a' Chaisteal   *The Mountain of the Castle*
Beinn Chaluim   *Malcolm's Mountain*
Beinn Cheathaich   *The Mountain of Mists*
Ben Chonzie   *The Mountain of the Cry of the Deer*
Beinn a' Chreachain   *The Mountain of the Clam Shell*
Beinn a' Chuirn   *The Mountain of the Rocky Heap*
Ben Donich   *The Brown Mountain*
Beinn Dorain   *The Mountain of the Otter*

Beinn an Dothaidh   *The Mountain of Scorching*
Beinn Dubh   *The Black Mountain*
Beinn Dubhain   *The Mountain of the Black Burn*
Beinn Dubhchraig   *The Mountain of the Black Rock*
Beinn Each (Beinn nan Eachan)   *The Mountain of the Horses*
Beinn Ghlas   *The Grey Mountain*
Ben Ime   *The Butter Mountain*
Ben Ledi   *The Mountain of the Gentle Slope*
Beinn (an) Lochain   *The Mountain of the Little Loch*
Ben Lomond   *The Beacon Mountain*
Ben Lui (Laoigh)   *The Mountain of the Calf*
Beinn (a') Mhanach   *The Monk's Mountain*
Ben More (Mhor)   *The Big Mountain*
Beinn Odhar   *The Dun-coloured Mountain*
Beinn nan Oighreag   *The Mountain of Cloudberries*
Ben Oss   *The Mountain of the Elk*
Beinn Ruadh   *The Red Mountain*
Beinn an t-Sithein   *The Hill of the Fairy Knoll*
Beinn Tharsuinn   *The Oblique Mountain*
Beinn Tulaichean   *The Knolly Mountain*
Beinn Udlaidh   *The Dark (or Gloomy) Mountain*
Ben Vane   *The White Mountain*
Ben Venue   *The Mountain of the Caves (or possibly The Mountain
    of Young Cattle)*
Carn   *cairn*
Carn Gorm   *The Blue Cairn*
Carn Mairg   *The Rust-coloured Cairn*
Ceann Garbh   *The Rough Head*
Clach Bheinn   *The Stony Mountain*
Cnoc Coinnich   *The Mossy Hillock*
Coille   *wood*
Coilessan   *The Wood of the Waterfalls*
Coire, corrie   *valley or hollow in the mountains*
Coiregrogain   *The Awkward Corrie*
Coire Daimh   *The Corrie of the Stags*
Coire Gaothaich   *The Corrie of Winds*
Coire Cheathaich   *The Corrie of Mists*
Craig, creag   *crag or rock*
Creag na Caillich   *The Crag of the Old Woman*
Creag Mhor   *The Big Crag*

Creag Tharsuinn   *The Oblique Crag*
Cruach Ardrain   *The High Heap*
Curra Lochain   *The Marshy Lochan*
Eas   *waterfall*
Fionn Choirein   *The Fair Corrie*
Garbh   *rough*
Garbh Mheall   *The Rough Hump*
Lairig, lairige, learg   *pass*
Leum an Eireannaich   *The Irishman's Leap*
Loch Achray   *The Loch of the Level Field*
Loch Ard   *The High Loch*
Lochan nan Cat   *The Little Loch of the Cat*
Lochan na Lairige   *The Little Loch of the Pass*
Meall   *rounded hill, lump or hump*
Meall Bhuidhe   *The Rounded Yellow Hill*
Meall a' Choire Leith   *The Round Hill of the Grey Corrie*
Meall a' Churain   *The Round Hill of the Stones*
Meall Corranaich   *The Round Hill of the Corrie of Bracken*
Meall na Dige   *The Round Hill of the Ditch*
Meall Dubh   *The Round Black Hill*
Meall Garbh   *The Rough Round Hill*
Meall Glas   *The Round Grey Hill*
Meall Greigh   *The Round Hill of the Cheek*
Meall Liath   *The Grey Lump*
Meall Luaidhe   *The Round Hill of Lead*
Meall an t-Scallaidh   *The Round Hill of the Sight*
Meall nan Tarmachan   *The Round Hill of the Ptarmigan*
Rowchoish (Rudha a' Chois)   *The Point of the Hollow*
Sgiath Chuil   *The Back Wing*
Stob   *peak, point or spur*
Stob a' Choin   *The Dog's Point*
Stob nan Clach   *The Stony Spur*
Stob Coire an Lochain   *The Peak of the Corrie of the Little Loch*
Stob Creagach   *The Rocky Point*
Stob an Eas   *The Point of the Waterfall*
Stob an Fhir-Bhoga   *The Spur of the Bowman*
Stob Garbh   *The Rough Peak*
Stuc a' Chroin   *The Peak of the Cloven Foot*
Stuchd an Lochain   *The Peak of the Little Loch*
Tom Molach   *The Tufty Hillock*
Uamh Bheag   *The Little Cave*

INDEX